T

A DAN JOSSELYN MEMORIAL PUBLICATION

# THE SWIFT CREEK GIFT

*Vessel Exchange on
the Atlantic Coast*

NEILL J. WALLIS

THE UNIVERSITY OF ALABAMA PRESS
*Tuscaloosa*

Copyright © 2011
The University of Alabama Press
Tuscaloosa, Alabama 35487-0380
All rights reserved
Manufactured in the United States of America

Typeface: Bembo

∞

The paper on which this book is printed meets the minimum requirements of American National Standard for Information Sciences—Permanence of Paper for Printed Library Materials, ANSI Z39.48-1984.

Library of Congress Cataloging-in-Publication Data

Wallis, Neill J.
   The Swift Creek gift : vessel exchange on the Atlantic Coast / Neill J. Wallis.
   p. cm.
   Includes bibliographical references and index.
   ISBN 978-0-8173-1717-1 (cloth : alk. paper) — ISBN 978-0-8173-5629-3 (paper : alk. paper) — ISBN 978-0-8173-8484-5 (electronic) 1. Swift Creek Site (Ga.) 2. Woodland culture—Atlantic Coast (South Atlantic States) 3. Indians of North America—Atlantic Coast (South Atlantic States)—Antiquities. 4. Indian pottery—Atlantic Coast (South Atlantic States)—Analysis. 5. Ceremonial exchange—Atlantic Coast (South Atlantic States)—History. 6. Social interaction—Atlantic Coast (South Atlantic States) 7. Social archaeology—Atlantic Coast (South Atlantic States) 8. Excavations (Archaeology)—Atlantic Coast (South Atlantic States) 9. Atlantic Coast (Ga.)—Antiquities. 10. Atlantic Coast (Fla.)—Antiquities. I. Title.
   E78.G3W25 2011
   975.8′225—dc22

2010031952

*For Michelle*

# Contents

List of Illustrations   ix
Acknowledgments   xiii
Introduction   1
1. What Is a Gift?   12
2. The Swift Creek Cultures   28
3. Cultural History and Archaeological Overview   53
4. Instrumental Neutron Activation Analysis: Patterns of Swift Creek Interaction   87
5. Petrographic Analysis: Patterns of Swift Creek Interaction   115
6. The Form, Technology, and Function of Swift Creek Pottery   137
7. The Swift Creek Gift   192
References   209
Index   241

# Illustrations

FIGURES

1.1. Primary distribution of Swift Creek pottery and sites mentioned in the text   7

2.1. Swift Creek design attributes characteristic of split representation   50

2.2. Split representation of birds in a Swift Creek design and a Haida design   51

3.1. Distribution of recorded Deptford and St. Johns I sites at their intersection on the Atlantic coast   57

3.2. Sites with Late Swift Creek pottery along the Atlantic coast   67

3.3. Swift Creek sites with paddle matches   78

3.4. Reconstructed design 34 and select paddle matches   79

3.5. Reconstructed design 36 and select paddle matches   80

3.6. Reconstructed design 38 and select paddle matches   82

3.7. Unnumbered design and select paddle matches   83

3.8. Reconstructed design 291 and paddle matches   84

3.9. Reconstructed design 151, sherds bearing this design from 9JD8, and a nearly identical design from 8DU43   85

4.1. Distribution of sites with assemblages used in the INAA study   91

4.2. Distribution of clay samples in the INAA study   92

4.3. Bivariate plot of chromium and calcium in assemblages from shell-bearing and shell-devoid sites   96

4.4. Inverse distance weighted (IDW) interpolation of calcium concentrations in both natural and archaeological clay samples   97

4.5. Biplot of the first two principal components along with the relative influence of each of the elemental variables   99

4.6. Bivariate plot of principal component 2 and principal component 4 for the clay samples   102

4.7. Bivariate plot of principal component 2 and principal component 4 for pottery group members and clay samples   103

4.8. Bivariate plot of chromium and cobalt showing separation of pottery groups and tentative clay groups   105

4.9. Inverse distance weighted (IDW) interpolation based on clay samples for cobalt and chromium   106

4.10. Bivariate plot of chromium and cobalt for unassigned samples   107

4.11. Bivariate plot of chromium and cobalt with paddle-matching samples plotted   111

4.12. Percentage of chemical group assignments, excluding charcoal-tempered vessels, from mound and midden sites on the Lower St. Johns River   113

5.1. Mineral constituents useful for distinguishing clay resource groups   125

5.2. Group assignments by quartz and chromium, cobalt   131

5.3. Group assignments by quartz and principal component 1, principal component 2   134

6.1. Open bowl profiles   150

6.2. Restricted bowl profiles   152

6.3. Restricted pot profiles   153

6.4. Open pot vessel profiles   155

6.5. Flattened-globular bowl profiles   157

6.6. Collared jar and collared bowl vessel profiles   159

6.7. Sooted collared jar with folded rim from Mayport Mound   160

6.8. Small cup and bowl vessel profiles   162

6.9. Small jar vessel profiles   163

6.10. Small jars with incising from Grant Mound E and Grant Mound A   164

6.11. Boat-shaped bowls from Low Grant, Floral Bluff, Grant, Mayport, and Dent   165

6.12. Double bowls from Beauclerc, Low Grant, and Point La Vista   167

6.13. Multi-compartment trays from Point La Vista, Grant E, Mayport, Dent, and Monroe   167

6.14. Beakers from Low Grant and Mayport   169

6.15. Double-globed jar from Grant Mound E   170

6.16. Rim profiles of small cups, bowls, and jars from midden contexts   177

6.17. Percentage of sooted vessels by orifice diameter   179

## TABLES

3.1. Calibrated radiocarbon assays for Early and Late Swift Creek contexts in northeastern Florida   62

3.2. Calibrated radiocarbon assays for Early and Late Swift Creek contexts in southern coastal Georgia   63

4.1. Site and type distribution of INAA pottery samples   89

4.2. Clay samples in the INAA study   93

4.3. Mean and standard deviation of elemental concentrations in each composition group   100

4.4. Pottery chemical group assignments by site   108

5.1. Site and type distribution of petrographic analysis pottery samples   117

5.2. Clay samples selected for petrographic analysis   118

5.3. Summary descriptions of variability in petrographic paste categories   120

5.4. Summary descriptions of variability in gross temper categories   122

5.5. Mineralogical paste categories by county and INAA group   126

5.6. Paddle-matching samples by INAA and petrographic groups   129

5.7. Percentage of quartz among chemical groups   130

5.8. R-squared value for the linear regression model and correlation between elements or principal components (PC) and quartz proportion   132

6.1. Vessel form summary statistics   146

6.2. Soot and mend hole frequencies in each vessel form   148

6.3. Frequency of vessel form by surface treatment and pottery type   149

6.4. Mound assemblage orifice diameter and rim thickness summary statistics   173

6.5. Midden assemblage orifice diameter and rim thickness summary statistics   174

6.6. Soot frequency grouped by orifice diameter   178

6.7. Aplastic constituents of gross paste categories   185

6.8. Frequency of gross paste groups by site   188

6.9. Rim thickness summary statistics by gross paste groups   189

# Acknowledgments

I have benefited tremendously from many people in the course of this research. This work was heavily reliant on existing collections, and I simply could not have carried it out without the generosity and helpfulness of all the people and institutions that made loans to me. For my use of these collections I must thank Frankie Snow (who also granted permission to reproduce his reconstructions of Swift Creek designs) at South Georgia College; Mark Williams at the University of Georgia; Ray Crook and Susan Fishman-Armstrong at the University of West Georgia Waring Laboratory; Brent Handley, Greg Hendryx, and Greg Smith at Environmental Services, Inc.; Bob Johnson at Florida Archeological Services; Christy Leonard at the Jacksonville Museum of Science and History; Donna Ruhl at the Florida Museum of Natural History; and Patricia Nietfeld at the National Museum of the American Indian. Travel to the National Museum of the American Indian was made possible by a grant from the Florida Archaeological Council. During my travels to various institutions I stayed with friends and family, including Michelle Amor; Michelle, Tom, Trisha, and Ann Fry; Tanya Peres and John Lemons; Rick, Mary Jane, Jordan, and Julia Taylor; and Jim and Marjorie Waggoner. I thank them all for their warm hospitality.

The use of raw clays was an important part of this research, and I was fortunate to have access to many samples that had already been located and collected. Clay samples were given to me by Vicki Rolland, Carolyn Rock, Brian Floyd, Keith Ashley, and Buzz Thunen. Fred Cook and Bill Stead came with me on an expedition along the Altamaha River to obtain clay samples from sources with which they were familiar. Ken Sassaman graciously offered his boat for this adventure. I thank all of these colleagues for their assistance in obtaining clay samples.

While at the University of Missouri Research Reactor (MURR), I gained valuable insights into the methods of instrumental neutron activation analysis (INAA), along with encouragement and expert guidance for my project from Mike Glascock, Matt Boulanger, Corinne Rosania, and Jeff Ferguson. Funding for this portion of the research came from the National Science Foundation (Grants #0504015 and #0744235). Ann Cordell performed the petrographic analysis at the Florida Museum of Natural History, was very helpful in interpreting mineralogical variation among samples, and shared great pictures of the thin sections. This work was also funded by the National Science Foundation (Grant #0744235).

I must also express my gratitude to many other individuals who helped shape, in various ways, my thoughts during this research, especially Ken Sassaman, Susan Gillespie, John Krigbaum, Jane Southworth, Keith Ashley, Deb Mullins, Asa Randall, and Jamie Waggoner. I also thank Judith Knight and the staff of The University of Alabama Press for their excellent work, and the anonymous reviewers for suggestions in improving this book. Most of all I thank my family, especially Michelle, for unwavering support in every step along the way toward publication.

# The Swift Creek Gift

# Introduction

Bronislaw Malinowski (1922) was the first to suggest that non-Western economies could be fundamentally different from Western markets in terms of how exchange systems were organized, how value was determined, and what motivated people to exchange. In his ethnographic work among the societies of the Trobriand Islands, which he perceived to be relatively uninfluenced by Western markets, Malinowski saw a system of "giving for the sake of giving" seemingly based on generosity rather than self-interest (1922: 175). What Malinowski observed in the Trobriands, the Kula ring, came to be known as the classic example in anthropology of a non-market gift economy that conformed to the rules of reciprocity. Theories of the gift continue to be focused on the perplexing questions of why people give gifts and what it is that obligates a return. The motivations for gift exchange have been variously explained as characteristic of primitive societies, as fundamental to the primeval nature of all humans in all societies, as a social phenomenon that creates important bonds between people, and as a mechanism of both social solidarity and competition (Levi-Strauss 1969; Malinowski 1922; Mauss 1925; Sahlins 1972).

Whatever its origins and many functions, gift exchange is concerned with creating, maintaining, or altering social relationships as much as it is about economic principles. Gifts can create bonds of equality, constitute social difference, or be used to threaten and cajole. Indeed, there can be menacing and destructive gifts (Parry 1986; Raheja 1988). In any case, a gift is never truly free, and although it is given with concern for social relationships, the intentions behind it are often not magnanimous. The organization, logic, and meanings of gift exchange ultimately depend on the specifics of historical and cultural contexts. Yet anthropologists have often interpreted the gift as evidence of a cross-cultural principle of reciprocity that operates mostly in kin-based societies and confounds the logic of self-interest in neoclassical economic theory. Marshall Sahlins's (1972) *Stone Age Economics,* a manifesto on reciprocity, has had a lasting effect on anthropology, particularly in archaeology. Sahlins (1972) discerned in "stone age" economies two forms of reciprocity corresponding with the domestic economy and political economy of small-scale, kin-based societies. Generalized reciprocity was understood to operate between kin within the domestic (immediate) economy of the household and was ostensibly altruistic. These gifts included everything from a mother's milk given to her child to the daily sharing of food among co-residents and kin. Alternatively, balanced reciprocity involved people of greater social distance in their attempt to forge social connections. This form of reciprocity constituted the political economies of small-scale societies, characterized by the give and take of gift exchange and attempts to engineer social relations. Following the influence of Malinowski (1922), these two economic domains can be seen as coupled with gendered divisions, with women typically confined to the internal workings of the domestic economy and men operating in the outreaching operations of the political economy (Weiner 1976:11–19).

These dichotomous ideas have been very influential in archaeological investigations of exchange in past societies without markets or standardized tribute systems. According to these conventional understandings, objects that are produced and consumed within the household tend not to be subject to exchange. This means that utilitarian items such as earthenware vessels, basketry, netting, or stone tools are generally not expected to be items of exchange in a gift economy. In contrast, especially exquisite or ornate examples of utilitarian items or objects that are rare, made of materials from far away, or produced with specialized ritual knowledge are particularly valuable items of exchange; and this is the material from which prestige is acquired in the political context of gift exchange. These two categories of material culture, utilitarian and ceremonial/prestige (i.e., exchangeable items), are therefore imagined as distinct, separate, and unshifting. According to this reasoning, domestic products are not regularly exchanged because they are ubiquitous, easily replaced, and are often the products of women, who are assumed to not be major players in the public political domain. These generalizations might be borne out in some social contexts in which highly valued and access-restricted objects were produced, but there is nothing inherent in an object that determines its value for exchange (*contra* Hayden 1995, 1998). Rather, objects are exchanged in the context of meanings that are embedded in social practice. Because all material technologies are constituted through culturally informed practices that are embedded with symbolic understandings, any category of object has some potential of becoming caught up in political struggles and systems of exchange, no matter how seemingly mundane and quotidian it appears to the archaeologist (Dobres 2000:116–117).

This book is concerned with one such class of material culture, pottery, that in its utilitarian form is rarely considered to have held any symbolic value, much less exchange value. By convention, long-distance transport and exchange should generally be limited to "luxury" or "ceremonial" vessels (e.g., Drennan 1985; Harry 2003; Struever and Houart 1972), while utilitarian vessels might be exchanged between close kin along with other subsistence or "maintenance" goods (e.g., David and Hennig 1972; Duff 2002; Fie 2000, 2006; Graves 1991). Perhaps explaining the distribution of vessels in some contexts, these unyielding categories of utilitarian and luxury objects, with their inherent measures of value, result in a myopic view of the materiality of exchange. In reality, objects of material culture often get "recontextualized" through different cultural milieus whereby value and significance shift in complex and unexpected ways (Meskell 2004; Miller 1995a; Thomas 1991). This is especially true of objects that are exchanged because they continually move in and out of different cultural contexts. Archaeologists have often been slow to recognize the potential for multiple and alternative symbolic capacities for individual objects, with some notable exceptions. In the southwestern United States, for example, widespread vessel exchange among Pueblo and ancestral Pueblo populations has been explained in terms of the biographies of vessels and with recognition of the multiple uses of individual vessels in both domestic and public performative contexts (Crown 2007; Duff 2002; Mills 2004, 2007; Walker 1995). However, archaeologists working in the Southwest often continue to use categories such as "undecorated" and "decorated," falling back on the Sahlins (1972) dichotomy to designate the former as "low-value utilitarian goods" exchanged informally between close kin and the latter as the material of "formal interaction among members of different communities" (Duff 2002:25–27). While these categories may very well explain Pueblo systems of exchange, by applying these conventions too broadly we risk masking the multiple ways that objects become mobilized through exchange.

Eschewing the presumption that utilitarian pottery carried less symbolic or exchange value than other artifacts, this study begins with the premise that all things have the potential to create bonds between people through exchange. This idea takes inspiration from Marcel Mauss's (1925) *The Gift*, perhaps the first work to outline how objects come to be entangled in social relationships through inalienable qualities that link them to persons and places in the context of exchange. It was Mauss (1925) who first demonstrated that the exchange value of objects is essentially contextual, often deriving from histories of association that imbue objects with cultural significance. The inherently arbitrary nature of symbolic signification, combined with continually developing social practices, makes for malleable values among objects, potentially exploding the ceremonial (political economic) and quotidian (domestic) analytical divide. Ultimately, even the material of daily practices, such as pottery associated with food preparation and eating, can be seen as linked to particular people, places, or ideas and thus can provide the substance through which social relationships are constructed and personhood is enacted in salient social contexts. For archaeologists, then, the challenge is to outline the everyday material practices of past populations in enough detail as to be able to identify contextual shifts in the use of objects that might indicate symbolic transformations that do not conform to preconceived categories. Based on the history of pottery production and use detailed in this study, along the Woodland period coast of present-day Georgia and Northeast Florida the exchange of utilitarian pottery appears to have been caught up in "ceremonial" contexts that indicate more than reciprocal exchanges of subsistence goods.

## Swift Creek Complicated Stamped Pottery and Social Interaction

During the second half of the Woodland period (ca. AD 100 to AD 850), Swift Creek Complicated Stamped pottery gained widespread popularity across much of the lower southeastern United States, eventually becoming common in assemblages throughout present-day Georgia and major portions of adjacent states. As with many archaeological types of pottery that are ubiquitous across the landscape, the historical reasons for the extensive adoption of complicated stamped pottery are poorly understood. However, unlike other types, Swift Creek Complicated Stamped pottery preserves tantalizing evidence of the social interactions that may have fueled its growth in popularity. Today, complicated stamped vessels and sherds yield definitive evidence of social interaction at an unparalleled level of detail, owing to distinctive vestiges of the manufacturing process (Snow 1998). To make the characteristic pottery, wooden paddles were carved with various motifs, some representing animals, plants, and faces, and were subsequently impressed into earthenware vessels before firing. The indelible impressions of the wooden paddles preserved inimitable signatures or "fingerprints," such as wooden cracks or asymmetrical design "flaws." These unique signatures allow archaeologists to identify paddle matches, that is, vessels sometimes hundreds of miles apart that were stamped with the same paddle. Hundreds of these paddle matches have been identified; therefore, either pots or the paddles that were used to stamp them were frequently carried across the landscape (Snow 1975, 1998; Snow and Stephenson 1998; Stephenson et al. 2002; Stoltman and Snow 1998).

Swift Creek pottery might also be unequaled in giving archaeologists a glimpse of Middle and Late Woodland symbolic representation in contexts where little else but pottery is preserved (Snow 1998, 2007). Indeed, well over 400 unique designs have been recorded pertaining to a variety of themes, and this is sure to represent only a small fraction of the immense corpus of designs. Although preserving the impressions of exquisite woodcarvings and coming in a variety of vessel forms, most Swift Creek pottery can be considered utilitarian. Made for cooking or storing food and, when broken, swept into village garbage middens, complicated stamped pottery is ubiquitous at many Swift Creek sites. Some therefore warn archaeologists to beware of mistakenly elevating the social importance of these everyday "humdrum" artifacts (Williams and Elliott 1998:10). Along these lines, evidence for the movement of both paddles and pots has received cursory explanation, mostly as the byproduct of social practices in which other objects were more important: marriage alliances in which mates were exchanged and economic transactions in which vessel contents were exchanged (Stephenson et al. 2002; Stoltman and Snow 1998).

In contrast, I submit that archaeologists must be attuned to the contextual details of pottery production, use, distribution, and deposition before discounting vessels as mere utilitarian tools with little symbolic value. Swift Creek Complicated Stamped vessels were made and used by populations that manifested a huge array of social diversity across a wide expanse of the southeastern landscape. In terms of cultural attributes, what constitutes Swift Creek in one area is not the same in another locale (Ashley and Wallis 2006); therefore, the ways in which complicated stamped pottery was embedded in social life certainly varied as well. Indeed, the social significance of complicated stamped vessels and the ways that individual designs were disseminated via pots or paddles may have been as variable as the Swift Creek social landscape itself, making multiple scales of analysis indispensable to studies of Swift Creek interaction. To understand Swift Creek culture on a global scale, we must venture to understand it on a local scale. This understanding is best pursued by detailing the range of variation within and between many assemblages from different kinds of sites in a region.

This book focuses on the material practices of pottery production, distribution, and use during the proliferation of complicated stamping on the Atlantic coast of present-day Florida and Georgia (Figure I.1). Swift Creek pottery came to the Atlantic seaboard through specific historical circumstances, adopted first along the Lower St. Johns River, Florida, around AD 200 and along the Altamaha River, Georgia, and intervening areas three centuries later (Ashley and Wallis 2006; Ashley et al. 2007). Swift Creek influences, whether due to migration, assimilation, or other social interactions, derived from different geographical areas in each river valley, from the Gulf Coast of Florida to the Lower St. Johns River and from central and south-central Georgia to the Altamaha River and Georgia coast. Perhaps as a consequence, cultural differences are observed between the two regions in the spatial structure of the built landscape of burial mounds and villages, in the modes of burial, and in the technological style of pottery. After AD 500, when complicated stamped pottery was being produced all along the coast from the mouth of the St. Johns River to the Altamaha River, paddle matches between sites became more abundant, not just between proximate sites but between river drainages separated by well over 100 kilometers. These contexts on the Atlantic coast therefore offer the potential to understand Swift Creek interaction as a historical process at the intersection of multiple temporal and spatial scales. Based on paddle matches, pottery was obviously involved in social interactions of some kind. In this research I attempt to determine more precisely how pottery was embedded in social practice and interaction by outlining a genealogy of the material practices of pottery production, use, distribution, and deposition along the Atlantic coast.

By using the term *genealogy,* I am referring to a record of temporal and spatial variation in earthenware vessel attributes that can be used to trace historical connections and disjunctures in material forms (cf. Gosden 2005). The record is developed in this research through empirical evidence of vessel provenance, function, use, and deposition that is situated within specific archaeological contexts that relate to distinctive social practices. Two different spaces, mortuary mounds and village sites, were inscribed onto the landscape and clearly reflect the materiality of particular actions and events. While mortuary mounds and village sites are widespread across the Eastern Woodlands, they take a variety of regionally distinct spatial configurations. Along the Lower St. Johns River, a series of low sand burial mounds, each constructed over the course of several centuries, stands separated from contemporaneous villages by hundreds of meters (Ashley and Wallis 2006; Wallis 2007). This mortuary landscape of continuous-use mounded cemeteries spatially segregated from habitation sites contrasts with the pattern of sites in coastal Georgia and along the Altamaha River, where village-adjacent mor-

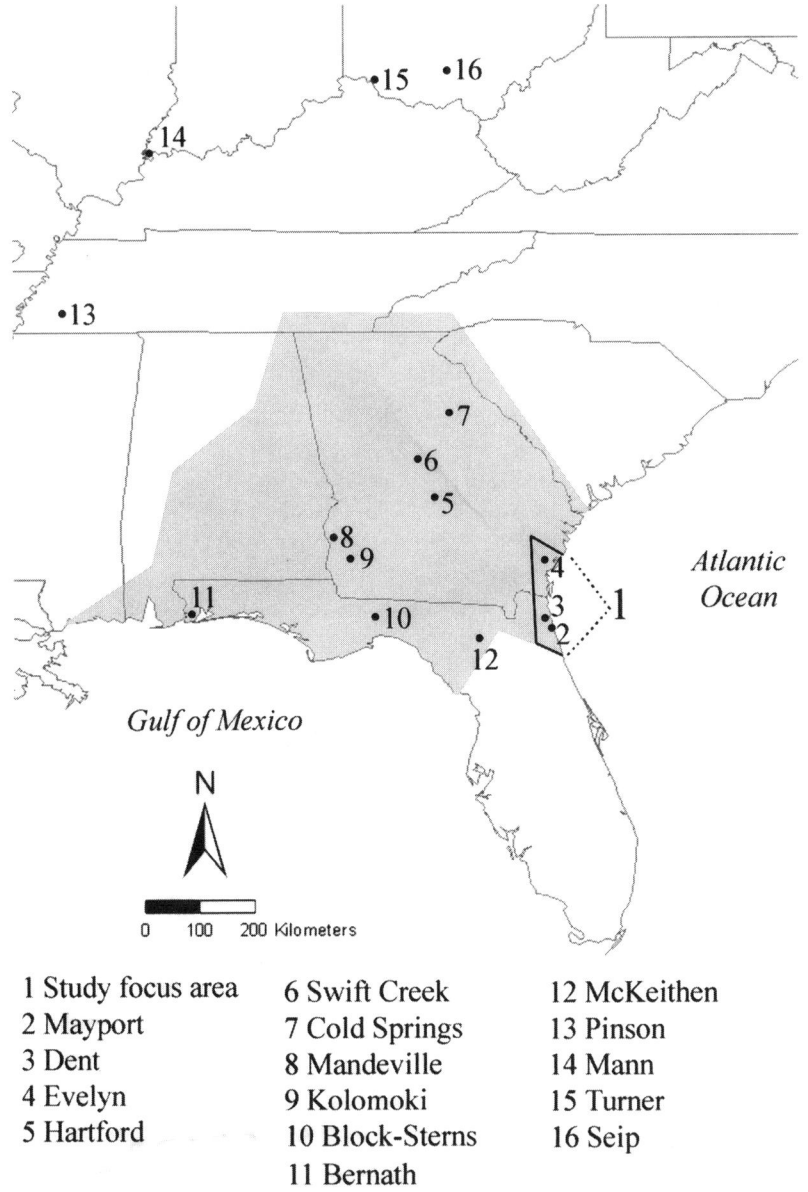

Figure I.1. Primary distribution of Swift Creek pottery (*shaded area*) and sites mentioned in the text. Modified from Williams and Elliott 1998:6.

tuary mounds are more common (Ashley et al. 2007). The separate cemetery and habitation spaces in both regions present the opportunity to discover how pottery production, use, and deposition varied with social context. In turn, these data can be used to reconstruct patterns of interaction and exchange.

I argue that the spatial distribution and technofunctional and stylistic attributes of nonlocal Swift Creek Complicated Stamped vessels are characteristic of gifts that were exchanged as important material for the constitution of social relationships, the most fundamental of which were marriage alliances. This conclusion is built on multiple lines of empirical data. Nonlocal vessels are identified by a robust sample of pottery and clays subjected to Instrumental Neutron Activation Analysis (INAA) and petrographic analysis. Chemical and mineralogical data indicate that nonlocal vessels were deposited almost exclusively at mortuary mounds and that they were predominantly complicated stamped. Technofunctional analysis reveals that village assemblages were nearly entirely comprised of domestic cooking vessels while mortuary mound assemblages included a diverse array of special-use ceremonial vessels in addition to cooking vessels. In the context of these many ceremonial vessel forms, a significant percentage of cooking vessels at mortuary mounds on the Lower St. Johns River was nonlocal, made somewhere along the Altamaha River. This distribution of nonlocal cooking vessels indicates that rather than the de facto refuse of moving people, complicated stamped vessels became important ceremonial material that was intentionally emplaced at mortuary sites, likely deriving symbolic importance from the fingerprinting capabilities of impressed designs. Finally, with faces and animals emblazoned on their surfaces, complicated stamped vessels that were distributed widely could have been used effectively to embody parts of a person linked across the landscape by matching designs. Consequently, I argue that simple cooking vessels from distant villages wound up in Lower St. Johns mortuary mounds as gifts used for honoring and renegotiating social relationships that were threatened in the event of a death, particularly marriage alliances between important descent groups living on the St. Johns and Altamaha rivers.

## Organization and Outline

This study begins by establishing a background in social theories of exchange and Swift Creek archaeological contexts, continues with presentation of the INAA, petrographic, and technofunctional data, and closes with a synthesis of Swift Creek exchange on the Atlantic coast. In chapter 1, I review theories of gift exchange and also draw more broadly on anthropological considerations of materiality to consider how and why objects are exchanged. I begin by focusing on the limitations of normative and functionalist conceptions of reciprocity that unrealistically limit the objects of exchange and reasons for transactions. I then review the various ways that material culture becomes entangled in social life, particularly in the context of exchange. Objects take on "social lives" through recognition of their biographies and as material extensions of social persons or as agentive persons themselves. The concepts of "index," "citation," and "distributed object" are introduced to give clarity to the symbolic potentialities that pertain especially to exchanged objects. Because the kinds of objects that become meaningful and that are exchanged are variable with context, I end by advocating a contextually based genealogy of material practice that details the range of variation in how a class of objects was made and used in order to infer the significance of their mobilization for exchange.

Chapter 2 is an overview of the Swift Creek archaeological culture that covered a vast expanse of the lower Southeast. I focus on the social and cultural diversity among populations who made and used complicated stamped pottery, suggesting that the meanings of Swift Creek carved designs and their role in social life were probably just as variable. Next I review available evidence and previous interpretations of Swift Creek social interaction at a variety of scales. While there is some evidence to suggest that both wooden paddles and earthenware vessels were moved considerable distances, previous explanations for interaction have been mostly decontextualized. Moreover, with few exceptions, the representational meanings of designs have been considered separately from their distribution on artifacts. Alternatively, I argue that the movement of designs via pots or paddles was likely critical to their meanings. Toward this end, I present my identifications of "split representation" in Swift Creek design execution that may support the contention that vessels and paddles were conferred degrees of personhood, which helps explain their dissemination.

Chapter 3 synthesizes current evidence of Swift Creek manifestations on the Atlantic coast. I begin with an outline of the ecological setting of the coastal sector, discussion of the pre–Swift Creek culture history of the Woodland period, and review of the Middle and Late Woodland culture chronology of the Atlantic coast. I then integrate Swift Creek site information along the coast to make important cultural distinctions between northeastern Florida and southeastern Georgia. I draw special attention to the mortuary landscapes of the Lower St. Johns River that consisted of a series of mortuary mounds segregated from contemporaneous villages. These distinctive mortuary landscapes provided important contexts for social interactions across considerable distances, as evidenced by paddle matches between sites. The chapter concludes with a review of known paddle matches along the Atlantic coast.

With this necessary background in place, the remaining chapters convey the major empirical contributions of the study. Chapter 4 presents new data derived from INAA of clay and pottery samples from the Atlantic coast. By discovering patterns in the chemical composition of samples, I use these data to determine the prevalence and locations of foreign-made vessels at each site. While a larger and more diverse sample would be beneficial, the current results are quite compelling. The frequency of nonlocal vessels within mortuary mound assemblages is significantly greater than among midden samples on the Lower St. Johns River. What these data indicate is that on the St. Johns River people were depositing foreign-made Swift Creek vessels at mounds but were not using or breaking foreign vessels very often at habitation sites.

I discuss in chapter 5 new mineralogical data from petrography of thin sections from a subsample of pottery and clays used in the INAA study. These data complement the chemical data to allow for better resolution in resource groups, firmly establishing the foreign manufacturing origins of some vessels. For instance, the combination of chemical and petrographic data shows that some vessels with paddle matches were likely made with the same clay source while others were made with slightly different clay sources from the same region. The mineralogical data also help assess the effect of quartz sand temper on the chemical composition of vessels. Because size of quartz temper closely corresponds with chemical group assignment, point count data were compared with elemental concentrations, showing that while some chemical differences may be due to the diluting effects of temper, other differences are almost certainly linked to variation among clay sources.

Chapter 6 presents the results of technofunctional analysis of pottery. I begin by reviewing how technofunctional data are important for understanding the practical functions of earthenware vessels and, by extension, their social significance. In what follows, I detail vessel form, function, and paste characteristics among assemblages from 30 sites. Using mortuary mound assemblages of reconstructed vessels, I identify 15 distinct vessel forms that were used for a variety of functions. Based on rim profiles and estimates of orifice diameter among assemblages, I infer that midden vessels are confined almost exclusively to cooking forms while mound assemblages have a wide range of formal variation that includes many special-function vessels. In addition, differences in rim thickness and paste constituents among Late Swift Creek vessels along the coast conform to a geographic pattern that likely corresponds with the long-lived traditions of different social groups. These differences lend further support to the idea that foreign vessels at Lower St. Johns River sites were made in Georgia by Georgia-local Swift Creek potters.

All of these data are brought to bear on an interpretation of Swift Creek interaction in chapter 7. The history of the adoption of Swift Creek Complicated Stamped pottery on the Atlantic coast is a story of cultural and historical distinction between the Altamaha River and St. Johns River regions. I explain that out of the specific context of these cultural distinctions grew systems of earthenware vessel exchange that became integral to the constitution of social relationships along the coast, namely, marriage alliances among descent groups. Based on the available evidence, I suggest that domestic cooking pots with complicated stamping were exchanged as a system of references to social persons, thus providing the material to forge and rework social relationships transcendent of the time and space of face-to-face interactions. Complicated stamped surface treatment was a technological innovation that imparted greater specificity to the representative meanings of material forms, and I suggest that these capabilities allowed for transformations of mundane cooking vessels into ceremonial material. Based on the distribution and apparent functions of vessels and specific qualities of designs, I argue that Swift Creek Complicated Stamped vessels had the symbolic capacity to give presence to important persons or social bodies, especially in ceremony. This research therefore negates the long-standing bias of anthropologists that utilitarian and mundane items are symbolically unimportant by detailing the specific ways that commonplace earthenware vessels became inextricably bound up in social and political processes. I close with a discussion of this study's limitations and the potential for further research.

# I

# What Is a Gift?

The gift has been a seminal idea in anthropology for the better part of a century, in its various guises informing considerations of economy, social solidarity, and human nature. Originally published in 1925, Marcel Mauss's *The Gift* is at once abstruse and rich with meaning, qualities that invite new readings of the work by each generation of anthropologists. In this way, interpretations of *The Gift* can be seen to follow, and in some ways shape, the contours of the discipline through time (Sykes 2005). The most recent spate of "Maussian revisionism" is foremost a critique of the anthropological considerations of gifts as the quintessential material of non-Western "primitive" economies that provide exception to the logic and motives of Western capitalism (Miller 2001; Sigaud 2002). Recent considerations of gifting have come to focus on the various ways that objects and people are engaged in processes of mutual constitution that give special impact and meaning to gift exchanges, not as a particular category of transaction that conforms to social classifications but rather as specific moments that are critical to the process of cultural construction in a variety of settings. The arbitrary nature of symbol-based behavior itself contradicts general models that attempt to predict what objects will take the form of gifts, the motivations for their exchange, or the significance of these transactions. In short, a gift is not a type of thing but part of a process by which things, social relationships, and persons are created. Accordingly, I do not view gifts as being characteristic of a particular type of economy (e.g., reciprocity) or type of society (e.g., small-scale) but as a process by which objects of exchange become variously integrated with social worlds in ways that are dependent on context. This chapter outlines the social process of gifting and important implications of theories of materiality in archaeological studies of exchange.

## The Legacy of Mauss

In *The Gift,* Mauss (1925) undertakes an explanation for prestations that are seemingly voluntary, spontaneous, and putatively munificent but that are, in fact, obligatory, premeditated, and carefully calculated. More specifically, Mauss attempts to explain why a gift obligates a return and what it is that structures the nature of the return gift. One answer that Mauss seems to offer is that the giving and receiving of gifts operates within a kind of original morality that stimulates systems of reciprocity. Indeed, Mauss's (1925) work has a distinctively evolutionary quality that betrays a deep concern with origins (Parry 1986), in which reciprocity can be understood as the primordial and inherently moral state of primitive economies. The idea of reciprocity in *The Gift* comes largely from Malinowski's (1922) work in the Trobriand Islands, from which Mauss drew heavily. Malinowski himself believed that the gift "from its very general and fundamental nature ... is a universal feature of all primitive societies" (1922:175). However, Malinowski presents an important difference: Mauss describes reciprocity as operating in all societies while Malinowski restricts its operation to a particular type of "primitive" society (Gudeman 2001:84). It has been the latter view that has garnered the most influence in anthropology until recent decades.

Claude Levi-Strauss (1969), Karl Polanyi (1944), and Marshall Sahlins (1972) were each influential in establishing what amounts to a law of reciprocity that conforms to evolutionary social typologies. Levi-Strauss (1969) made the claim that exchange was the primary fundamental phenomenon of social life, making reciprocity the very foundation of society. Polanyi (1944) introduced a three-part typology of economies that was implicitly arranged on an evolutionary scale: reciprocity was practiced in societies dominated by kinship concerns, redistribution pertained to "ancient" societies where religious and political authority were established, and market exchange occurred in modern capitalist contexts. In many ways Sahlins (1972) combined aspects of the work of Mauss (1925), Levi-Strauss (1969), and Polanyi (1944) to devise a typology of "stone age" economies based on social distance, with reciprocity as its foundation. Sahlins described generalized reciprocity as exchange that was ostensibly altruistic between kin, balanced reciprocity as less personal and "more economic" gift exchange between non-kin, and negative reciprocity as barter and theft. Each of these types of exchange was a version of reciprocity at its core but was defined by different levels of social distance, with negative reciprocity characterized by the greatest social distance and the least personal form of transaction.

Largely through the influence of these works, Mauss's idea of the gift enjoyed somewhat of an invented legacy in anthropology as it came to represent part of a dichotomy between reciprocity and market exchange that is probably best codified in the work of Chris Gregory (1982). Through perspectives that were deeply rooted in colonialist economics and politics, critics argue, the "gift" ultimately came to be synonymous with "reciprocity," understood as the natural, primitive, and inherently moral state of the economy of the ethnographic other, who stood in opposition to Western market economies (Hart 2007; Sigaud 2002; Weiner 1992, 1994). Mauss himself actually viewed the gift as a total social fact, a common reality that pervades all of society and all institutions, economic, political, religious, and aesthetic, instead of as a dichotomy between disparate economic systems (Hart 2007). For Mauss the purely altruistic gift was indeed the polar opposite of pure self-interest, but "gift" exchange systems are not purely altruistic, nor are capitalist markets based purely on self-interest. In fact, Mauss conceived of the "archaic" gift as a mixture of these two modes of exchange and rarely used the term "reciprocity" (Hart 2007).

Whatever Mauss's original intent, the idea of reciprocity as an inherent regulatory mechanism in "primitive" societies devoid of ownership, legal codes, or political hierarchy has confounded anthropological efforts to understand what motivates gift exchange. Other research has demonstrated a more calculative dimension among societies otherwise described as only concerned with solidarity (Appadurai 1986; Bourdieu 1977; Weiner 1992, 1994). For example, Weiner (1992, 1994) refocused the question of why a gift obligates a return by focusing on the inalienable qualities of exchanged objects. Mauss described "the spirit of the gift," most famously in the Maori *hau,* as a way that things create bonds between people by retaining inalienable qualities of the giver's person in the context of exchange. Gifts essentially embody the "nature," "substance," and "spiritual essence" of a person and thus become powerful, dangerous, alive, and personified (Mauss 1925:10). Weiner develops this idea further to argue that inalienability itself is the thrust of systems of exchange as people engage in a process of "keeping while giving" (1992:150). Weiner (1992) outlines how, through exchange of other objects, persons or social groups attempt to conserve their most valuable possessions that establish differences between themselves and other persons or groups. These items, such as Samoan fine mats or Kwakiutl coppers, are ranked against one another according to their relative "symbolic density," and some rarely circulate (Weiner 1994). In this way the exchange of fine mats or coppers is as much about the objects that are being offered as about the ones that are being kept out of exchange. These are the items that Mauss described as "immeuble," immovable objects that are heirlooms because of their close links to "soil, clan, the family, and the person" (Weiner 1992:46). Thus, according to Weiner, it is the "radiating power of keeping inalienable possessions out of exchange" that fuels reciprocal exchange networks (1992:150).

While invaluable items may be literally "kept," according to Weiner (1992), the other related implications of inalienability have to do with the qualities of place and person that adhere to an object even through changes in possession and geography. In this sense objects are inalienable not because they cannot be given away but because they represent linkages that are inextricable from their material form. Recognition of the spirit of the gift in terms of the entanglement of things and persons opens opportunities to understand specific social contexts in which objects are mobilized as more than their material parts. Indeed, some things matter in the profound sense that they are critical to the process of self-construction (Miller 1995b). As theories of material culture have long demonstrated, social worlds are constituted by the object world, not just the other way around (Appadurai 1986; Bourdieu 1977; Miller 1987, 1995b, 2005). Rather than reducing material culture to essentialized models of the social world, materiality can be seen as integral to the process of sociality. Things inevitably become "entangled" in peoples' lives in ways that bind them to particular ideas, meanings, memories, places, and persons and confer to them various degrees of agency (Thomas 1991:16). Therefore, objects mediate social agency in ways that are contextually specific and historically situated. Although this realization is deceptively simple and far from new, anthropological research invested in this perspective of materiality, as the mutually constituting dialectic of people and things, arguably brings us closer to studying "the social" as a process in a continual state of becoming rather than focusing on analytical abstractions such as "society" and "culture" (e.g., DeMarrais et al. 2005; Meskell 2004, 2005; Miller 2005; Thomas 1999). No less important, a materiality perspective with a focus on the engagement of objects within social worlds enhances the relevance of archaeology, transforming the discipline from an ineffectual attempt to understand past societies through the vestiges of long-gone thoughts and behaviors to resurrecting some of the very substance through which past socialities were constituted and transformed.

## The Social Life of Things: Object Biographies

As Appadurai (1986) describes, material things have social lives in the sense that they are inextricably bound up in social process, perhaps most significantly in the intertwining of the biographies of persons and things. The concept of object biographies has become popular among anthropologists and, particularly, archaeologists, who often outline the life cycle of objects (e.g.,

Schiffer 1975, 1976; Schiffer and Skibo 1997). However, Appadurai (1986) was interested not just in the cultural biography, or individual life histories of objects, but also in the social history of things, the collective history of a particular class of objects and how it was imbricated with social life. In an effort to understand the relationship of material things to human actors, such a project is necessarily deeply contextual.

Because symbols are not inherently meaningful but depend on specific social practices (e.g., Leach 1976), there are different kinds of object biographies that pertain to particular social and cultural contexts. Chris Gosden and Yvonne Marshall (1999) distinguish between objects that gather biographies to themselves and those that serve mostly to contribute to the biography of a ceremony or body of knowledge. Some objects have the ability to accumulate histories, deriving significance from the people, places, and events to which they are connected. Most famously, Kula valuables in the Trobriands have this quality, maintaining links with named persons who possess and transact each object. The direct relationship between a person and an object is retained through each subsequent possession by another person, setting up a process whereby social relations and persons become defined by exchanged objects. John Chapman (2000) refers to this process as "enchainment," invoking an image of material linkages that bind identities and forge social relations through the distribution of objects. In the context of the Kula, the identities of people and objects are mutually created as objects gain value through their associations with powerful people and people build reputations through their possession of famous objects. Not only its attachment to people, but also where something is from (or perceived to be from) is a significant part of its biography. An object may be valued because of its procurement from an important place or simply because it comes from far away (Helms 1988). As "pieces of places" (Bradley 2000), objects can be seen to materialize distant places, events, and persons and, in their exchange, thereby constitute social connections and define social differences (Thomas 1999).

Objects that accrue biographies can also be distinguished by the level of specificity in their recognized histories. Gosden and Marshall (1999) point to Kula valuables as examples of objects that have very specific histories of association with named persons. In contrast, *tabua,* which are whales' teeth that are circulated (singly) throughout Fiji, take on value through a rather generic understanding of their age. Over time, tabua become darker in color due to the oil from people's hands in contact with them. The darker the tabua, the older and more valuable it is, but this biographic quality is not linked to particular named owners or places, making its story generic compared to famed Kula valuables.

In contrast to objects with accumulative biographies, some objects hold little inherent meaning outside of performative contexts. For example, among the Kwakwaka'wakw on the Northwest coast of North America, carved wooden masks were a means through which ceremonial privileges could be manifested in material form. However, possession of the mask itself was not significant because its meaning was tied to the context of performance. It was the act of showing the mask that was central to its power and meaning. Thus, in material form the masks were alienable and the Kwakwaka'wakw were not wary of selling them to outsiders. However, neighboring Nuxalk groups to the north understood and performed the relationships between masks and people much differently, making their sale as commodities much more problematic (Seip 1999). Hence, the biographic qualities of objects are historically and culturally contextual to the extent that the same class of artifact used in similar ways can have quite different biographic capabilities.

## Object Extension and Personhood

One productive way to explore contextual variations in the social lives of objects is in thinking about an artifact's extension in social space and time. This focus returns to the idea of a social history of things proposed by Appadurai (1986), recognizing that objects have a social habitat, a correct place and time of use (Robb 2005). Material objects are part of culturally specific practices that are associated with particular social roles for practitioners, a corpus of knowledge including bodily knowledge and comportment, and symbolic significance (Robb 2005:134). A common way that objects function in the social worlds of Melanesia is as extensions in time and space of the social life of a person or lineage (Munn 1983, 1986, 1990). Kula valuables that are associated with a person's name are viewed as representations of his physical presence, knowledge, age, and intelligence; and a Kula operator must carefully calculate how these parts of his self are distributed (Gell 1998:230–231). Objects such as these have referential qualities of personhood and of thoughts, intentions, and mental states; Alfred Gell refers to these as "indexes" (1998:231–232), thus conjuring up the complex webs of both systematic and implicit citations that connect written texts. Through the indexical qualities of objects, Gell argues that the "Kula system as a whole is a *form of cognition,* which takes place outside the body, which is diffused in space and time, and which is carried on through the medium of physical indexes and transactions involving them" (1998:231–232). In this way the Kula necklaces and arm-shells transacted by a Kula operator are a "distributed object," an object having many spatially separated parts with different micro-histories and with each disparate part connected to a whole through indexical qualities. By way of the dissemination of various parts of this indexically linked whole, the person who sets the objects in motion becomes a "distributed person," extended through time and space (Gell 1998:221). The Kula system is, in effect, an objectified social world in which social relationships between persons can occur beyond the face-to-face interactions of biological individuals.

The extension of persons is not a capability restricted to Kula valuables, but is also typical of many of the objects employed in mortuary ceremony. For example, in the Trobriands, when someone died their possessions (earrings, armbands, clan-associated feathers for men or skirts and earrings for women) or even bones from their body were carried for up to a year by members of the matrilineage of the spouse or father of the deceased. In an interview with Fred Myers and Barbara Kirshenblatt-Gimblett (2001), Annette Weiner convincingly interprets these actions as extending the social life of persons after their death, specifically by maintaining relationships between lineages that had been forged through marriage. By carrying part of the material identity of the deceased, reciprocal obligations originally forged by marriage were continued, and women's skirts and banana leaf bundles were subsequently given by the deceased person's lineage. The extension of the deceased person through exchanges maintained social relationships between lineages in anticipation of a new marriage between them in the future.

The Sabarl axe in the southern Massim area of Papua New Guinea goes even further to extend personhood in time and space (Battaglia 1983, 1990). According to symbolic representations, Sabarl axes are conceived as bodies, with particular named body parts that are correlated with human body parts: the blade represents the right hand or genitals, the shaft is an arm with a crook that represents an elbow, and so on. These axes are animated by the reproductive potential of a person, called *hinona,* which is embodied in the "heat-generating" greenstone blade that represents the genitals and the right hand that guides exchange. Significantly, the shape of the axe is also a material metaphor for exchange relations and the movement of gifts in mortuary exchanges as well as a representation of two different aspects of the person (clan member and individual) united in a single form. In the event of a death, five axes are presented by the paternal clan to the maternal clan of the deceased. The maternal clan then uses these axes, along with food, to constitute the "corpse" of the deceased. Once the mortuary ceremony is over, the axe corpse is deconstructed by "reproducing" axes, in effect killing the dead person and severing links between clans while at the same time creating an ancestor. The axes not only serve as substitutes for a person in this case, but also can be seen to act as persons because they participate in the same social actions as persons: they gather at mortuary ceremonies and have the power to reproduce new people, new objects, and new social ties through exchange.

These examples of objects conceived as persons or as parts of persons are consistent with Marilyn Strathern's (1988) descriptions of Melanesian personhood. Rather than individuals, Strathern (1988) argues that Melanesian persons are conceived as "dividuals" who have partible components. Every person is multiply authored and created out of relations between others, starting with both parents. Therefore, each person is a composite of the substances and actions of others, encompassing constituent things and relations received from other people. These relationships may be condensed into physical substances or objects; and, through partibility, some parts can be extricated from a person. This partibility can be important for a number of reasons, such as allowing a person to remove parts of their dividual self that are the same as others in the community for the purposes of marriage (Mosko 1992). Through the extrication allowed by partibility, the partible person becomes "a partial *version* of that person, in which the extracted part is presented as the whole" (Fowler 2004:25). For example, a pig in the Highlands of New Guinea is multiply authored—it is produced through the labor of a man and his wives. However, in offering a pig as a gift, a man temporarily presents it as a unitary version of himself, standing in for his family in the process. Consequently, it is the man's person who enters into the exchange relationship and it is the man who garners prestige from the transaction. In this way a person can fluctuate between their dividual nature, constituted by various relations, and their partible nature in which parts of themselves, which are also multiply authored, can be extricated and given away (Fowler 2004:31).

The concepts of a fragmented and multiply constituted person and the consequent person-like qualities of objects have been employed by archaeologists studying patterns of exchange in many parts of the world. It is perhaps the lack of individual or biographic specificity in Strathern's (1988) work, along with it being one of the most thorough negations of the bounded Western individual, that has made her ideas so popular for prehistoric archaeologists (Meskell 2004:55). Indeed, the concepts of personhood developed through ethnographic work in the Trobriands and Papua New Guinea have become so pervasive among some researchers as to give the European Neolithic a "Melanesian flavour" (Jones 2005:195). Of course, the partibility of persons does not pertain to all times and places because their definition and creation is contextual. As Edward LiPuma (1998) argues, both individual and dividual modalities of personhood exist in all cultures, but one of the aspects is masked according to different contexts. Generally speaking, in Western cultures the multicomponent, dividual parts of the person are masked while the individual is emphasized. The opposite is true in Melanesian contexts. It is out of this tension between dividual and individual aspects of personhood that social persons emerge (LiPuma 1998:57). In essence, people are configured in historically and culturally specific ways, and the criteria for defining exactly who or what may or may not be a person is contextually variable. Rather than simply populating the prehistoric past of Europe or North America with Melanesian models of personhood, archaeologists must attempt to define the contextual world of objects and how they interrelate with human lives. Andrew Jones (2005:126) points to other possibilities derived from Mayan (Gillespie 2001; Houston and Stuart 1998; Joyce 1998, 2003; Meskell and Joyce 2003) and Andean (Allen 1998) examples in which less emphasis is placed on object exchange as the most salient medium for the production of persons. Instead, persons emerge primarily through bodily practices, ritual practice, and the inhabitation of architectural spaces. Yet in all events persons can be located in the sum of their relationships, which are archaeologically accessible through the relations between people and things, between people and architectural spaces, and, more generally, with their landscape and environment (Jones 2005:199). Deciphering the process by which materiality helps constitute the social world, including personhood, is principally based on a concern with context.

## Genealogies of Objects, Genealogies of Practice

Chris Gosden's (2005) focus on the genealogy of objects is relevant here. The genealogy of objects refers to a historical concern with descent lines of material forms and their modifications through time and space, paying particular attention to how things of different origins and histories are put together in coherent ways. Gosden (2005) is foremost interested in how things shape people and argues that rather than focus on meanings, per se, that we should first focus on the effects of object worlds. The agency of objects, defined as their social effect on people, is in the combination of their forms, historical trajectories, and perceived sources. Gosden's (2005) compelling example comes from the incorporation of the British Isles into the Roman Empire, in which changes in form and attributions of source among pottery vessels and metal fibulae and brooches with demonstrable influences from the continent resulted ultimately in the construction of new and locally distinctive types of people. These were not "Romans," but locally unique persons who were constituted out of new combinations of material practices and their simultaneous transformation.

There is a commonality in Timothy Pauketat and Susan Alt's (2005) approach to genealogies of practice that examines the socially constituting qualities of materiality. In their study of "agency in a postmold," Pauketat and Alt (2005) argue that physical objects such as posts used in house construction can be the catalyst through which social change happens or continuity is secured. In pre-Mississippian times, house construction was initiated with posts that were secured in individually dug holes that made necessary the coordination and collaboration of labor among familial or communal groups. The necessity for community cooperation in the construction of each house was later obviated by a new kind of house, introduced from the political center of Cahokia, that included wall trenches and possibly prefabricated walls. These houses could be constructed by a single person. Even in the midst of adopting these new house construction techniques, however, some farmers continued to dig individual posts beneath the trenches, presumably referencing the symbolic importance of the communal effort of building houses. Concurrently, the erection of large "marker" posts in the plazas of ceremonial centers can be seen as an inversion of the familial-communal basis of the post-setting practices that once were used for building houses. Given the frequent resetting and replacement of marker posts, it was the communal practice of setting posts rather than just the physical post itself that was important. Through the genealogy of the practice of post-setting in various contexts, we can begin to see how the materiality of posts came to shape the lives of people.

Thus, objects can be agents in the sense that they have social effects. The quite influential idea of object agency has been explored in detail by Bruno Latour (1999) and Alfred Gell (1998). Latour emphasizes the fact that just like people, objects cause actions and their effects have real social consequences. This can be true of objects that are perceived by people to be animate and have agency as well as those that are not. Latour (1999) uses the term "actant" to describe all people and things with agency in a symmetrical and equal way, thereby entirely dissolving the theoretical opposition of agentive subjects and inanimate objects. Gell (1998) is somewhat less willing to grant full agency to objects, instead creating a category of "secondary agency" that describes the effect of human agency through objects. In effect, Gell proposes that primary agents create secondary agents through the process of objectification. The extreme position of Latour (1999), though perhaps philosophically coherent, introduces the danger of asserting object agency to the exclusion of keeping track of how objects were important in particular times and places.

The agency of objects certainly does not always pertain; and, as Meskell argues, "theories of object agency are most efficacious when they enhance our understandings of *people's* intentions and practices" (2004:5, my emphasis).

In archaeological terms, such an understanding of past social practice only comes from a deep concern with historical, social, and cultural contexts, as described by Gosden (2005) and Pauketat and Alt (2005). In essence, a focus on the genealogy of objects or the genealogy of practice (as it is implicated in materiality) can provide the robust understanding of context through which to infer the social ramifications of changes in materiality. These genealogies provide the basis for the identification and interpretation of "recontextualizations," whereby objects move through various social contexts. Nicholas Thomas (1991) uses the idea of recontextualization to describe the transformation of ethnographic "art" objects through their movement into transnational commodity markets, museum exhibitions, and the holdings of private collectors. However, the term can be usefully applied to the movement of any object through various social contexts that redefine its referential meaning. What is more, when viewed at a larger scale, recontextualization can refer to the transformation of a corpus of material practices over time, as in the case of "Roman" pottery in Britain (Gosden 2005) or the changing use of posts in a variety of domestic and ritual settings (Pauketat and Alt 2005).

In agreement with the procedural agenda set forth by Pauketat and Alt (2005), I believe the most efficacious way to study past social practice is through an understanding of three related aspects of materiality: the genealogy of objects (the corpus of a class of material culture, including its range of variation in time and space), the genealogy of practice (how objects, including architecture, were made and used through time), and, finally, the interrelations of practices as they were implicated across various classes of material culture. These avenues of study refer to the indexicality (Gell 1998) and citational (Jones 2005) capabilities of objects and social practice. Drawing on the function of citations in texts, which refer to other texts and in the process reiterate their importance, we can view social practice itself as embedded in a network of citations (Butler 1993; Derrida 1982). For example, Judith Butler (1993) and Rosemary Joyce (1998, 2000a) discuss how actions are gendered with reference to prior gendered performances that thereby build and accentuate their social connotation. Similarly, the object world is enmeshed in referential fields of material citations (akin to what Gell [1998] calls "indexes") as each action through materiality makes reference to and acquires its meaning from past and present objectifications. Importantly, social practice through material referential fields, or "citational fields," as Andrew

Jones (2001, 2005) calls them, is not necessarily conservative. Rather, the citation of past or spatially removed events and actions in new social contexts or in innovative combinations enables the constitution of new and different meanings (Jones 2005). When based on corpuses of material culture that are specific to particular contexts, the concept is therefore useful in understanding how material practices were used to create social worlds and how these practices were changed or transformed through time. The work of Gosden (2005) and Pauketat and Alt (2005) is above all a focus on the transformations of material practices, the most obvious of which are transformations in the form, temporality, and space of material production, use, and deposition; but by inference these correlate also with changes in the constitution of persons and communities.

## The Contexts of Exchange

The forms and reasons for exchange in the past are best understood by situating acts of exchange within the broad social contexts of materiality outlined above. While all material culture is a citation in one way or another, at the very least referencing the practices that engage objects of the same kind, individual exchanged objects are often particularly important citations that bridge multiple and significant distances in social space and time. Approaching the indexicality of exchanged objects as citations or extensions requires the sort of contextual genealogies that allow us to be attuned to instances of transformation. This is an empirical enterprise that necessitates leaving behind the received wisdom of evolutionary social typology and its corresponding economic categories. As Nicholas Thomas (1991:39) argues, "the transformations and contextual mutations of objects cannot be appreciated if it is presumed that gifts are invariably gifts and commodities invariably commodities."

This contextual approach runs counter to many archaeological studies of exchange in the Eastern Woodlands of North America, studies that have been mired in categories of social organization and types of exchange, thereby often overlooking actual past human practice. In general, modes of exchange have been differentiated according to a dichotomy that opposes group mechanisms of integration and the fulfillment of economic requirements with individuals' tendencies to aggrandize power and wealth. Exchange among the smallest and most mobile social groups has been most often interpreted as generalized reciprocity, argued to be both economically practical (or necessary) and socially integrative (Sahlins 1972). These functionalist interpretations of social interaction and exchange foreground the economic and biological needs of small-scale societies, ranging from the biological imperative for mate exchange to insurance against periodic food production shortfalls (e.g., Anderson 1995; Anderson and Hanson 1988; Braun 1986; Braun and Plog 1982; Brose 1994; Clay 1998; Dye 1996; Jefferies 1996; Walthall and Koldehoff 1998). This "risk management" perspective, ultimately supported by the work of behavioral ecologists with hunter-gatherers in marginal environments, posits that the function of exchange and associated practices, such as feasts among hunter-gatherers, is to build alliance networks and redistribute wealth and subsistence goods, thereby pooling economic risks (Brown 1985; Kelly 1995:168–201; Wiessner 1982). Thus, recognized periods of heightened exchange are assumed to correspond with amplified social and economic risk associated with changes in climate, population size, and subsistence systems (Braun and Plog 1982).

In contrast, theories for exchange among larger, more socially complex, and typically agricultural social groups have focused on its sociopolitical function, namely, the development and maintenance of hierarchical power through unequal access to goods and information networks and the "prestige goods" or "primitive valuables" trafficked through them (e.g., Brown et al. 1990; Peregrine 1991; Welch 1991). The concept of a prestige good, however, presents a confounding tautology within archaeological interpretation, as *prestige* is somehow defined by what is gained through the possession and use of prestige goods, and prestige goods are those whose use gives one prestige (Robb 1999:6). Indeed, defining whether prestige or the prestige good came first is problematic, as some researchers argue that power and domination would have been necessary to orchestrate the widespread and sometimes high-volume exchange networks evident at large "ceremonial centers" or "gateways," yet others see power as derived from the products of these very networks (e.g., Gibson 1996; Smith 1986). The actions of elites are not always interpreted as the consequence of individual political ambition alone, but also attributed to economic adaptations. Thus, a dichotomy between "functional" and "exploitative," "adaptationist" and "political," and, ultimately, "corporate" and "network" strategies lends dynamism to elite behavior and its social contexts (e.g., Blanton et al. 1996; Brumfiel and Earle 1987; Gilman 1981; Saitta 1999). Even still, prestige-goods models arguably condense and limit the kinds and scales of social relationships created or maintained by the use, display, or exchange of different objects.

These interpretations of non-capitalist exchange derive explicitly and implicitly from the economic typologies proposed by Sahlins (1972) and Polanyi (1944). In fact, various models used to explain the same archaeological context can sometimes be seen to embody several typological categories.

Hopewell exchange, characterized by the long-distance movement of a variety of artifacts and raw materials throughout much of North America, has been interpreted in a variety of ways that can be grouped into three categories. First, exchange of Hopewell objects has been construed as part of a system of centralized redistribution that implies a chiefdom-like tribute system (Griffin 1965). Second, Hopewell objects are understood as prestige goods that became significant markers of status and were exchanged between high-ranking individuals in a network with important elements of competition (Braun 1986; Brose 1979a, 1979b; Struever and Houart 1972). Finally, exchange is argued to be part of alliance-building strategies that were not necessarily competitive and did not only involve elites (Braun and Plog 1982; Seeman 1995). Although archaeologists now recognize that Hopewell interaction was comprised of many distinct social processes (Carr 2006a; Seeman 1995), the differences in interpretation described here are drawn as much from typological assumptions as they are from archaeological data. In many of these models, the exchange of subsistence or utilitarian materials is viewed as ancillary to prominent formal exchanges. Thus, formal exchanges paved the way for beneficial exchanges of goods that either provided insurance against food shortages or fostered elite control of those goods to bolster political power.

These are good examples of how long-distance exchange has been generally interpreted among small-scale and middle-range societies. The use of types of exchange that ostensibly correspond with social variation are problematic because interpretations tend to be decontextualized and either uncritically accept some sort of "law" of reciprocity or give suspiciously Western economic and political readings to gifts, reciprocity, authority, and gender (Weiner 1994). Consequently, researchers using exchange models rooted in economic theory and social typology not only posit the value of objects a priori but also predetermine which items are significant for the purposes of exchange. For example, outside of standardized tribute or market exchange systems, pottery is nearly always considered to be locally made and not exchanged. The reasons for this assumption usually include the wide availability of materials, the consequent ubiquity of pottery production across the landscape, and the tendency for vessels to be bulky and heavy, making them cumbersome to transport compared to most preciosities (Fie 2006). More importantly, earthenware vessels are presumed not to have been exchange items because they are understood to be a product of the domestic economy and particularly the immediate labor of women, who are assumed to not be major players in the public domain.

However, if we take seriously the transformative capabilities of objects, all things have the potential to become important items of exchange depending on the social context. As Melanesian ethnography repeatedly shows, the products of women's labor are often quite critical objects of exchange (e.g., MacKenzie 1991; Strathern 1988; Weiner 1992). Ultimately, even the most common materials of daily practice can be seen as linked to particular people or qualities of people and thereby can be constitutive of social relationships. Maure MacKenzie's (1991) description of *bilums* made by women in Papua New Guinea is a prominent example of a utilitarian item with significant exchange value deriving, in part, from biographic qualities of the objects. Bilums are string netbags used by men, women, and children for the utilitarian tasks of storing or carrying a wide range of objects. Netbags are therefore functionally useful, but they also have aesthetic value as an ornament that is worn on the body, and a variety of styles serve as markers of cultural and social identity. What is more, bilums are symbolically linked to the womb and reproduction, and they are central to much of social life, marking individual achievements, clan membership, and transitions in the life cycle, as well as maintaining ritual and kinship ties and serving as items of wealth (Tilley 1999:64). The netbags themselves are produced by women, but men take some of them and add additional features such as feathers in the context of initiation ceremonies, in the process claiming the bilums as products of their own labor. However, this elaboration of the netbag does not erase the woman's relationship to it. Rather, the bilum "stands for detachable aspects of a woman's identity that are still indelibly linked to her" (Tilley 1999:66). Thus, a man's bilum is the product of multiple authorship, and as it passes through various stages of production and use it acquires a biography that embodies relationships between men and women. As exchange items that accumulate biographies, bilums mediate relationships between men and women and different social groups, sometimes serving as payments of bride wealth.

Thus, meaningful exchange objects emerge out of a corpus of material practices that help constitute the social world. In a generic sense, objects acquire value because they embody memory and knowledge (Hendon 2000), and it is the task of the researcher to investigate the various functions served by a class of objects that reveal its contributions to the ongoing process of cultural construction. In archaeological research, this is best accomplished by tracing genealogies of material practice over time and space and analyzing potential contextual transformations. Rather than be limited by functionalist platitudes, such an endeavor can lend specificity, in terms of actual social and cultural process, to explanations for observed variations in patterns of exchange. Indeed, archaeological evidence in the Americas has already indicated that pre-Columbian exchange was exceptionally variable in terms of what, how often, and in what social context it took place (Earle 1994:420). Moreover, most archaeologists also recognize that exchange is contingent upon variable social and historical factors so that the forms and scales of exchange do not dependably correspond with structural aspects of social or political organization (Saitta 2000).

The present study is concerned with two commonplace and widespread classes of material culture that were each routinely moved across the landscape among Woodland period Swift Creek cultures: carved wooden paddles and earthenware vessels. Removed from the specificities of context, a number of social practices might all potentially explain the distribution of these objects, including migrations, seasonal rounds, post-marital residence patterns, pilgrimages, and various kinds of exchange. Of course, deciphering among these alternatives is possible only through detailed contextual analyses that attempt to reconstruct historical, social, and cultural circumstances. With enough data, a genealogy of material practice can reveal how these objects were employed in daily life and how practices varied over time and space, thereby presenting the opportunity to understand how and why the objects were moved. Identification of variation and transformations in material practice ultimately depends on definitions of scale, and the most thorough understandings derive from tacking back and forth between multiple scales of analysis (Nassaney and Sassaman 1995; Pauketat and Alt 2005). Our understandings of the Swift Creek archaeological culture are impoverished without situating the phenomenon within the context of the various local social groups that made and used complicated stamped pottery, as well as vice versa. Indeed, Swift Creek Complicated Stamped pottery appears as a veneer across the lower southeastern landscape and seems to have connected a variety of distinct social groups with unique histories (Ashley and Wallis 2006). The reasons for the adoption of Swift Creek pottery, the use of complicated stamped vessels, and, ultimately, the movement of individual carved or stamped objects grew out of unique (though connected) historical and social circumstances that require analytical attention. In what follows in subsequent chapters, multiple lines of evidence indicate that earthenware vessels were exchanged as significant gifts that constituted social relationships across considerable distances along the Atlantic coast. This conclusion emerges out of a reconstruction of object worlds and the specificities of past practice at local levels that can be situated within the global-scale phenomenon that is Swift Creek culture. As a point of departure, I now turn to the Swift Creek archaeological culture.

# 2
# The Swift Creek Cultures

The Swift Creek archaeological culture is defined almost exclusively by the production and use of complicated stamped pottery across the Woodland period lower-southeastern United States. Specifically, Swift Creek Complicated Stamped pottery became popular circa AD 100 and continued to be produced until around AD 850 in present-day Georgia and portions of adjacent states (see Figure I.1 in introduction) (Stephenson et al. 2002:318). Although the term *Swift Creek* has often been used to designate both a type of pottery and an archaeological culture, an explanation for the fluorescence and persistence of complicated stamping must begin with recognition of the apparent social diversity that existed among the people who made and used this type of pottery (Anderson 1998:275; Ashley and Wallis 2006:5). Indeed, as Jerald Milanich indicates, "like . . . its taxonomic siblings, Swift Creek has proven to be a handful. When it comes to its role as a ceramic assemblage, it is well behaved. But when Swift Creek is used to designate a single culture, it can be a schizoid problem" (1999:704). This chapter summarizes previous research of "Swift Creek" contexts and highlights the archaeological diversity that the term encompasses with focus on technology, chronology, social and cultural attributes, social interaction, and the meaning of designs. At the end of the chapter, I explore new interpretations of Swift Creek interaction based on the representative techniques evident in designs and their spatial distribution on vessels.

The Middle Woodland period (ca. 200 BC to AD 400) saw extensive long-distance exchange and interaction networks which culminated in the "Hopewell Interaction Sphere" that spanned most of the Midwest and surrounding regions (e.g., Caldwell 1964). With artifacts and raw materials of chert, copper, galena, marine shell, mica, and obsidian exchanged or carried long distances across the landscape, Hopewell interaction imparted a semblance of cultural and religious continuity among many otherwise distinct Middle Woodland societies (Caldwell 1964; Struever 1964). The fluorescence of long-distance exchange and earthen mound building in some areas, along with the preferential treatment of some individuals in burial, arguably reflects the rise of more powerful descent groups that vied for increasing political influence (Anderson and Mainfort 2002:10; Smith 1986:48). While cultural connections were indeed far-reaching, many Middle Woodland societies were comparatively insular and apparently did not participate in exchange networks or manifest power disparities among kin groups to a significant degree (Anderson and Mainfort 2002:10). In fact, materials derived from Hopewell interactions were overwhelmingly concentrated at major ceremonial mound centers, especially the geometric earthworks and large conical burial mounds in southern Ohio and west-central Illinois. Likewise, connections further afield, such as in the lower Mississippi valley, northern Alabama, and western Georgia, were also restricted to earthen mound centers, where mortuary regimes and exotic materials indicate Hopewell influence (Cobb 1991:176). Hopewell materials were brought south to the Swift Creek cultures at mound centers in western areas of Georgia and Florida; and, moving in the opposite direction, Swift Creek pottery was deposited at Hopewell sites toward the north (Brose 1979a; Kellar 1979; Smith 1979). Swift Creek cultures toward the east were somewhat less connected to Hopewell exchange networks (Seeman 1979).

Like Hopewell, Swift Creek complicated stamping seems to have been implicated in social connections across various distinct societies rather than being the trademark of a monolithic and insular culture. Some of the earliest complicated stamping is associated with Deptford contexts in northwestern Florida and southwestern Georgia (Knight and Mistovich 1984:217–220; Stephenson et al. 2002:335). As the popularity of complicated stamping proliferated across large portions of present-day Florida, Georgia, and Alabama, as well as the edges of South Carolina and Tennessee, broad regional connections became apparent. There is a strong association between Weeden Island cultures and Late Swift Creek Complicated Stamped pottery in southwestern Georgia and northwestern Florida (Milanich 1994:166; Sears 1962; Willey 1949:396–409). Charles Fairbanks referred to the relationship between Swift Creek, Weeden Island, and earlier pottery series as one of "merging" between groups in southern Georgia and northern Florida (1952:289). Going further, William Sears (1956) equated pottery directly with people to suggest that Weeden Island pottery indicated activity areas of an elite class in contrast to a subservient Swift Creek pottery-using group. This correlation is unlikely, but the Swift Creek series is known to have generally preceded the production of Weeden Island pottery and then continued to be produced alongside Weeden Island wares in northwestern Florida and southwestern Georgia.

While the eastern panhandle Late Swift Creek populations between the Aucilla and Apalachicola rivers are associated with Weeden Island culture, Early Swift Creek west of the Apalachicola River shows similarities to the contemporaneous Marksville archaeological culture of the lower Mississippi valley. Western panhandle Swift Creek manifestations are different enough to receive a different appellation, Santa Rosa–Swift Creek (or Florida Marksville). Santa Rosa–Swift Creek sites include both Swift Creek Complicated Stamped and Santa Rosa series pottery, the latter consisting of many types that are considered Marksville variants, such as Alligator Bayou Stamped, Basin Bayou Stamped, Santa Rosa Stamped, and Santa Rosa Punctated (Milanich 1994:152; Stephenson et al. 2002:334; Willey 1949:372–378).

There are other affinities expressed on the various geographic peripheries of the primary Swift Creek pottery distribution. Pickwick Complicated Stamped pottery in the Tennessee River Valley is recognized as a variant of Swift Creek and tends to be a minority ware on multicomponent sites (Elliot 1998). In areas of northern and western Georgia, Swift Creek Complicated Stamped pottery is found among Cartersville assemblages, while Deptford sites in eastern Georgia and South Carolina sometimes contain complicated stamped sherds (Anderson 1998:277). On the Lower St. Johns River, in Florida, Swift Creek assemblages often include Weeden Island, St. Johns, and Deptford series sherds. Late Swift Creek sites in particular seem to include St. Johns Plain pottery as a minority ware, with the highest frequencies at mortuary mounds (Wallis 2007).

Swift Creek Complicated Stamped pottery has also been found at many important Middle and Late Woodland period sites far outside its primary distribution. These include various sites in southern Florida and Hopewell sites in Ohio and Indiana (Milanich 1994:142; Ruby and Shriner 2006; Stephenson et al. 2002:349). Clearly, complicated stamped pottery often served as the material for social connections in the Woodland period Southeast, and the diversity of contexts in which it is found may reflect an intricate history of various kinds of interaction between social groups.

## Swift Creek Technology: Wood and Earthenware

Swift Creek pottery is defined by the stamped impressions of "complicated" designs on the exterior surfaces of vessels. These designs were achieved by impressing a paddle into the surface of still-wet vessels before drying and firing. These paddles followed a long-lived tradition of pottery-manufacturing technology in the Eastern Woodlands, in which various simple-stamped, check-stamped, and fabric-impressed surface treatments were used in some of the earliest Woodland period pottery traditions (Chase 1998:49). Almost always made of wood, paddles had lines carved into them or were wrapped with fabric or cordage and stamped into vessels to achieve the desired effect. Complicated stamping appears to be a departure from the technology of the previous millennium only in the content of the designs carved into the paddles. Rather than being limited to pottery, the intricate and sometimes ornate designs found on Swift Creek pottery may, in fact, be a mere glimpse of a prolific wood-carving tradition that culminated in entire object worlds being engraved (e.g., Williams and Elliott 1998:10).

Owing to the unlikelihood of preservation, no carved wooden paddles have ever been reported, although at least one earthenware complicated stamped paddle has been found (Milanich 1994:146). Impressions on vessels that show the grain of the wood and characteristic cracks indicate that the paddles were primarily wooden. Frankie Snow (1998:71) suggests that the long axis of the wooden paddles was oriented parallel to both the wood grain and the cracks that sometimes developed on the paddle face. Judging from stamped impressions, the faces of the paddles themselves appear to have been roughly rectangular (Snow 1998:70) and generally about 10 to 15 centimeters in length and 10 centimeters or less in width. Both sides of the paddle head may have been carved, but, interestingly, only one example of a vessel stamped with two designs has ever been documented (Snow 1998:71). There are also rare examples of negative impressions of known designs, indicating that complicated stamped sherds were occasionally used as a substitute for carved paddles (Snow 1998:67). Snow calls these sherds "convenience paddles" and documents paddle (positive) and sherd (negative) matches at the same site in central Georgia (1998:67).

The technique for impressing designs into vessels appears to have been somewhat variable and may have been context specific (Wallis 2007:215). Snow (1998:72), who has analyzed more Swift Creek designs than any other researcher, argues that the primary purpose for paddle stamping was to bind clay coils during manufacture. This assertion is based on a number of attributes common to Swift Creek Complicated Stamped pottery. First, the whole design, as it would have appeared on the wooden paddle, is almost never registered on a vessel. Instead, the extremities of the paddle, particularly the proximal end, seem to have rarely had contact with the wet clay surface. Second, design orientation is variable on vessels. Representative figures such as "masks" or animals, although they are almost always oriented with the head toward the distal end of the wooden paddle, are turned a number of directions on vessel surfaces. Third, overstamping is common, resulting from the frequent overlapping of paddle impressions. Finally, stamped impressions were often smoothed over prior to drying and firing. All of these characteristics seem to indicate that clear, unadulterated design impressions were not intended, but that overlapping designs covering the vessel achieved the desired effect (Snow 1998:72).

In contrast to Snow's (1998) assertion, Bettye Broyles (1968:54) argues that the primary purpose of Swift Creek paddle stamping was to transfer designs onto vessels. Analyzing vessels primarily from Kolomoki, Fairchilds Landing, Mandeville, and the Quartermaster site, Broyles observed a general lack of overstamping and the prevalence of spaces between stamping impressions. If the carved wooden paddles were used to shape the vessels, Broyles reasoned, then "overstamping . . . would necessarily result from pounding the vessel into shape" (1968:54).

I believe the divergent conclusions of Snow and Broyles are due, in part, to their analysis of different assemblages and the contextually variable role of carved paddles in the manufacturing process (Wallis 2007:215). Like Broyles (1968), I find it unlikely that carved paddles were always used to form vessels into their final shapes, unless the un-carved sides of the paddles were used or the vessels were smoothed before final design application. At the same time, the seemingly haphazard and overlapping placement of paddle impressions, and prevalence of smoothing on some vessel surfaces, demonstrates that crisp and complete designs were often not desired. In short, carved paddle stamping may have been applied after vessels had been formed into their desired shape but the resulting surface treatment was somewhat variable in its execution. The practice of stamping a vessel with a carved paddle may have been more significant than the quality of the design registered on the final product.

While there are some general trends in vessel attributes that lend themselves to fine seriation (as discussed below), the overall morphology and function of "Swift Creek" vessels was variable. In fact, Swift Creek complicated stamping seems to have been used on vessels of many shapes, sizes, and tempers. Indeed, in many regions Swift Creek complicated stamping appears to have simply replaced the earlier Deptford check stamping on a similar suite of vessel forms (Sears 1952:103).

## Chronology

Swift Creek Complicated Stamped was formally defined as a pottery type by Jesse Jennings and Charles Fairbanks (1939) one year after Arthur Kelly (1938) had published a preliminary report of excavations at the Swift Creek type site near Macon, Georgia. Based largely on Kelly's (1938) stratigraphic excavations in Mound A, Early, Middle, and Late Swift Creek types were defined. Early Swift Creek pottery is characterized by weakly impressed designs with narrow lands, the prevalence of rectilinear designs, tetrapodal basal supports, and very small rim folds or notched or scalloped rims. Middle Swift Creek pottery tends to have more curvilinear motifs, stamped impressions are better registered, and rim folds are more prominent. Finally, Late Swift Creek pottery has "carelessly" applied designs, designs applied in restricted zones (usually the top third of the vessel), and very large rim folds. This chronology has been generally interpreted as the rise, culmination, and decline of a pottery style (Caldwell 1958:37).

Outside of central Georgia, the "Middle" Swift Creek designation has been rarely used. Based on stratigraphic analysis of Swift Creek on the Gulf Coast of Florida, Gordon Willey (1949:378) independently defined Early and Late Swift Creek varieties. Many of the attributes used to differentiate Early and Late Swift Creek on the Gulf Coast were consistent with Kelly's (1938) findings, including the differences noted in rim form, design style, and stamping execution. However, Willey (1949) found no evidence of Middle Swift Creek in northwestern Florida, a disparity that may be due to the limited date range of the Swift Creek type site. In comparison to other assemblages from northwestern Florida and southern Georgia, Mound A at the Swift Creek site primarily dates to the Early and Middle Swift Creek phases with very few examples of Late Swift Creek pottery (Fairbanks 1952:288; Price 2003). Throughout the geographic distribution of Swift Creek pottery, chronological trends have been noted not only in the execution of stamping but in the designs themselves, with Early Swift Creek designs generally less complex in comparison to Late Swift Creek designs (Anderson 1998:277; Fairbanks 1952:288). However, these labels are subjective and the trends may be locally specific, making rim forms more reliable time markers than stamping designs.

Vernon Knight and Timothy Mistovich (1984) offered a refinement of Kelly's (1938) chronology, based on work in the Chattahoochee River drainage in southwestern Georgia and southeastern Alabama. Their Mandeville, Kolomoki, and Quartermaster phases, based on pottery from each of these respective sites in the region, roughly correspond with Kelly's (1938) Early, Middle, and Late Swift Creek chronology. A 50-year gap between Mandeville and Kolomoki phases was inferred by Knight and Mistovich (1984), but this temporal gap is filled by pottery from the submound midden at Hartford in central Georgia (Snow and Stephenson 1998; Stephenson et al. 2002:342). However, outside of the Chattahoochee River area, the Knight and Mistovich (1984) chronology is rarely used. In northwestern Florida, for example, Kolomoki-phase pottery is simply called Late Swift Creek (Smith 1999).

## The Diverse Social Landscape

The Middle and Late Woodland periods saw major earthen mound-building projects, numerous multi-house circular villages, and widespread long-distance exchange and interaction. However, there was also much social and cultural diversity across the Southeast during this time, and some populations were comparatively unconnected and apparently chose not to participate in these cultural trends. Some of the societies that made up the Swift Creek archaeological culture were undoubtedly significant players on the social landscape, but the spatial distribution of complicated stamped pottery also encompasses an impressive amount of diversity in monuments, settlement, mobility, and interaction. The broad range of this diversity necessitates an emphasis on particular contexts and highlights the problems associated with treating Swift Creek as a coherent "culture."

As with many archaeological cultures of the Eastern Woodlands, Swift Creek culture and cultural history were constructed primarily through pottery typology and seriation and, more recently, through absolute dating of carbon attached to or associated with pottery. This regional trend results from the ubiquity of pottery in the archaeological record, particularly at sites with poor preservation, where little else is found. However, the failure to incorporate other archaeological data in the construction of archaeological cultures has sometimes led to interpretive problems in considering social interaction and culture change, or worse, the uncritical conflation of ceramic types and actual cultural or ethnic groups. Archaeological cultures are admittedly necessary abstractions that archaeologists must use to structure the heterogeneous archaeological record, yet uncritical use of these devices harbors the corresponding tendency to mask archaeological differences among assemblages, sites, and landscapes, especially when they are based on a single class of artifact (Binford and Sabloff 1982).

At the very least, variation in subsistence, technology, and settlement patterns among regions provides the basis for differentiating subgroups within widespread archaeological cultures. For example, the Deptford archaeological culture, which stretches across much of the same expansive lower southeastern region as Swift Creek culture, has been recently reconstructed based on new archaeological evidence that indicates considerable cultural diversity corresponding with geographical and ecological regions. Deptford was first defined as a coastal culture by excavations at the type site (9CH2) near the mouth of the Savannah River (Caldwell 1952; Waring and Holder 1968) and by subsequent research by Milanich (1971) on Cumberland Island. A year-round coastal tradition that was based on maritime resources was indicated by the predominance of shellfish and fish in middens and the discovery of both winter and summer houses (Milanich 1971, 1994:124–215). Sites with Deptford series pottery on the interior coastal plain, much smaller than most coastal sites, were assumed to indicate short-term occupation of inland forests, probably hunting and foraging expeditions that targeted deer, hickory nuts, and acorns (Fradkin and Milanich 1977; Milanich 1994:120–123; Tesar 1980:688–794). However, this model of coastal settlement with only periodic forays inland was complicated by the discovery and excavation of substantial, year-round "Deptford" sites on the interior coastal plain (Anderson 1985; Brooks and Canouts 1984; Stephenson et al. 2002). Although these sites contain check-stamped pottery characteristic of the Deptford series, the assemblages are qualitatively different, with a much higher frequency of linear check-stamping decoration on pottery (Milanich 2004). In addition, so-called Deptford in western Georgia appears more closely related to other archaeological cultures with check-stamped pottery to the north and west, such as Cartersville (Smith 1975; Stephenson et al. 2002:331–332). Moreover, inland "Deptford" sites contain consistently greater numbers of stone and bone tools in combination with a subsistence regime focused on deer (Milanich 2004). Due to these differences, and because there is little convincing evidence that inland and coastal populations were connected beyond the popularity of check-stamped pottery, separate archaeological complexes and different developmental sequences are recognized, including Gulf, Atlantic, and Interior/Riverine Deptford (Milanich 2004; Stephenson et al. 2002).

The Swift Creek archaeological culture is in need of similar revision in order to emphasize the temporal and cultural variation that the term encompasses. As Milanich argues, "It does not make a great deal of sense to label as Swift Creek an A.D. 100 shell midden site on the panhandle coast of Florida, an A.D. 700 site near Macon, Georgia, and a site of unknown antiquity near Brunswick, Georgia" (2002:371). In fact, similar Gulf, Atlantic, and Interior/Riverine Swift Creek subregions might be usefully recognized based on different subsistence and settlement patterns. Santa Rosa–Swift Creek sites are overwhelmingly located on the "coastal strip," on or near the coast (Stephenson et al. 2002:342). Swift Creek sites along the Atlantic seaboard are also primarily within the coastal sector, and subsistence remains from sites in both regions indicate an almost exclusively maritime diet of fish and shellfish (Byrd 1997; deFrance 1993; Fradkin 1998; Reitz and Quitmyer 1988). Among Santa Rosa–Swift Creek sites, at least three configurations of middens have been identified: ring middens, linear middens with long axes oriented along the coastline, and small dumps (Milanich 1994:144–145; Stephenson et al. 2002). The same configurations have also been identified along the Atlantic coast (Ashley and Wallis 2006; Saunders 1998).

Riverine-focused Swift Creek groups occupied central and southern Georgia with an entirely different subsistence and settlement strategy. Subsistence data from the interior coastal plain are woefully underrepresented because of a persistent preservation bias. However, data from a few well-preserved contexts in the "pine barrens" indicate that deer overwhelmingly made up the bulk of the Woodland period diet (Carder et al. 2004). At the Hartford site (9PU1) near the Ocmulgee River, deer comprised 35 percent of the MNI and nearly 95 percent of the biomass in the vertebrate assemblage (Carder et al. 2004:31). Birds and other mammals made up most of the remainder of the assemblage, with almost negligible meat weights coming from freshwater fishes and turtles. Settlement data come primarily from the nearby Ocmulgee Big Bend region from Snow's (1977) extensive pedestrian surveys. In this area the settlement pattern consisted mostly of small seasonal resource-extraction sites with a few larger sites serving as central or base sites (Snow 1977; Stephenson et al. 2002:345). The implication is that communities were relatively mobile on a seasonal basis as part of an adaptive strategy that focused on deer hunting. This degree of mobility stands in contrast to the more permanent settlements evident on the Gulf and Atlantic coasts. However, the Ocmulgee Big Bend data should not be used as generalizations for the entire interior of Georgia since many large and more permanently settled sites (including Hartford) existed within the interior as well.

In contrast to the Deptford evidence, where cultural relationships between subregions are somewhat tenuous, design matches on Swift Creek pottery indicate that artifacts were carried between coastal and inland villages (Ashley et al. 2007; Kirkland 2003). Thus, diverse cultures across the lower Southeast were connected via carved paddles or stamped pots but often with little other evidence of cultural influence across subregions. Swift Creek pottery-producing cultures appear to have embodied the entire range of cultural and social diversity that existed during the Woodland period, ranging from small groups of mobile hunter-gatherers to larger and more centralized populations that undertook major mound-building projects. Even with this range of diversity, however, the proliferation of ceremonial mound centers and circular villages are important topics of discussion for their apparent connections to Swift Creek pottery-producing cultures.

## Ceremonial Centers

More than merely a "precocious" pottery tradition of otherwise simple societies (Caldwell 1958:44), Swift Creek Complicated Stamped pottery is associated with large monuments that were once assigned to the Mississippian period. Platform mounds were constructed for the first time on a large scale during the Middle Woodland period (Jefferies 1994; Lindauer and Blitz 1997; Mainfort 1988; Pluckhahn 2003; Thunen 1998). Many Woodland period platform mounds were associated with the Swift Creek archaeological culture, including at the sites of Swift Creek, Kolomoki, Mandeville, Annewakee Creek, Cold Springs, and probably Evelyn in Georgia, Garden Creek in western North Carolina, and McKeithen and possibly Block-Sterns in Florida (Anderson 1998:290). These mounds generally lack evidence of buildings on their summits and probably functioned as ceremonial stages, access to which might have been restricted to privileged factions (Jefferies 1994; Lindauer and Blitz 1997). Many of the mounds, which vary in size and scale, were built in stages over time, indicating that the functions and meanings of the monuments were continually changing through recurrent practice (Jefferies 1994; Lindauer and Blitz 1997). For example, the Swift Creek Mound A was initially constructed as a low earthen platform but became an accretional mound with at least seven "midden" layers that maintained a platform shape at various stages of accretion (Jefferies 1994:72; Kelly and Smith 1975).

Anderson (1998) suggests that sites with platform mounds were positioned as gateways or trading centers to take advantage of the exchange of shell and other items into the interior of the Eastern Woodlands. This idea is consistent with a common Middle Woodland theme of dispersed populations living in scattered households or small villages and coming together periodically at regional centers (Anderson 1998:283). However, some platform mounds were also bordered by villages with resident populations. Kolomoki's Mound A, the largest example of a Middle Woodland platform mound (ca. 17 meters high), had a substantial village population (Pluckhahn 2003). The function of platform mounds may also have varied. At McKeithen, a Weeden Island village site with three mounds, the platform mound was apparently built to support the residence of a high ranking "big man" (Milanich et al. 1997). It is also possible that mound complexes with associated villages were ceremonial centers for surrounding social groups as well, but the association of ceremonial practice with a select resident group may have been distinctly different from the practice of converging at "vacant" ceremonial centers.

In northern Georgia, Mark Williams and Jennifer Freer Harris (1998) noted an even spacing among Swift Creek mound sites, about 30 kilometers apart. These sites appear to have been mortuary mounds without associated villages and very little associated midden. Furthermore, these sites are often located on the tops of high ridges, away from the river floodplains that are comparatively richer in subsistence resources. Williams and Harris (1998) label these mound sites as "shrines," substantiating the idea that Middle Woodland populations gathered at vacant ceremonial centers.

Other sites that lack platform mounds are also likely to have been "civic-ceremonial" gathering centers for disparate populations, including sites such as Little River, Milamo, Fortson Mound, and Hartford (Stephenson et al. 2002). At the Hartford site (9PU1), excavation within a submound midden revealed a large structure with an interior hearth (Snow and Stephenson 1998). At 12.5 meters across, this structure was larger than might be expected for Middle Woodland domiciles (cf. Anderson 1985; Pluckhahn 2003). The site is at the confluence of major historic Indian trails and was apparently a crossroads during the Woodland period as well. The site contained exotic marine fauna and other nonlocal materials such as quartz crystals, mica, hematite, graphite, galena, copper-bearing silver, and chert from the Ridge and Valley province (Carder et al. 2004). Faunal analysis of the hearth contents also indicates the preferential selection of choice cuts of deer meat. All of this evidence led researchers to conclude that the Hartford submound context represents a ceremonial center where groups gathered periodically (Carder et al. 2004; Stephenson et al. 2002).

Elsewhere, permanently nucleated villages constructed their own mortuary and ceremonial spaces sometimes without obvious contributions from populations living beyond the immediate region, in some cases perhaps corresponding with more insular or alienated people (Knight 2001; Milanich 1994; Milanich et al. 1984, 1997). Residential sites with adjacent mortuary mounds, for example, are not uncommon on the Florida Gulf Coast (Willey 1949). However, even relatively modest mounds and the village ring middens themselves frequently contain Hopewellian "prestige items" that show connections to the Midwest (Seeman 1979; Stephenson et al. 2002:242–243). In fact, baked clay figurines are not uncommon within Santa Rosa–Swift Creek and Swift Creek middens along the Gulf Coast and are presumed to be associated with the Hopewell Interaction Sphere (Keller and Carr 2006; Milanich 1994:148). In general, Hopewell Interaction Sphere items seem to be concentrated at Early Swift Creek and Santa Rosa–Swift Creek mortuary sites in western Florida and Georgia, with the largest sites containing the most numerous exotic items (Seeman 1979). Although there is still much to understand about the social structure and practice that was manifested at mound centers, the variations in the size and orientations of locations on the built landscape may reflect major differences in both the mobility and the degree of connectivity of various social groups across the lower Southeast.

## Swift Creek Villages

Many large Swift Creek sites appear to have been organized according to a similar, basically circular community plan, showing continuity with Archaic and Early Woodland site structure. Circular and horseshoe-shaped middens in Swift Creek contexts have been frequently interpreted as village sites corresponding to the arrangement of houses around a central plaza (Bense 1998; Bense and Watson 1979; Stephenson et al. 2002:346; Thomas and Campbell 1993; Wallis 2007). At some sites numerous postmolds and even substantial fragments of burned daub near the perimeter of these predominantly shell-constituted rings support the interpretation of these sites as villages, although no posthole patterns have been recorded (Stephenson et al. 2002:346). Considerable morphological variability exists among the Swift Creek ring middens in Florida and Georgia. A continuous midden of dense shell occasionally over a meter high or a series of discrete middens arranged in an arc are both common configurations of the village perimeter. Both complete, closed circles and semi-circular or horseshoe shaped middens have been observed. The orientations of the openings of the semi-circular middens are variable and do not conform to any pattern (Stephenson et al. 2002:346).

Based on seasonality studies and radiocarbon assays, many Swift Creek circular villages appear to have been occupied for long periods of time or were returned to repeatedly over many years. At the Horseshoe Bayou site near Choctawatchee Bay, Florida, for example, the species of fish represented in the faunal assemblage suggest occupation during every season, while radiocarbon results indicate that the duration of Swift Creek activity may have been protracted over more than two centuries (Bense 1998:253–255).

The size of Swift Creek circular villages seems to have been at least interregionally variable. Judith Bense (1998:257) reports an average diameter of approximately 100 meters for Santa Rosa–Swift Creek villages, but villages may be as small as 50 meters in diameter on the Atlantic coast of Florida (Smith and Handley 2002; Wallis 2007). Plazas are generally characterized as swept clean (Stephenson et al. 2002:342; Thomas and Campbell 1993); however, a notable exception was discovered at the Bernath site in the western panhandle of Florida, where more than 300 individuals were estimated to have been interred within the central space (Bense 1998). Another plaza cemetery, perhaps comprised of a very low mound in the center of a circular village, may have been discovered in northeastern Florida at Greenfield site no. 8/9 (Johnson 1998). Burials at ring middens may be more common than currently understood due to inadequate sampling within "sterile" plazas (Bense 1998:269), but adjacent or nearby mounds seem to have served as mortuary repositories for most Swift Creek village populations (Stephenson et al. 2002:345). An alternative pattern is recognized in northeastern Florida, where village sites normally appear to have been situated some distance away from mortuary mounds (Ashley and Wallis 2006; Wallis 2008).

The consistency with which Swift Creek villages were organized according to a circular plan is indeed striking, showing continuity across thousands of miles and hundreds of years. Regardless of their consistency, however, circular villages are not a uniquely Swift Creek trait, having been popular among Archaic cultures (e.g., Stallings) and many contemporary and adjacent Woodland cultures (e.g., Deptford, Weeden Island, Marksville) as well (Milanich et al. 1984:53–54; Phillips 1970:265–353; Sassaman 2006). Regardless of the specific social and structural implications of circular village design, these site-plan data are important for establishing that Swift Creek groups commonly lived in multi-household villages that were oftentimes permanent or semi-permanent settlements.

## Swift Creek Interaction

Swift Creek cultures were important participants in the various far-reaching interactive networks of the Hopewell Interaction Sphere. The "Hopewell Interaction Sphere" is characterized by the long-distance movement of raw materials and finished artifacts, in the past interpreted as various unitary phenomena, including a trade network, mortuary cult, shared religion, and interaction of a peer polity (Braun 1986; Caldwell 1964; Carr 2006b; Struever and Houart 1972). However, more recent research has recognized separate and geographically distinct patterns in the distribution of "Hopewell" artifacts, patterns that are likely to have corresponded to different and distinct practices (Carr 2006a; Seeman 1995). The Hopewell Interaction Sphere is thus beginning to be deconstructed into its constituent parts in a way that beguiles the old unifying synthetic concepts that celebrated a monolithic Hopewell society across the landscape. Carr defines "Interregional Hopewell" as "a composite of multiple, diverse kinds of practices, ideas, and symbols, which had their origins in multiple, differing regional traditions and were shared or operated at multiple, different supraregional scales" (2006a:53). Caught up in this complex web of material distribution and exchange, Swift Creek cultures were on both giving and receiving ends of material exchanges and influence (Kellar 1979; Seeman 1979; Smith 1979). Copper panpipes, cymbal ornaments, stone plummets, and gorgets, along with other ostensibly Hopewellian artifacts, are found in variable frequencies at Santa Rosa–Swift Creek, Swift Creek, and other Middle Woodland sites in the Deep South and Gulf Coast (Kellar 1979; Sears 1962). Conversely, conch shells were procured from the Gulf coastal areas inhabited by Swift Creek populations and distributed as far north as Michigan and New York (Carr 2006b). In a more limited way, shell from the Atlantic coastal plain was also distributed north, as evidenced by Altamaha spiny mussel shells (*Elliptio spinosa*) with Hopewell engravings recovered from a mound site in Indiana (Farnsworth and Atwell n.d.). Swift Creek Complicated Stamped pottery is also found at several Hopewell sites in Ohio and Indiana (Ruby and Shriner 2006; Stephenson et al. 2002).

Swift Creek cultures were certainly participants in various Hopewellian networks; however, the heyday of Hopewell interaction (ca. 200 BC to AD 400) predates many of the Swift Creek cultures that thrived until at least the ninth century. The temporal extent of Hopewell manifestations is well defined in William Sears's (1962) definition of the Yent and Green Point ceremonial complexes along the Gulf Coast of Florida. Based on the sites of Crystal River, Pierce, and Yent, the "Yent Complex" dates to the Deptford phase and exhibits a long list of Hopewellian ceremonial traits. The related but later "Green Point Complex," defined by four Swift Creek phase sites, demonstrates comparatively fewer Hopewellian traits. While the coherency of Sears's (1962) complexes is questionable, they provide a description of the extent and timescale of Hopewell influence along the Gulf Coast. Hopewell traits were on the wane during Early Swift Creek times and were completely absent by the Late Swift Creek phase. However, Swift Creek interaction, as broadly defined below, mostly seems to have operated independently of Hopewell interactive networks and continued long after the demise of interregional Hopewell interaction. As with recent deconstructions of Hopewell interaction, Swift Creek interaction might be explained by various social practices that operated at differing geographical scales.

Researchers have long noticed patterns in the distribution of Swift Creek Complicated Stamped designs. Bettye Broyles (1968) pioneered the study of Swift Creek design distribution through her painstaking reconstruction of designs that facilitated their identification at multiple sites. This work was taken up primarily through the efforts of Frankie Snow (1975, 1977, 1998, 2007), who has outlined many of the attributes necessary for identifying vessels that were stamped with the same wooden paddle. These attributes include design "flaws," or idiosyncratic and non-symmetrical elements, and cracks in the wooden paddle that are evident in stamped impressions. Using these attributes as part of the "fingerprint" of each design, Snow has identified many hundreds of paddle matches that link sites across Georgia and adjacent states. Over the course of more than three decades of research, Snow (2007) has compiled an impressive database of Swift Creek designs and lists of sites where each has been found. An important limitation of the database, however, is that the bulk of the designs derive from pottery from south-central Georgia. This has resulted in more paddle matches being linked to south-central Georgia sites than to sites in any other region.

Major gaps in our knowledge of Swift Creek designs include the Gulf and Atlantic coasts of Florida. Snow has reconstructed a limited number of designs from these regions. There are also some records of design elements (Moore 1894, 1895; Saunders 1986; Wallis 2007; Willey 1949), but these have somewhat limited utility compared to Snow's (2007) robust database of south-central Georgia complete designs.

An exception to the general dearth of design data from outside south-central Georgia is southwestern Georgia, where a fair number of complete or nearly complete designs have been recorded. Both Broyles (1968) and Snow (2007) have reconstructed designs from some of the most important sites in the region, including Kolomoki, Mandeville, Quartermaster, and Fairchilds Landing. This more limited inventory of designs has allowed for the identification of several paddle matches, most notably with sites in south-central Georgia (e.g., Snow and Stephenson 1998).

Paddle matches between Swift Creek sites provide direct evidence of some form of social interaction (Snow and Stephenson 1998). On a regional scale, the identification of paddle matches or merely Swift Creek pottery outside of its primary distribution can be combined with petrographic and neutron activation analyses to help determine whether pots or paddles were carried across the landscape (Mainfort et al. 1997; Ruby and Shriner 2006; Smith 1998; Stoltman and Snow 1998). Each of these studies that attempt to explain the dissemination of Swift Creek designs deserves careful consideration as important background to the present research.

Using a fairly robust sampling strategy, James Stoltman and Frankie Snow (1998) analyzed 69 petrographic thin sections from 11 sites, including 22 thin sections from vessels that had paddle-matching designs linking them to two or more sites. The samples came primarily from the near-piedmont site of Hartford (n = 19) and the coastal plain site of Milamo (n = 15). Most of the remaining samples (n = 24) came from sites near Milamo in the coastal plain of south-central Georgia. Using a paddle match between the Hartford site and three sites in the coastal plain, the authors argue that the identification of metamorphic rock temper in all matching vessels indicates that vessels were moved from the piedmont into the coastal plain. Further, another paddle match between Hartford and a small site on the Oconee River showed enough paste similarity to indicate the movement of a vessel from the piedmont.

An alternative explanation is offered for five other designs that were identified as paddle matches linking Milamo to various sites, including Hartford, Kolomoki, and several sites in the coastal plain. The variability in paste constituents among these vessels led Stoltman and Snow to conclude that paddles were moved between sites and that vessels were made with local materials. However, the authors acknowledge that the ranges of variation in paste composition overlap between many of the sites and in most cases sample sizes are inadequate (Stoltman and Snow 1998:149–151). Therefore, the number of paddle matches attributed to paddle movement and local production may be inflated. Whatever the case, the petrographic analysis was successful in identifying both instances in which paddles were carried across the landscape and examples of when vessels were moved.

In a separate study, Betty Smith (1998) used Neutron Activation Analysis (NAA) to identify nonlocal vessels at Mandeville, Swift Creek, and Block-Sterns using 75 samples from earthenware sherds and figurines. Conducted in 1975 at the University of Georgia, this early NAA study unfortunately suffered from a number of limitations. Only 8 elements were recorded (compared to the standard 33 elements at the University of Missouri Research Reactor [MURR]), and some of the most powerful multivariate statistical methods were not employed to analyze the results. Combined with the incomplete publishing of results, these data are therefore incomparable with other NAA research. Based on a cluster analysis and comparisons of summary statistics, Smith (1998) concluded that at least one sherd from Swift Creek and one from Mandeville was nonlocal. In addition, three ceramic figurines were identified as probable nonlocal productions.

Robert Mainfort and colleagues (1997) conducted INAA at MURR on a sample of sherds from the Pinson mounds. Along with other presumably nonlocal types, there was a total of 74 Swift Creek Complicated Stamped sherds recovered during Mainfort's excavations at Pinson. Mainfort and colleagues (1997) irradiated 163 samples from Pinson, including 4 Swift Creek sherds. Based on the chemical data, all of the Swift Creek samples were assigned to the same statistical group, "3A," which was judged to be comprised of only locally produced pottery. Thus, in this case a Swift Creek carved wooden paddle appears to have been carried to Pinson mounds or manufactured there. Later, Stoltman and Mainfort (2002) objected to this finding with reference to petrographic analysis of these Swift Creek sherds. The authors argued that slight "textural differences" between the Swift Creek sherds and a limited number of presumably local specimens from Pinson (n = 32) and other nearby sites (n = 16) provided "suggestive but not conclusive evidence of nonlocal status" (Stoltman and Mainfort 2002:16). Given the preponderance of the data from the INAA study, I view these Swift Creek sherds as likely local productions.

Finally, Bret Ruby and Christine Shriner (2006) attempted to assign a source to Swift Creek pottery at the Mann site. The Mann site, a large Middle Woodland habitation site in southwestern Indiana, is known to contain copious amounts of Swift Creek Complicated Stamped pottery. Judith Rein (1974) analyzed a sample of 984 complicated stamped sherds from Mann and suggested that they were very similar to Early Swift Creek designs from central Georgia. Further, Rein argued that three of the designs found at Mann were identical to central Georgia examples (i.e., they may be paddle matches). To help explain the unusually high frequency of Swift Creek pottery at Mann and five other habitation sites within a 40-kilometer radius, Ruby and Shriner (2006) combined petrography with a number of other analytical methods, including scanning electron microscopy, x-ray diffraction, and sherd refiring. Of the 80 petrographic thin sections included in the study, 11 were derived from Swift Creek Complicated Stamped sherds. Based on the similarity of clays and paste constituents, Ruby and Shriner (2006) concluded that all of the Swift Creek samples were produced locally. In fact, of all the pottery analyzed for the project only five simple stamped sherds were judged to have been manufactured nonlocally in the Southeast.

In sum, paddle matches between sites can be explained by both paddles being carried across the landscape and vessels being moved. Alternatively, the occurrence of Swift Creek Complicated Stamped pottery at more distant sites like Pinson and Mann appears to be the result of local pottery production only. Several explanations pertain to the distribution of local and nonlocal Swift Creek pottery at sites. First, group residential mobility might explain the movement of both paddles and pots across the landscape as groups carried them during seasonal rounds and other migrations. Snow (1977:22; Stoltman and Snow 1998:152), for example, has noted that many Swift Creek sites in the Ocmulgee Big Bend region of southern Georgia appear to be "small campsites used intermittently from year to year," with some found on the floodplain and others on oak-hickory sand ridges, perhaps indicating a seasonal round. Paddle matches between these sites, evident on both locally made and imported vessels, likely indicate that both paddles and pots were carried among residential sites.

Paddle matches between more distant sites and the occurrence of Swift Creek pottery far outside its primary distribution may call for other explanations. Long-distance paddle matches with local paste have been hypothesized to correspond with patterns of post-marital residence among presumably female potters who curated their wooden paddles (Snow and Stephenson 1998; Stoltman and Snow 1998). Alternatively, nonlocal paste among Swift Creek vessels may be the result of gift giving and feasting (Ashley and Wallis 2006; Stoltman and Snow 1998). Of course, both of these explanations could pertain to related parts of a coherent social process; they are not mutually exclusive. If Swift Creek descent groups formed marriage alliances, then we might expect to find both the movement of objects owned by women with their changes in residence and gifts given to foster these relationships and repay associated debts. Further, the "marriage alliance" and "gift" explanations have been posited with implicit assumptions about the social context of wooden-paddle and earthenware-pot production and use. Most fundamentally, wooden paddles are assumed to have been owned and used exclusively by female potters, though this was not necessarily the case. Instead, paddles may have been produced and owned by wood-carving specialists or owned by descent groups rather than individuals. Evidence for the movement of wooden paddles does not necessarily correspond with the movement of individuals, married women or otherwise, since paddles may have been objects of exchange (Saunders 1998; Wallis 2006a).

Identifying what kind of social interaction resulted in the dissemination of Swift Creek designs in general and paddle matches in particular is inseparable from an understanding of Swift Creek materiality: specifically, the way that paddles, vessels, and designs were embedded in social life. Identifying the locations and frequencies of individual paddle designs is a prudent start toward this goal. For example, Snow and Keith Stephenson (1998) identify the place where a paddle "resided" based on the comparatively high frequency of its design on vessels at a site. These sorts of design distribution studies can be profitably combined with painstaking analysis of the archaeological contexts of Swift Creek paddle matches. In particular, a more complete understanding of the social context of paddle production, use, and movement can come from a detailed analysis of large assemblages in which paddle matches are identified. With this objective in mind, in the chapters that follow I present the results of my analysis of many large assemblages.

## Intrasite Design Distributions

There have also been attempts to identify patterns in the distribution of designs within sites. Bettye Broyles (1968:50) and Betty Smith (1998:113) observed possible sacred and secular dichotomies in designs at the Swift Creek and Kolomoki sites, with some designs restricted to pottery in either burial mounds or midden areas. More recently, Thomas Pluckhahn (2007) employed symmetry analysis to compare the designs that are differentially distributed at Kolomoki. Pluckhahn (2007) identified a higher frequency of symmetry in mound assemblages, compared to nearby village contexts, and interpreted this difference as an active strategy of social incorporation in ceremonial contexts.

Alternatively, Rebecca Saunders (1998) recorded patterns, in design distributions at village sites, that might represent kin group affiliations. At the Kings Bay site (9CM171a), Saunders (1998) recognized that particular designs were circumscribed within either the northern or southern half of the arc-shaped village midden while other designs were found throughout the site. Saunders (1986, 1998) employed a concept of design hierarchy to argue that all of these designs were representations of group affiliation, with those more restricted in space signifying lineages, clans, or moieties and those more widely distributed representing a larger social group or polity. In her comparison of stamping designs between Kings Bay and the nearby Mallard Creek site (9CM185), Saunders (1998) concluded that the same population inhabited both sites, perhaps for different purposes.

At the Swift Creek village area at Greenfield site #8/9 (8DU5544/5), I identified a minimum of 22 individual carved paddle designs stamped into a minimum of 187 vessels (Wallis 2007). Of the seven paddle designs with conclusive intrasite paddle matches, vessels with the same design were distributed widely across the site in ostensibly separate "household" middens. Consequently, I argued that if designs represented clans or lineages, then they were shared among these household groups. This spatial distribution does not negate the possibility that Swift Creek designs were used as emblems or totems because their circulation on vessels may have been a significant practice in constituting relationships between descent groups (Wallis 2006a). I approach the interpretation of the meaning of Swift Creek designs by combining two independent sets of data, the designs themselves and their distribution. The former is discussed below and data pertaining to the latter is the subject of subsequent chapters.

## Representational Meaning of Swift Creek Designs

Many Swift Creek designs seem to incorporate variations on a limited number of common elements: spirals, concentric circles, ladders, and chevrons, to name a few. In addition to these common elements, a robust database of reconstructed whole designs reveals common motifs, some seemingly abstract and unrecognizable and others suggestive of plant, animal, and human representations (Broyles 1968; Snow 1975, 1977, 1998, 2007). Designs generally appear to represent birds, animals, flowers, and various anthropomorphic and zoomorphic faces. Further, Snow (1998) speculates that some designs may have attributes suitable for making more specific inferences, tentatively identifying rabbits, serpents, mosquitoes, buzzards, woodpeckers, horned owls, roseate spoonbills, and mythological beings that have characteristics of multiple animals. Among the designs that appear to be faces or "masks," Snow (1998) identifies a wolf, owl, bear, and long-nosed god. These are potentially important observations for tracing the historical trajectory of particular representations. For example, the eye, circle-in-cross, and long-nosed god motifs are important Mississippian and historical-period symbols in the Southeast that may be traceable back through the Woodland period in Swift Creek art (Snow 1998).

Interpreting the representational meaning of Swift Creek designs is nearly impossible without an understanding of the rules of representation that seem to dominate Swift Creek art. There is an undeniable grammar to the structure of Swift Creek designs, and Frankie Snow has outlined many of its principles. First, Snow (1998) has recognized general geometric similarities, such as the particular prevalence of a quadripartite symmetry within designs. Bilateral symmetry and particular geometric transformations are also common (Pluckhahn 2007). In addition, there are often purposefully asymmetrical elements incorporated into otherwise perfectly symmetrical designs. A second observation of Snow (1998) is that particular elements appear to be interchangeable between designs. For example, the concentric circle ("sun/fire") and "eye" elements appear in largely identical contexts and may therefore be interchangeable and have similar meanings. Third, Snow (1998) has identified particular elements that are normally associated with one another. For example, spirals often are present in association with the supposedly moving parts of represented bodies, such as the legs of a bear or the wings of a bird.

Drawing on some of Snow's observations, I have advocated an inductive and formal analytical framework for assessing the constituent parts of Swift Creek styles (Wallis 2006b). This framework could be profitably modeled on the work of Dorothy Washburn (1995), who delineated a corpus of representational transformations for categorizing and interpreting "decorative styles" within their cultural contexts. Her premise is that visual images are more often structural descriptions of relationships rather than iconic pictures and that these representations rest on a culturally informed repertoire of geometric and metric transformations (Washburn 1995). Structural transformations are a necessary tool for artists who attempt to render three-dimensional images onto two-dimensional surfaces, and a relatively conservative corpus of these transformations is assumed to make up an artistic tradition with limited degrees of freedom for individual artisans working within it (Washburn 1995). The essential points are that transformational rules inform artistic styles, that these rules can be systematically understood by archaeologists, and that rules of representation and transformation may reflect structural aspects of a society.

## Split Representation

An important trend in Swift Creek representation that I have observed primarily concerns designs that appear to depict faces (or "masks" using Snow's [1998] terminology), but also animals and other beings (Wallis 2006b). Although these faces do indeed have characteristics that make them distinct and might differentiate them according to different animals or persons, an equally profitable focus of inquiry concerns the strict rules of representation to which these designs conform. These images are unlike Western graphic representational art with conventions for representing three dimensions on a flat surface, where depth perspective is achieved by interposition, relative height and size, linear perspective, texture gradient, and shadow. Instead, these faces are "flattened" by split representation, as defined by Franz Boas (1955) and Claude Levi-Strauss (1963).

Split representation is a convention whereby a three-dimensional object is imagined as cut into parts and spread onto a flat surface, often with only one end of the object cohering. In its simplest form, split representation corresponds to two profiles conjoined at a central point, thus showing both sides of a face or a body at once. More complex split representation can be used as well, depending on the number and orientation of the "cuts" through a body. The desired effect in all split representation is to display at once multiple sides of a three-dimensional body in two dimensions. The use of split representation may reveal important structural relationships within a culture. For example, Levi-Strauss (1963) and Alfred Gell (1998) argue that this technique is exclusively employed when the artwork itself *constitutes* a person or animal rather than merely representing or referring to one. In other words, to the culturally informed subject, split representation does not just render an image that looks like an animal or person, the image or object is actually conferred a degree of personhood. The same has also been argued in regards to the representation of *faces* (irrespective of split representation) in contradistinction to *heads*. As Gilles Deleuze and Félix Guattari (1987:167–191) argue, heads are normally conceived of as connected to a body and are coded by the body in the sense that they are part of a complete organism. In contrast, giving an object a face and an expression dispenses with these corporeal coordinates and arguably lends a subject to or behind the face (e.g., personhood). If correct, these interpretations would be essential for interpreting the movement of Swift Creek designs across the landscape.

There are at least three attributes of Swift Creek designs that reveal them to be structured by the principles of split representation. First, a flattened face in split representation often appears wide because the profiles have been spread apart (Figure 2.1A). Indeed, like the Haida and Maori examples referenced by Boas (1955:242–247) and Levi-Strauss (1963:plate VII), Swift Creek faces are often nearly as wide or wider than they are long. Second, the splitting of the face into two halves only joined in limited places frequently results in the appearance of a depression between the brows, as the forehead is cut down the center and spread to each side (Figure 2.1B). Finally, an exceptionally wide mouth is typical of split representation, as it is spread apart in the process of "splitting" (Figure 2.1C). Each of these traits can occur either in combination or in isolation within each Swift Creek design. Thus, the overall similarity of many Swift Creek faces to those that are rendered by split representation indicates that they may have been conceived by similar principles.

In addition to faces, whole bodies of animals might also be represented by split representation. A Swift Creek design depicting birds (Snow 1998:94) is very similar to a Haida design illustrated by Boas (1955:226), differing primarily in the parts that are cohering, the head in the former and the tail feathers in the latter (Figure 2.2). Through split representation, both the Haida design and the Swift Creek design do not represent two birds; rather, they represent at once two sides or profiles of a single bird that has been cut in half and spread apart. There also exist much more complex forms of dislocation and recombination of body parts within traditions of split representation, and this could potentially explain some of the rotation and complex symmetry in other Swift Creek designs.

There are significant social implications for split representation in Swift Creek art, more than simply denoting a recognizable non-Western representative technique. As Levi-Strauss (1963:263) indicates, split representation is used when social factors prevent the dissociation of graphic two-dimensional and plastic three-dimensional images. This is most commonly the case when the plastic component consists of the face or human body along with the painted or tattooed decoration that is applied. In other words, when socially constitutive indelible forms are inscribed onto the body, neither the body nor the design can be graphically represented without the other. This inextricable link between the design and the human face or body, in turn, implies the strict conformity of persons to their social roles (Levi-Strauss 1963:264). Split representation is especially associated with "masking cul-

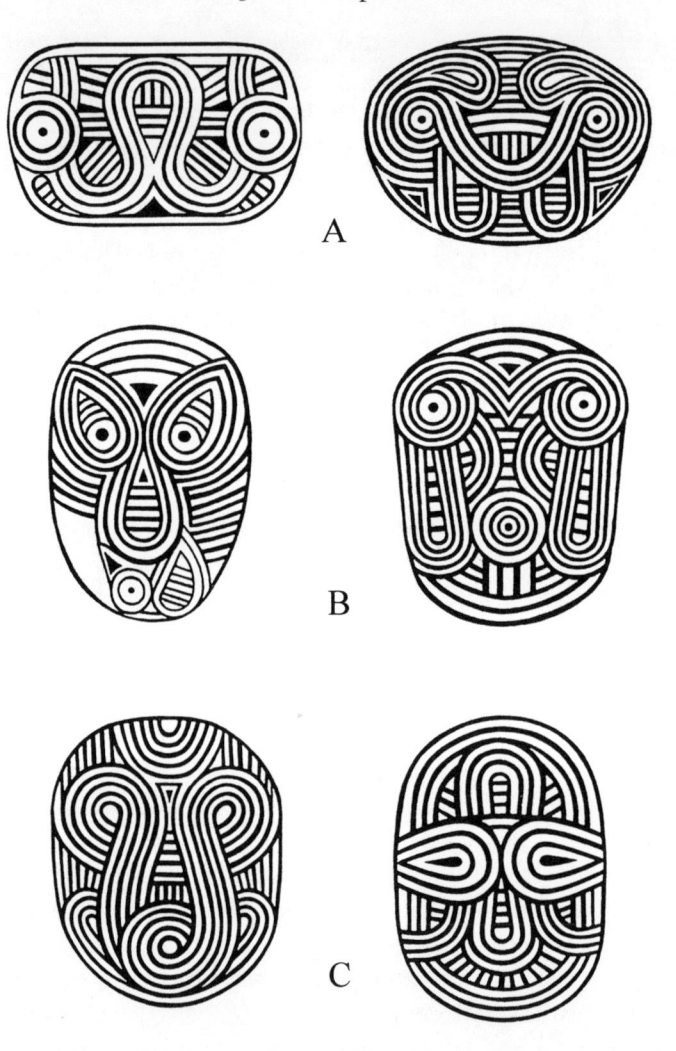

Figure 2.1. Swift Creek design attributes characteristic of split representation: (A) wide faces; (B) depression between brows; (C) wide mouths. Reconstructions by Frankie Snow.

tures" in which the person and mask are permanently linked, often achieved by indelible means such as tattooing (Gell 1998:195). While "masks," for example, frequently enable persons to temporarily become sacred beings during particular ceremonial occasions, the use of split representation implies that the "mask" identity is not temporary. Thus, split representation is necessary when motifs are critical to and inextricable from the constitution of so-

Figure 2.2. Split representation of birds in a Swift Creek design (*left,* by Frankie Snow) and a Haida design (*right,* from Boas 1955, 226, figure 226) described as "tattooing representing a duck" (note the singular).

cial persons and, therefore, often corresponds with prestige struggles and rivalry among ranked lineages as ancestral identity is understood as embodied in living persons.

The foregoing interpretation may provide a useful framework for answering the question of why Swift Creek designs were carved into small wooden manufacturing tools. As others have surmised, paddle designs were probably part of a prolific wood-carving tradition that included other artifacts that may have carried more importance than paddles (Williams and Elliott 1998). However, we should not downplay the social importance of carved paddles that were easily transported and, more importantly, that provided an efficient way to disseminate images on a broad scale. Given the prominence of the dissemination of pottery and paddles that are archaeologically visible via matching stamp designs on different vessels, complicated stamping may have been an effective way to extend social relationships and further the renown of the descent group or person that ultimately claimed ownership of the design. If the principles espoused by Levi-Strauss (1963) and Gell (1998) apply to Swift Creek designs, then objects bearing designs (including vessels) may have been conferred degrees of personhood or may have acted as extensions of persons. Consequently, the ownership, movement, and exchange of paddles and pots with Swift Creek designs might have been directed by their qualities of inalienability, perhaps as embodiments of social persons such as important ancestors claimed by particular descent groups. Exchanges of artifacts with these designs might reflect heightened concerns with social rank constructed and legitimated through "myths, ritual, and pedigree" that are typical of societies that use split representation (Levi-Strauss 1963:264). Of course, determining the symbolic importance of Swift Creek Complicated Stamped vessels depends not only on understanding the principles of design representation, but also on the entanglements of vessels in social practice that can be evaluated with context-specific studies of provenance and techno-function. In subsequent chapters, I present data that show nonlocal complicated stamped cooking vessels were restricted mainly to mortuary contexts, which, I argue, demonstrates that designs conferred symbolic density to vessels in a way that made them appropriate material for negotiating relationships between kin groups.

## Summary and Conclusions

Identified by the wide distribution of complicated stamped pottery across the lower Southeast, the Swift Creek archaeological culture encompassed a diverse array of Woodland period cultures with unique traditions and histories. Consequently, the social connections evinced by the identification of complicated stamping at sites across the region were probably as variable as the social groups who made and used Swift Creek pottery. Swift Creek pottery gained and maintained popularity throughout the lower Southeast through interactive networks that doubtless connected groups in various ways, leading some to share other cultural features beyond complicated stamped pottery that lent a "semblance of pan-regional cultural equivalence" (Ashley and Wallis 2006:5). What constitutes "Swift Creek" in one area, however, is not necessarily the same as Swift Creek in other places. In order to begin to explain the widespread distribution and promulgation of Swift Creek pottery, an exploration of the nuances of local archaeological contexts is essential. Keeping with the idea of materiality as a dialectic of people and things, I am most interested in understanding the way that the material world was bound up in social relationships and, specifically, in the case of Swift Creek pottery, how objects became "extended" artifacts (Robb 2005:134). A general aspect of an artifact's extension is in the sense of its positioning within social space and time—the normal or correct social context for an object's production and consumption. With this in mind, I explore "Swift Creek" object worlds with focus on the socially prescribed uses of pottery, in general, and complicated stamped pottery, in particular. It is to the material worlds of Swift Creek pottery makers on the Atlantic coast to which I now turn.

# 3
# Cultural History and Archaeological Overview

This chapter presents an overview of Woodland period archaeology on the Atlantic coasts of Georgia and Northeast Florida, focusing on local manifestations of the Swift Creek archaeological culture. In many ways, the coastal sectors of Georgia and Northeast Florida were different from one another in environment and culture throughout the Woodland period, but these distinctions converged around the area of the Lower St. Johns River. With its long history as a "boundary" or "transitional" zone (Russo 1992:107), the region that includes northeastern Florida and southeastern Georgia seems to have been a consistent location of intercultural interaction. In terms of archaeological visibility, and ostensibly past practice as well, these interactions culminated with Middle and Late Woodland period Swift Creek cultures. This chapter begins by outlining the ecological setting of the Atlantic coast and reviewing the pre–Swift Creek culture history of the Woodland period. Building on this background, a review of the Middle and Late Woodland culture chronology of the Atlantic coast follows, focusing on the distinctions between northeastern Florida and southeastern Georgia. I draw special attention to the mortuary landscapes of the Lower St. Johns River that consisted of series of mortuary mounds segregated from contemporaneous villages. These distinctive mortuary landscapes were important inscriptions of descent-group identity and loci of social interactions across considerable distances, as evidenced by paddle matches between sites. The chapter concludes with a synthesis of important Swift Creek sites and a review of the evidence for social interaction in the form of paddle matches.

## The Ecological Setting

The Georgia and northern Florida coasts occupy a central portion of the Georgia Bight, or Georgia Embayment, the long, westward-curving shoreline that extends from Cape Hatteras, North Carolina, to Cape Canaveral, Florida. Along portions of this stretch of shoreline are a series of barrier islands that front the open ocean waters of the Atlantic and protect a network of tidal estuaries and wetlands that thrive between the mainland and leeward side of the islands. The islands themselves consist of a series of Pleistocene and Holocene barrier islands that formed through marine deposition and erosion during fluctuations in sea levels, with some of them now combined to form large composite islands (Pilkey and Fraser 2002:245). Variations in the shape of these coastal plain islands, which in large part determine the character of the nearby estuaries, are also defined by differences in the forces of tide and waves along the length of the Georgia Bight. The contours of the coastline cause tidewaters to accumulate toward the center of the Georgia Bight, giving the shoreline in Georgia extreme tidal fluctuations, more than three meters, and trending toward more minimal tides of less than a meter toward the northern (Hatteras) and southern (Canaveral) capes (Davis 1997:158). In addition, the Georgia coast abuts a very wide and shallow continental shelf that diminishes the size of waves through friction with the seafloor, resulting in the lowest waves on the eastern coast of North America (Pilkey and Fraser 2002:248). This distinctive tide–wave energy balance results in a series of sea islands in Georgia (as well as one each in South Carolina and Florida) backed by wide and deep tidal inlets and extensive tidal flats and marshes many miles wide (Davis and Hayes 1984). Based on sea level data, essentially modern coastal conditions began to be established by around 2,500 years ago, when rapid sea level rise gave way to much more modest rates of rise (Davis 1997:157–158; Depratter and Howard 1981; Gayes et al. 1992).

The estuarine environments of the Georgia and northeastern Florida coasts sustain a rich and diverse maritime ecosystem. The salt marshes, comprised of a thick mat of salt-tolerant grasses on mudflats that are repeatedly submerged in saltwater, provide nursery areas in the life cycles of many marine vertebrates and invertebrates. These marshes also supply nutrients to the surrounding estuarine and open waters as they drain with each ebbing tide (Pilkey and Fraser 2002:72–73). The marshes are punctuated by small islands, many of them relict barrier islands covered by maritime oak hammocks, and an intricate network of tidal creeks. Maritime forest comprised mainly of live oak also dominates the mainland and barrier island shorelines that face the marsh, while further inland the high sand hills are covered by pines and turkey oaks

(Wharton 1978). This landscape is periodically interrupted by several large rivers with freshwater sources. From north to south these rivers include the Savannah, Ogeechee, Altamaha, Satilla, St. Marys, Nassau, and St. Johns. The first three of these rivers ultimately drain the piedmont while the latter four all originate in the coastal plain. The low gradient of all of these rivers subjects their flow to heavy tidal influence at their lower reaches, typically resulting in a flooded estuary. Tidal influence and estuarine habitats are thus able to reach further inland at these rivers, compared to the salt marshes limited to areas between the mainland and barrier islands. The St. Johns River has an exceptionally low gradient so that tidal effects may reach as far south as Lake George, over 100 miles upstream, but true estuarine habitats do not occur much beyond 15 miles of the coast (Anderson and Goolsby 1973:1–2; Ashley 2003:62).

The coastal network of estuaries, salt marshes, and maritime hammocks supports extensive wildlife populations. Zooarchaeological studies indicate that Woodland period populations particularly targeted coastal areas for fish and shellfish, along with a diverse array of terrestrial and marine vertebrates, including turtles, snakes, alligators, deer, opossum, rabbit, raccoon, and numerous species of birds (Fradkin 1998; Reitz 1988; Reitz and Quitmyer 1988). Paleobotanical research is conspicuously absent, but wild plants are assumed to have made up an important part of the diet as well. Coastal sector ecology is affected by fluctuations in temperature, rainfall, salinity, wind, and tide, which would have made resource availability somewhat variable at least on a seasonal basis (Hackney et al. 1976:273–276). The subtropical climate of the Georgia and northern Florida coasts is comprised of warm, humid summers and short, mild winters, with water temperatures in the estuaries ranging from below 10 degrees C to above 30 degrees C (Reitz and Quitmyer 1988:96). Consequently, these fluctuating conditions result in patterns in the presence and distribution of particular species of fish within the estuary. Based on the relative frequencies of various species of fish, along with seasonality data collected from *Mercenaria* clams, the Woodland period coastal sector seems to have been occupied during every season, and perhaps permanently year-round (Reitz and Quitmyer 1988:105–106). This subsistence regime, focused on year-round exploitation of estuarine habitats, is likely to have continued throughout the Woodland period and beyond, through various cultural changes.

## Pre–Swift Creek Culture History

The first half of the Woodland period in eastern Georgia and Northeast Florida was dominated by two archaeological cultures (Figure 3.1). From roughly 800 BC to as late as AD 500, Deptford sites pervaded along the coast as far south as the Lower St. Johns River (Milanich 1971, 1994:112–115; Stephenson et al. 2002). The St. Johns I culture thrived toward the south of this Deptford distribution, occupying most of the eastern half of the Florida peninsula from at least 500 BC to AD 750 (Milanich 1994:244). These archaeological cultures are each defined primarily by differences in pottery. Deptford series pottery along the coast is tempered with sand or grit with various surface treatments of check stamping, linear check stamping, simple stamping, cord marking, and, at late sites, complicated stamping. In contrast, St. Johns I pottery is mostly plain and occasionally incised, with a distinctive sponge spicule temper that gives vessel surfaces a "chalky" feel. In addition to these differences in pottery assemblages, the two archaeological cultures may be usefully distinguished by variation in mortuary ceremonialism and subsistence regime.

Atlantic Deptford populations are presumed to have built low sand burial mounds less than a meter high, although the paucity of diagnostic artifacts at mortuary sites of this time period makes assignments of cultural affiliation somewhat tenuous (Stephenson et al. 2002:327). David Thomas and C. S. Larsen (1979) excavated nine mounds on St. Catherine's Island, Georgia, most of which are presumed to be Deptford. Some of these mounds contained up to a few hundred Refuge and Deptford series sherds while others produced virtually no pottery at all and few other artifacts. Nonetheless, a series of radiocarbon assays from these artifact-poor mounds confirms that most were constructed during a Deptford time period (Caldwell 1970; cited in Milanich 1973:55; Thomas and Larsen 1979:138–143). Thomas and Larsen's (1979) extensive fieldwork seems to demonstrate that Deptford mortuary regimes were consistently limited in terms of burial accoutrements. These material restrictions appear particularly austere when juxtaposed with other Middle Woodland burial treatments across the Eastern Woodlands that incorporated the largess of the Adena and Hopewell traditions. Both primary-extended and secondary-bundled burials are present in Deptford mounds, usually with fewer than 25 individuals in each mound. The preponderance of female burials in the mounds led Thomas and Larsen (1979) to propose a matrilineal society among the Atlantic Deptford.

To the south, St. Johns I populations built low sand burial mounds around a meter high, although a few are more than three meters high (Milanich 1994:260). Most information about these mounds comes from C. B. Moore's (1894, 1895) early excavations, summarized by John Goggin (1952). The preparation of bodies for interment may have been largely identical to Deptford practices, with both primary and secondary burials present. Most mounds

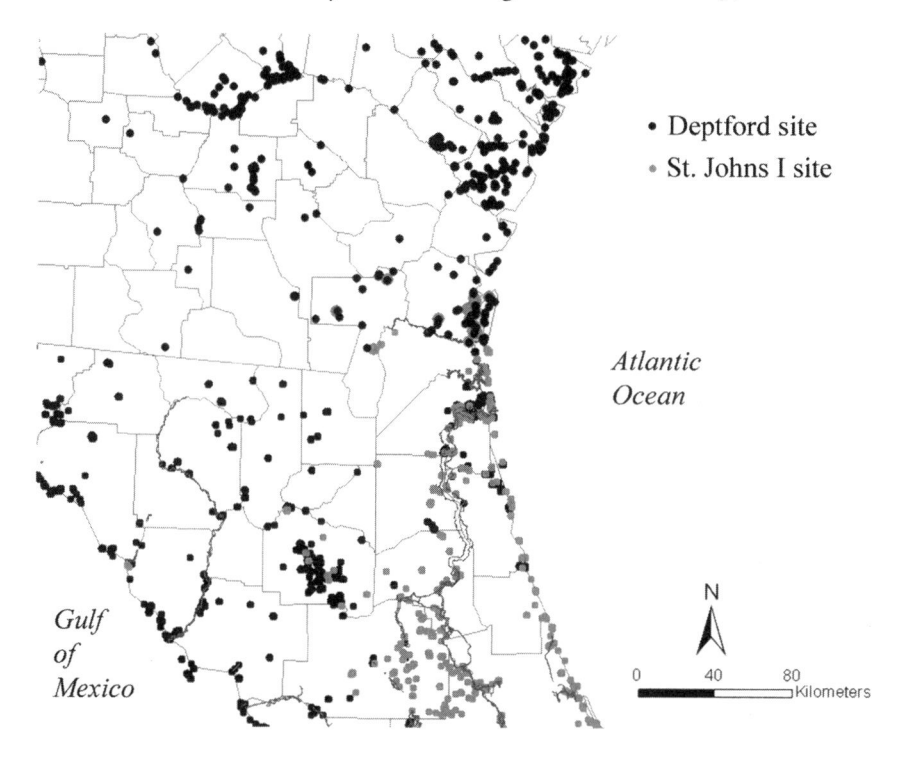

Figure 3.1. Distribution of recorded Deptford and St. Johns I sites at their intersection on the Atlantic coast, based on Florida and Georgia state site file data.

contain less than 25 individuals, although a few mounds contain up to 100. The distinguishing feature of the St. Johns burial regime, compared to Deptford, is in the quantity and types of material culture found at mounds. While Deptford mounds can be characterized by the paucity of material culture, St. Johns I mounds contain artifacts in abundance. Locally produced vessels of St. Johns Plain and Dunns Creek Red, a red-painted ware most common in ceremonial contexts, are ubiquitous at mounds. Mounds also contain Deptford, Swift Creek, and Weeden Island vessels of foreign manufacture, or locally made copies, and earthenware plant and animal effigies (Milanich 1994:247). Extralocal influence is further evident in nonlocal mineral, metal, and stone (Seeman 1979) as well as occasional log-lined tombs reminiscent of Hopewellian burial treatments (Bullen et al. 1967; LaFond 1983). In sum, St. Johns mortuary ritual was rich in material accoutrements and demonstrates pervasive connections with many contemporary Woodland period cultures.

Differences between Deptford and St. Johns I cultures are also evident in subsistence regime, with the two cultures having been primarily adapted to distinct ecological zones. In fact, the extent of estuarine and freshwater ecosystems along the Atlantic coast may have been influential in the formation of cultural boundaries. There seems to be a strong correspondence between the distribution of Deptford and St. Johns I sites and particular ecological zones (see Figure 3.1). Atlantic Deptford populations were adapted to the especially wide and extensive estuaries that back the sea islands of the southern South Carolina, Georgia, and northeastern Florida coasts. Notably, these estuaries become much narrower and, eventually, intermittent further toward the south. Only the two northernmost islands in Florida (Amelia and Fort George) are true barrier islands with natural inlets and an extensive saltwater estuary behind them (Pilkey and Fraser 2002:70). With a more wave-dominated environment toward the south, barriers are long, inlets are unstable, and tidal influence is limited, leading to lagoons behind barriers in eastern Florida that are essentially freshwater (Davis 1997:159). Indeed, before the dredging and blasting of channels to the ocean during the last century, freshwater ecosystems near the central and southern Florida coast were much more common. Perhaps as a partial consequence, Deptford sites are uncommon south of the St. Johns River mouth, where estuarine environments are more limited. Atlantic Deptford populations seem to have been overwhelmingly focused on the exploitation of oyster and saltwater fish while making only periodic special-use camps for the procurement of upland resources (Espenshade et al. 1994).

Alternatively, the St. Johns I culture was centered on the exploitation of aquatic freshwater resources with the Upper and Middle St. Johns River as its heartland. Freshwater banded mystery snails (*Viviparus georgianus*), fish, and turtles make up the bulk of middens along rivers and lakes (Wing and McKean 1987). While there are also St. Johns I sites that clearly show extensive maritime adaptation (Russo et al. 1989), these estuarine environments south of the mouth of the St. Johns River were smaller and more isolated than their counterparts to the north in Georgia and northeastern Florida. As such, freshwater ecosystems were a subsistence mainstay for many St. Johns I populations. As among Deptford sites, no large St. Johns I sites have been located any distance away from major rivers, lakes, or coastal estuaries. Smaller extractive camps exist in the piney flatlands, bottomland swamps, and cypress domes between the St. Johns River and Atlantic Ocean (Hardin and Russo 1987; Hardin et al. 1988; Sigler-Eisenberg et al. 1985).

The extensive estuarine habitats of the north and widespread freshwater environments of the south meet dramatically at the mouth of the Lower St.

Johns River in northeastern Florida. Here, the 310-mile river empties into the ocean to become part of a huge, flooded estuary. This is also the area where Woodland period typological distinctions begin to break down, creating difficulties for archaeologists attempting to construct culture histories. Based on the published work of C. B. Moore (1894), John Goggin (1949, 1952:36) included the Lower St. Johns River in his definitions of St. Johns I and II cultures of the St. Johns River valley, largely ignoring the typological complexity of the northern fringes of the region. In his estimation, St. Johns I was a "predominantly plain chalky ware period," with subperiods defined by minority wares of extralocal origin (Goggin 1952:47). However, William Sears's (1957) later stratigraphic excavations along the southern bank of the Lower St. Johns River failed to yield any Woodland period sites with predominantly St. Johns Plain pottery. Instead, Sears's (1957) work produced assemblages dominated by sand-tempered plainwares, with only minor occurrences of St. Johns Plain. Interpreting the Lower St. Johns as a "boundary between the Georgia coast and Northern St. Johns culture areas," Sears (1957:2) defined a locally specific Woodland period chronology that began with Deptford, followed by a long sand-tempered plain "period" that included minority occurrences of Swift Creek Complicated Stamped wares and ended with the sherd-tempered series known as Colorinda (Ashley 2003:67).

Despite Sears's (1957) attempt at reformulating a chronology tailored to the Lower St. Johns River area and the taxonomic difficulties encountered in other excavations (Bullen and Griffin 1952; Wilson 1965), Goggin's (1952) culture areas and chronology were subsequently repeated by Milanich and Fairbanks (1980) in their synthesis of Florida archaeology. As Ashley (2003: 66–74) argues, Milanich and Fairbanks's (1980) gloss of the Lower St. Johns River region was the chronological framework used for many contract archaeology projects that ensued in the following decades. Consequently, the Florida Master Site File is filled with sites from the Lower St. Johns River that are labeled "St. Johns I" even when only a few, or even just one, St. Johns Plain sherd was recovered among a large assemblage of sand-tempered plain pottery (Ashley 2003:69). To this day only one site along the Lower St. Johns River, the Wood-Hopkins Midden (8DU9185), has produced a preponderance of St. Johns Plain pottery (Johnson 1994:52–69). This small freshwater snail (*Viviparus georgianus*) midden, located just 15 kilometers west of the Atlantic Ocean, may represent a rare foray of Middle St. Johns groups into the area (Ashley 2003:72). The site is anomalous in terms of both pottery assemblage (all St. Johns Plain) and shell species (mostly *Viviparus* with some oyster), in an area where St. Johns Plain pottery is rare and middens are dominated by oyster.

Michael Russo (1992) was the first after Sears (1957) to attempt to refine the problematic chronology by proposing a separate culture area for the Lower St. Johns River locale: the St. Marys region. As Russo (1992) envisioned it, the St. Marys region included the area along the Atlantic coast between the Lower St. Johns River and the Satilla River in southeastern Georgia. Drawing primarily on extensive survey work from the Timucuan Historic and Ecological Preserve, near the mouth of the St. Johns River, Russo (1992; Russo et al. 1993) provided a new view on the complex chronology of the local Woodland period. Like Sears (1957), Russo emphasized that sand-tempered plain pottery was often dominant on Woodland period sites, with Deptford, Swift Creek, St. Johns, and Colorinda also occurring in varying amounts. Due to the multicomponent nature of the sites he excavated, Russo (1992) was unable to connect the ubiquitous sand-tempered plainwares to a specific archaeological culture or develop a Woodland period chronology with the few temporally diagnostic pottery types.

In the decade that followed Russo's (1992) work, a healthy database of Woodland period radiocarbon dates was developed. Ashley (2003:81) compiled these radiocarbon assays and found that they largely substantiated Sears's (1957) original attempt at a chronology through seriation of midden pottery. As Ashley (2003:74) observes, Deptford series pottery began the Woodland period chronology and was produced from roughly 500 BC to AD 1 (Kirkland and Johnson 2000). Following Deptford, a 500-year period ensued in which sand-tempered plain pottery dominated assemblages along with minor occurrences of check stamped and complicated stamped (Early Swift Creek) surface treatments. St. Johns Plain pottery was made locally in limited amounts or brought in from the Middle St. Johns River. Charcoal-tempered plain and complicated stamped pottery was produced at this time as well, from roughly AD 300 to 500. After AD 500 to roughly AD 850, sand-tempered pottery continued to dominate assemblages but Late Swift Creek Complicated Stamped became more prevalent than any previous minority ware. Finally, Colorinda pottery concluded the Woodland period chronology, produced for a short time between AD 850 and 900 (Ashley 2003:74–75). This most recent chronology provides the basis for a more detailed discussion of typology and chronology of Swift Creek contexts on the Atlantic coast.

## Swift Creek Radiocarbon Chronology, Typology, and Culture History

While Swift Creek Complicated Stamped pottery was produced for almost a millennium across the southeastern United States, the specific temporal range of its production varied considerably across the region (Stephenson et al. 2002; Williams and Elliott 1998). This is true along the Atlantic coast itself, where complicated stamping appears on the Lower St. Johns River several centuries earlier than along the estuaries of southeastern Georgia. As with many areas of the Southeast, Swift Creek pottery in northeastern Florida can be partitioned into Early and Late varieties based on attributes such as rim and lip form as well as quality of design execution and application (e.g., Kelly 1938; Kelly and Smith 1975; Phelps 1969; Willey 1949). In southeastern Georgia, Deptford pottery persisted through Early Swift Creek occupations of northeastern Florida, and only the Late variety of Swift Creek pottery is found at coastal Georgia sites. Complicated stamping continued well into the ninth century in both southeastern Georgia and northeastern Florida. Along the Atlantic coast, a total of 43 radiocarbon assays have been recorded from 13 sites (Tables 3.1 and 3.2). This series of dates confirms that Early Swift Creek pottery is restricted to northeastern Florida while Late Swift Creek pottery is contemporaneous along much of the Florida and Georgia coasts.

Early Swift Creek contexts in northeastern Florida are represented by six radiocarbon dates from three sites (Table 3.1). Four of these are accelerator mass spectrometry (AMS) assays derived from soot samples on Early Swift Creek charcoal-tempered plain and complicated stamped vessels from the Dent and Mayport mounds. Another comes from soot on a complicated stamped sponge-spicule-tempered vessel from the Tillie Fowler (8DU17245) village site (Hendryx and Wallis 2007). Finally, one date comes from a charcoal sample from a fire pit 60 centimeters below the ground surface at the Mayport Mound (Wilson 1965:31). Calibration of the entire series of assays indicates a conservative time span of circa AD 30 to 600 for Early Swift Creek pottery. However, both the earliest AMS assay from the Dent Mound and the radiocarbon date from charcoal at the Mayport Mound should be viewed with caution. As an anomalous outlier among AMS dates from soot on charcoal-tempered pottery, the Dent assay may be a result of the old-wood problem, in which the wood used as fuel was much older than the cooking activity that caused soot to adhere to the vessel surface (Ashley and Wallis 2006:8). Alternatively, the cultural affiliation of the Mayport charcoal sample is uncertain because Rex Wilson (1965) did not provide a record of material culture from this feature, although this assay may well relate to the earliest stages of mound construction. Although more assays from Early Swift Creek contexts are needed, the current suite supports a conservative, calibrated date range of AD 200 to 600.

Presently, 37 Late Swift Creek radiometric dates have been recorded from 13 sites along the Atlantic coast between the mouth of the Altamaha River

Table 3.1. Calibrated radiocarbon assays for Early and Late Swift Creek contexts in northeastern Florida

| Site | Beta # | Material | Measured C14 age (BP) | C13/C12 ratio (o/oo) | Conventional C14 age (BP) | Calibrated 1 Sigma (AD) with intercept | Calibrated 2 Sigma (AD) | Reference |
|---|---|---|---|---|---|---|---|---|
| *Early Swift Creek* | | | | | | | | |
| 8DU68 | 182333 | soot | 1930 ± 40 | −24.2 | 1940 ± 40 | 30 (65) 95 | 30 BC–135 | Stephenson et al. 2002 |
| 8DU96 | GX315* | charcoal | 1865 ± 95 | −25.0 | 1865 ± 95 | 55 (130) 250 | 50 BC–395 | Wilson 1965 |
| 8DU17245 | 217829 | soot | 1830 ± 40 | −26.7 | 1800 ± 40 | 150 (230) 250 | 120–340 | Hendryx and Wallis 2007 |
| 8DU68 | 182332 | soot | 1690 ± 40 | −24.7 | 1690 ± 40 | 330 (385) 410 | 250–430 | Stephenson et al. 2002 |
| 8DU96 | 168177 | soot | 1560 ± 40 | −24.5 | 1570 ± 40 | 430 (460, 480, 520) 540 | 410–580 | Stephenson et al. 2002 |
| 8DU96 | 190255 | soot | 1510 ± 40 | −25.3 | 1510 ± 40 | 530 (560) 610 | 440–640 | Wallis 2004 |
| 8DU96 | 169421 | soot | 1450 ± 40 | −22.8 | 1490 ± 40 | 540 (580) 620 | 460–480 and 520–560 | Stephenson et al. 2002 |
| *Late Swift Creek* | | | | | | | | |
| 8DU68 | 169420 | soot | 1330 ± 40 | −18.4 | 1440 ± 40 | 580 (600) 650 | 550–660 | Stephenson et al. 2002 |
| 8DU81 | 181303 | oyster | 1460 ± 70 | −3.6 | 1810 ± 70 | 540 (610) 670 | 440–710 | Ashley 2003 |
| 8DU5545 | 163598 | oyster | 1390 ± 60 | −3.2 | 1390 ± 60 | 600 (660) 690 | 540–740 | Smith and Handley 2002 |
| 8DU5545 | 163597 | oyster | 1350 ± 60 | −2.3 | 1350 ± 60 | 620 (670) 700 | 560–770 | Smith and Handley 2002 |
| 8NA32 | 190666 | oyster | 1340 ± 60 | −1.6 | 1340 ± 60 | 640 (680) 720 | 580–780 | Handley et al. 2004 |
| 8DU5545 | 168176 | soot | 1290 ± 40 | −24.5 | 1300 ± 40 | 670 (690) 770 | 660–790 | Stephenson et al. 2002 |
| 8NA32 | 190665 | oyster | 1310 ± 60 | −1.8 | 1310 ± 60 | 660 (700) 770 | 590–850 | Handley et al. 2004 |
| 8DU68 | 182334 | soot | 1270 ± 40 | −25.0 | 1270 ± 40 | 685 (720, 745, 760) 780 | 670–870 | Stephenson et al. 2002 |
| 8DU81 | 182335 | soot | 1250 ± 40 | −25.4 | 1240 ± 40 | 705–815 (775) 840–855 | 680–885 | Stephenson et al. 2002 |
| 8DU68 | 54645 | oyster | 1250 ± 70 | −2.7 | 1610 ± 70 | 695 (775) 865 | 655–955 | Ashley 1995 |
| 8NA709 | 126313 | oyster | 1180 ± 60 | 0.0 | 1590 ± 60 | 730 (800) 875 | 685–945 | Dickinson and Wayne 1999 |
| 8NA910 | 159964 | soot | 1150 ± 40 | −23.4 | 1180 ± 40 | 790 (880) 900 | 770–970 | Hendryx 2004 |

*From Geochron Laboratories, Cambridge, Massachusetts. All others from Beta Analytic, Miami, Florida.

Table 3.2. Calibrated radiocarbon assays for Early and Late Swift Creek contexts in southern coastal Georgia

| Site | Beta # | Material | Measured C14 age (BP) | C13/C12 ratio (o/oo) | Conventional C14 age (BP) | Calibrated 1 Sigma (AD) with intercept | Calibrated 2 Sigma (AD) | Reference |
|---|---|---|---|---|---|---|---|---|
| 9CM171 | 2122 | oyster | 1490 ± 90 | 0.0 | 1891 ± 90 | 415 (515) 615 | 295–680 | Adams (ed.) 1985 |
| 9CM171 | 4005 | oyster | 1470 ± 80 | 0.0 | 1871 ± 80 | 430 (545) 632 | 330–690 | Adams (ed.) 1985 |
| 9CM171 | 4421 | oyster | 1410 ± 70 | 0.0 | 1811 ± 70 | 515 (605) 670 | 420–720 | Adams (ed.) 1985 |
| 9CM171 | 4418 | charcoal | 1470 ± 100 | −25.0 | 1470 ± 100 | 450 (605) 665 | 385–765 | Adams (ed.) 1985 |
| 9MC360 | nr | charcoal | 1450 ± 50 | −25.0 | 1450 ± 50 | 560 (620) 650 | 450–680 | Wayne 1987 |
| 9CM171 | 4420 | charcoal | 1440 ± 80 | −25.0 | 1440 ± 80 | 550 (625) 670 | 420–760 | Adams (ed.) 1985 |
| 9CM171 | 3994 | charcoal | 1420 ± 80 | −25.0 | 1420 ± 80 | 555 (640) 675 | 435–775 | Adams (ed.) 1985 |
| 9CM171 | 3996 | charcoal | 1410 ± 140 | −25.0 | 1410 ± 140 | 530 (645) 760 | 360–955 | Adams (ed.) 1985 |
| 9MC372 | 82086 | bone | 1280 ± 60 | −17.1 | 1400 ± 60 | 620 (650) 675 | 560–760 | Cook 1995 |
| 9MC233 | 157590 | soot | 1400 ± 40 | −25.2 | 1400 ± 40 | 630 (650) 660 | 600–680 | Kirkland 2003 |
| 9CM171 | 3989 | charcoal | 1360 ± 80 | −25.0 | 1360 ± 80 | 620 (665) 755 | 540–875 | Adams (ed.) 1985 |
| 9CM171 | 4010 | oyster | 1330 ± 60 | 0.0 | 1730 ± 60 | 610 (670) 715 | 530–800 | Adams (ed.) 1985 |
| 9CM171 | 3988 | charcoal | 1340 ± 80 | −25.0 | 1340 ± 80 | 630 (675) 770 | 550–885 | Adams (ed.) 1985 |
| 9CM171 | 4417 | charcoal | 1330 ± 70 | −25.0 | 1330 ± 70 | 645 (675) 770 | 580–880 | Adams (ed.) 1985 |
| 9CM171 | 4000 | charcoal | 1320 ± 80 | −25.0 | 1320 ± 80 | 645 (680) 780 | 565–895 | Adams (ed.) 1985 |
| 9CM171 | 3993 | charcoal | 1320 ± 60 | −25.0 | 1320 ± 60 | 655 (680) 770 | 605–880 | Adams (ed.) 1985 |
| 9CM233 | 157591 | soot | 1300 ± 40 | −26.4 | 1280 ± 40 | 680 (710) 780 | 660–860 | Kirkland 2003 |
| 9CM171 | 4429 | quahog | 1250 ± 60 | 0.0 | 1650 ± 60 | 670 (720) 805 | 610–900 | Adams (ed.) 1985 |
| 9CM171 | 3995 | charcoal | 1260 ± 130 | −25.0 | 1260 ± 130 | 655 (760) 950 | 545–1020 | Adams (ed.) 1985 |
| 9CM171 | 4004 | oyster | 1220 ± 90 | 0.0 | 1620 ± 90 | 675 (760) 880 | 590–995 | Adams (ed.) 1985 |
| 9CM171 | 4012 | oyster | 1190 ± 60 | 0.0 | 1590 ± 60 | 705 (790) 885 | 665–975 | Adams (ed.) 1985 |
| 9CM171 | 4015 | oyster | 1180 ± 60 | 0.0 | 1580 ± 60 | 715 (800) 895 | 670–985 | Adams (ed.) 1985 |
| 9GN6 | 225771 | soot | 1100 ± 40 | −25.2 | 1100 ± 40 | 890 (970) 990 | 880–1020 | Ashley et al. 2007 |

and the mouth of the St Johns River (Tables 3.1 and 3.2). This series of dates indicates that Late Swift Creek contexts have a time span of roughly AD 500 to 850, with the seventh and eighth centuries particularly well represented. Nearly half of the assays come from the Kings Bay site (9CM171) in southern Camden County, which itself spans the entire temporal range of Late Swift Creek occupation along the coast (Adams 1985:358–359). The sixth century was a time of transition in pottery production, indicated by the overlap in the temporal ranges of Early and Late Swift Creek radiometric dates in northeastern Florida. Along the Lower St. Johns River, charcoal tempering and early notched rim forms appear to have gradually diminished to give way to the ubiquity of sand tempering and late folded rims. In southeastern Georgia, Late Swift Creek pottery production began during the sixth century but enjoyed its greatest popularity in the following two centuries. While Early and Late Swift Creek manifestations clearly overlap according to radiometric assays, for convenience I have divided the transitional sixth century in half for my outline of Swift Creek culture history along the Atlantic coast. By circa AD 850, a shift in pottery production occurred and was accompanied by other cultural changes. These waning Late Swift Creek manifestations, labeled the Kelvin culture by Fred Cook (1979), are represented by two radiometric dates from extreme northeastern Florida and possibly one more from the Evelyn site on the Altamaha River (Ashley et al. 2007; Hendryx 2004).

## Early Swift Creek (ca. AD 200 to 550)

In northeastern Florida, Early Swift Creek assemblages consist of locally produced plain and complicated stamped wares, with rim treatments that include simple rounded and flattened lips as well as hallmark forms such as notched, nicked, scalloped, and crenulated (Ashley 1992:130–131, 1998:204; Sears 1959:155). Although sand tempering seems to predominate at many Early Swift Creek sites, early vessels are often charcoal tempered. Charcoal-tempered pottery contains quartz sand and charcoal inclusions that range from very common to sparse. While the production of charcoal-tempered pottery seems to have been mainly restricted to sites near the mouth of Lower St. Johns River, it has been recorded in limited quantities as far upstream as the River Point site (8SJ4790) on the St. Johns, as far south along the coast as the Shannon Road Midden site (8SJ3169), and as far north as the Sadlers Landing site (9CM233) in Camden County, Georgia, a straight-line distance of about 90 kilometers (Ashley and Wallis 2006:8). Charcoal tempering seems to have been a local, spatially circumscribed tradition among groups making Early Swift Creek pottery. At both mortuary mounds and trash middens, plain charcoal-tempered sherds outnumber complicated stamped versions, but sand-tempered plain represents the dominant type in most Early Swift Creek assemblages (Ashley 1998:200; Russo 1992:115; Sears 1957:29).

The technological tradition of charcoal tempering has been interpreted through the results of petrographic analysis by Ann Cordell and Lee Newsom (Wallis et al. 2005). In general, most extant charcoal particles in the paste tend to exhibit little shrinkage from vessel firing and cooking, indicating that predominantly charcoal, rather than wood, was added as temper. On both the interior and exterior surfaces of vessels, charcoal particles often appear to have been burned to ash, leaving holes or voids (Ashley 1998:202; Russo et al. 1993:35–36). These are the characteristic holes that Sears (1957, 1959) and Wilson (1965) identified to designate "hole-tempered" and "limestone-tempered" pottery, respectively. Petrographic analysis reveals the prevalence of charcoal, crushed bone, and grog inclusions in the paste of many vessels, supporting the possibility that these materials were hearth contents added to the clay during paste preparation. In addition, the consistent size of temper particles, ranging from medium to coarse on the Wentworth scale, suggest that charcoal was consistently pounded and sieved before being added to the raw clay.

Designs on Early Swift Creek pottery tend to be "sloppy" in execution, differentiating them from Late Swift Creek varieties (Ashley and Wallis 2006:8). Paddle impressions typically cover the entire exterior surface of vessels, which are predominantly sub-conical pots and bowls. The apparent prevalence of overstamping and smoothing has generally hindered attempts to reconstruct Early Swift Creek designs, although they are presumed to be similar to those of the Gulf Coast of Florida (Ashley and Wallis 2006:13). One exception is the diamond and raised dot design characteristic of the Sun City Complicated Stamped type, which has been identified at Swift Creek sites in the Florida panhandle as well as on charcoal-tempered vessels in northeastern Florida (Hendryx and Wallis 2007; Thomas and Campbell 1993:571; Willey 1949:437).

### Late Swift Creek (ca. AD 550 to 850)

Late Swift Creek pottery has a much broader distribution than the early variety, being prevalent at sites along the Atlantic seaboard from just south of the St. Johns River to the north side of the Altamaha River (Figure 3.2) (Ashley et al. 2007; Ashley and Wallis 2006:9). Rim treatments include hallmark thick rim folds as well as simple rounded or flattened lips. Temper among Late Swift Creek assemblages is typically sand, with vessels from the Georgia coast and northernmost Florida coastal islands (e.g., Amelia Island, Martin Island) having coarser (i.e., larger) quartz temper than Lower St. Johns River vessels (Ashley and Wallis 2006:9). Two other temper variants have also been noted with some frequency. First, bone tempering, which typically consists of bone crushed into fine particles, has been observed in limited amounts among classic sand-tempered Late Swift Creek assemblages. Second, grog tempering, almost always crushed into very fine particles, occurs within some Late Swift Creek vessels as well. In fact, grog tempering is characteristic of the waning Late Swift Creek tradition that Cook (1979) labels Kelvin (Ashley and Wallis 2006:9). Thus, grog tempering may be a temporal marker in the latest Swift Creek sherds, its use signifying a precursor to the grog particles of the terminal Late Woodland cultures of Colorinda and Kelvin (Ashley and Wallis 2006:9). Sand-tempered plain continues to dominate assemblages throughout Late Swift Creek and waning Late Swift Creek contexts.

Designs on Late Swift Creek Complicated Stamped vessels appear more carefully executed than on Early Swift Creek vessels. Complete stamping all over the vessel continued, but zoned stamping also became popular. Zoned stamping is also coincident with new vessel forms, particularly collared jars and bowls that are not present among Early Swift Creek assemblages. At the same time, sub-conical pots and bowls continue to be common. Paddle matches and design similarities on Late Swift Creek pottery along the Atlantic coast demonstrate cultural connections among populations of northeastern Florida and southeastern Georgia (Ashley and Wallis 2006:12–14). By the end of the ninth century, carved paddle designs became more simplistic and paddle impressions were more "sloppy" in execution. Nested chevron designs, often typed as Crooked River Complicated Stamped, became a persistent surface decoration on vessels, dominating some assemblages. Rim folds became uncommon and were replaced by an incised line or "false fold" below the lip. These characteristics define the waning Late Swift Creek or Kelvin pottery assemblages that seem to have continued into the tenth century.

## Swift Creek Site Types

Swift Creek pottery is common in small amounts at many sites on the Atlantic coast (Ashley 1992; Ashley et al. 2007; Russo 1992; Russo et al. 1993). The widespread occurrence of a few complicated stamped sherds in assemblages dominated by other types is perhaps testimony to the breadth of social interactions mediated through Swift Creek material culture. However, Swift Creek sites, defined by the predominance of complicated stamping in assemblages (usually following sand-tempered plain), essentially consist of three types: small artifact scatters, large shell middens, and low sand mortu-

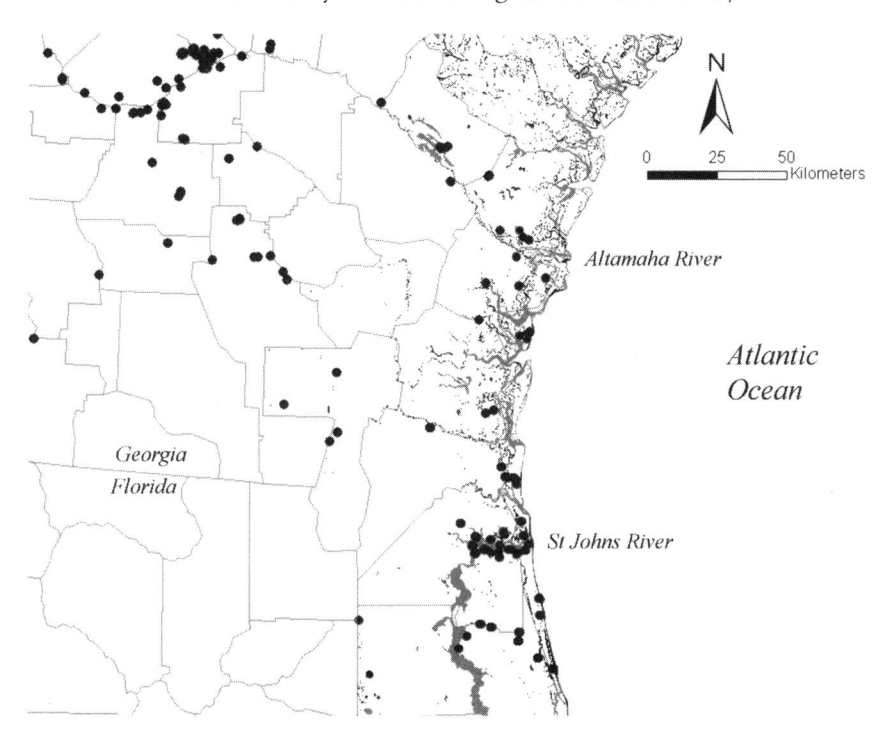

Figure 3.2. Sites with Late Swift Creek pottery along the Atlantic coast.

ary mounds. The distribution of these types of archaeological sites and their relationship to one another is variable across the landscape. Along the Lower St. Johns River in northeastern Florida, a series of mounded cemeteries stand segregated from the multi-household villages represented by extensive shell middens (Wallis 2008). In contrast, mortuary mounds are scarce along the Georgia coast, perhaps as the result of both site destruction and different burial practices (Ashley et al. 2007:22). At sites where mounds are present or likely to have been present in coastal Georgia, villages were located nearby. Therefore, even with the sampling bias that may pertain, the built landscapes among local Swift Creek populations were different along the Lower St. Johns River and the Georgia coast.

## Village Middens

It is difficult to infer the structure of Swift Creek settlement from complicated stamped pottery found in hundreds of small artifact scatters and many dense multicomponent sites (Ashley 1998; Ashley et al. 2007). However, large single-component sites seem to correspond with multi-household villages and many reveal patterns in community structure. A conspicuous feature of many shell middens along the coast is their circular or semi-circular arrangement, presumably corresponding with the circular shape of villages, although other configurations are also noted. The failure to discover clear architectural features at arcuate arrangements of middens may indicate that houses were located adjacent to middens, perhaps inside the shell ring. These areas, which tend to be mostly devoid of artifacts, have received very limited excavation coverage. At the same time, the lack of shell in these areas makes preservation of cultural features very unlikely. The shallow nature of many of these shell middens suggests seasonal rather than extended year-round site occupancy. Thus, Swift Creek populations on the coast were probably at least seasonally mobile. Subsistence data along the coast indicates a diet overwhelmingly dominated by maritime resources, especially fish and shellfish. Further inland, beyond the saltwater habitats of oysters and clams, poor faunal preservation has resulted in a paucity of subsistence data. Below is a brief review of the largest Swift Creek middens along the coast that are interpreted as village sites.

## Northeastern Florida

Work in the last two decades has greatly expanded our knowledge of Swift Creek habitation in northeastern Florida. Presently, there are at least five sites that represent substantial villages from the east bank of the St. Johns River near downtown Jacksonville to Amelia Island near the Georgia border. These sites represent a range of ecological settings, adaptations, and village structure.

On the eastern bank of the St. Johns River, across from Jacksonville, numerous Swift Creek deposits have been identified (Ashley and Hendryx 2008; Hendryx and Wallis 2007). Small amounts of Swift Creek Complicated Stamped pottery are widely scattered at sites along the water's edge and a hundred or more meters inland on the sand ridges that flank the eastern and southern banks of the river (Ashley 1998:215). These sites are commonly quite small, but a significant Swift Creek component was recently excavated at the Tillie Fowler site (Hendryx and Wallis 2007). The northern portion of the Tillie Fowler site (8DU17245) was comprised of two distinct loci of artifact concentration primarily dating to the Early Swift Creek phase. Along a portion of the river too brackish for freshwater snails and too fresh for saltwater oysters and clams, the site contained almost no shellfish, which resulted in very poor preservation of artifacts and features. Even with the paucity of non-ceramic artifacts and cultural features, the density of the pottery deposits and their spatial distribution covering nearly one hectare very likely correspond with a village. As elsewhere along the river, Swift Creek pottery has also been recovered from contexts closer to the water's edge, such as at the nearby Dolphin Reef Site (8DU276), where more than 200 Swift Creek and many presumably contemporaneous sand-tempered plain sherds were documented (Ashley and Hendryx 2008).

Moving east from Jacksonville along the St. Johns River toward the Atlantic Ocean, there are many sites that indicate intensive Swift Creek occupation. At least four multicomponent sites (8DU62, 8DU66, 8DU5602, 8DU5611) with appreciable quantities of Swift Creek pottery have been tested in the vicinity of Mill Cove (Ashley 1998; Johnson 1988) and near St. Johns bluff (Sears 1957, 1959). The limited nature of testing at these sites frustrates attempts to interpret their Woodland period components (Ashley 1998:216). However, three single-component sites further to the east, on the Greenfield peninsula, provide a compelling view of Swift Creek occupation.

The Greenfield peninsula is bordered by salt marshes that extend from the St. Johns River to the north, Greenfield Creek to the west, and San Pablo Creek (intracoastal waterway) to the east. Situated between 50 and 200 meters away from the present western shoreline, Greenfield site 7 (8DU5543) consisted of three hectares of sparse midden debris interspersed with several small areas of dense shell midden (Ashley 1998; Florida Archeological Services 1994). Of the five areas of dense shell identified, three were intensively investigated and subsequently interpreted as "household refuse" middens (Florida Archeological Services 1994:121). These middens contained a "solidly packed," homogeneous oyster shell matrix averaging 10 to 15 centimeters thick and with abundant vertebrate faunal remains and pottery. Two adjacent middens, measuring 2 × 7 meters and 6 × 12 meters in plan view, contained exclusively Early Swift Creek Plain and Early Swift Creek Complicated Stamped pottery. The third and smallest (3 × 5 meters) midden investigated, roughly 120 meters southeast of the others, contained only Late Swift Creek Plain and Late Swift Creek Complicated Stamped pottery. Combined, these three middens produced approximately 1,000 sherds, which were equally divided between complicated stamped and plain varieties. Notably, Early Swift Creek and Late Swift Creek contexts were discrete at the site, with no mixing of diagnostic wares in any of the excavated features or shell middens.

Although only five shell midden concentrations were identified, and only three of these were intensively investigated, the site clearly represents two chronologically distinct occupations that were both substantial. The form of these occupations may have been either solitary houses or multi-household villages but is more likely the latter. As the authors note, "it is highly probable that undemonstrated refuse heaps exist within the site boundaries" because these features were smaller than the shovel-testing interval used across much of the site (Florida Archeological Services 1994:121). The spatial orientations of these villages, however, cannot be determined from available evidence.

A clearly circular Late Swift Creek village was located nearby. Roughly in the middle of the Greenfield peninsula, the Swift Creek Middens Area at Greenfield site #8/9 (8DU5544/5545) was a non-mounded horseshoe-shaped shell midden approximately 50 meters in diameter with two interior "household middens" rife with faunal remains and sherds (Smith and Handley 2002:49; Wallis 2007). Although few posts and no definitive evidence of structures were identified, the spatial configuration of midden deposits is consistent with many other Swift Creek ring middens interpreted as circular villages (Stephenson et al. 2002:346). Three radiocarbon assays put occupation of the site solidly in the seventh century and possibly the eighth. The pottery assemblage consisted almost exclusively of sand-tempered plain and complicated stamped sherds; however, microscopic analysis identified charcoal tempering in a few sherds (Wallis 2007). Because the charcoal-tempered sherds were recovered from various depths throughout the dense shell midden, they are likely to be contemporaneous with the Late Swift Creek occupation of the site and represent the last waning years of the tradition of charcoal tempering.

The Swift Creek Middens Area represents a discrete Late Swift Creek village, perhaps the best example of one in northeastern Florida. Another Late Swift Creek ring midden was recorded on the same site (8DU5544/5545) just 175 meters to the east (Johnson 1998). This roughly arcuate midden (Midden A) is notable not only for its large size, at 120 meters across its long axis, but also for its probable plaza cemetery. Five test units were excavated in the center of the arc-shaped site with human remains and Swift Creek pottery encountered each time. This area was labeled Mound C, described as a low, barely perceptible 30-centimeter rise with an oval shape "cradled" by Midden A (Johnson 1998:71). However, the recorded relative elevations of the surface of Midden A and Mound C reveal that the apex of the "mound" stood only 10 centimeters above the highest portions of the midden (Johnson 1998:22, 64). Thus, Mound C may not have been a mound, per se, but rather a plaza cemetery akin to the Bernath Place Swift Creek village on the Gulf Coast, where dozens of individuals were recorded (Bense 1998). Whether mounded or not, the cemetery–village complex at Greenfield #8/9 is unique in a region where solitary mortuary mounds were more common during Swift Creek times (Ashley and Wallis 2006).

To the north of the Greenfield peninsula, multicomponent sites at Cedar Point (8DU81), Crane Island (8NA709), and Amelia Island (McArthur Estates, 8NA32) indicate substantial Swift Creek occupations, but little information about village structure can be discerned (Ashley 2003; Dickinson and Wayne 1999; Handley et al. 2004). At McArthur Estates (8NA32) numerous postholes and widespread pit features filled with domestic refuse likely correspond with a Late Swift Creek village, yet no spatial patterns are apparent. Radiocarbon assays from Swift Creek pit features date the site to the seventh and eighth centuries.

Another Amelia Island site shows more clearly an approximately circular village layout. Ocean Reach (8NA782) was a Late Swift Creek site consisting of 22 discrete shell middens (Johnson et al. 1997). These middens, averaging between 3 meters and 4 meters across and uniformly between 10 and 20 centimeters in thickness, were interpreted as individual household refuse deposits. Three clusters of individual middens were apparent at the site, with each forming roughly the corner of a triangle about 80 meters on a side. An important distinction at Ocean Reach was that the shell middens were comprised primarily of quahog clam (*Mercenaria* spp.), as opposed to oyster (*Crassostrea virginica*), which dominates most Swift Creek shell middens.

## Southeastern Georgia

Large Swift Creek components in coastal Georgia are mainly confined to southern areas, between the St. Marys River and just north of the Altamaha River. While there are more than 60 sites that contain Swift Creek pottery along the coast (Ashley et al. 2007:7), at present 7 sites that have been investigated are likely to represent village sites.

In Camden County, Georgia, three Swift Creek sites correspond with substantial habitation sites. Two large village complexes at the Kings Bay locality were excavated by the University of Florida during the 1970s and 1980s (Adams 1985; B. Smith 1986; R. Smith 1978; Smith et al. 1981; Smith et al. 1985). The first was the Kings Bay site (9CM171), which included a series of discrete shell middens arranged in an arc on a bluff overlooking the salt marsh. While this area of the site was interpreted as the location of a village with individual household middens, evidence of a structure and hearths/trash pits at two adjacent locales were interpreted as special processing areas (Saunders 1986:17–18). Seasonality data indicated occupations during all seasons of the year, perhaps denoting year-round residency (Quitmyer 1985:89; Reitz and Quitmyer 1988). The Mallard Creek site (9CM185), located 1.5 kilometers inland from Kings Bay (9CM171), exhibited a settlement structure entirely different than the typical arcuate-shaped arrangement of middens. Instead, the site consisted of a single "centralized refuse disposal area" with domestic activities apparently confined to its periphery (Smith et al. 1985:140). An analysis of quahog clam growth rings points to a spring season of occupation (Saunders 1998:163).

The Sadlers Landing site (9CM233), located 8 kilometers north of the Kings Bay site, included numerous discrete oyster shell middens, but their spatial arrangement was not clearly arcuate (Kirkland 2003:122). In one area of the site partial, multiple, and primary burials were also encountered along with red ochre, stone celts, deer antler fragments, a bear tooth, and mica sheets. While no evidence of a mound was encountered during excavation, there is a strong possibility that one existed at the site but had been razed by plowing (Kirkland 2003:152). The dense shell middens recorded nearby may be evidence of a village directly adjacent to the site of the former mound. Based on the field map, discrete clusters of shell midden also were recorded between approximately 150 meters and 600 meters from the human remains (Kirkland 2003:122). Two AMS assays date the site between AD 600 and 800, firmly within the Late Swift Creek phase.

To the north, significant Swift Creek sites exist at Cumberland Harbor Shell Midden (9CM249) on the northeast end of the Point Peter peninsula as well as Pike's Bluff Shell Midden (9GN200) on the west side of St. Simons Island, but reports of excavations at these sites have yet to be released (Ashley et al. 2007:24). Further to the north along the Altamaha River and its tributaries, numerous important sites have been investigated, most notably Evelyn (9GN6), Cathead Creek (9MC360), Sidon (9MC372), and Lewis Creek (9MC16).

The Evelyn site includes seven mounds across about 200 acres overlooking the tidal marsh on the southern side of the Altamaha River. A Swift Creek shell midden covering more than an acre is situated just north of Mound B, a platform mound, and Mound C, a conical burial mound, both of which have been demonstrated to be Swift Creek (Ashley et al. 2007:14–15; Chance 1974; Waring and Holder 1968:140). Surface collecting and very limited subsurface testing have revealed that the midden is Late Swift Creek with a probable Kelvin component, and Keith Ashley and colleagues (2007:14) suggest that further investigation may reveal an arc-shaped habitation area. With further work, the Evelyn site may reveal a substantial Swift Creek village directly adjacent to both a conical burial mound and platform mound.

Roughly across the river from Evelyn at the confluence of Cathead Creek and the Darien River is the Cathead Creek site (9MC360). This site is known solely through mitigation efforts that were focused on narrow utility corridors. This spatial restriction and the multicomponent nature of the site made delineations of site structure difficult, yet concentrations of Swift Creek pottery suggest the possibility of an arc-like settlement pattern (Wayne 1987: 59). The Swift Creek components of the site included both shallow and deep pits as well as shell middens. One calibrated radiocarbon age dates Swift Creek occupation of the site to the sixth or seventh century. A face-down burial was also discovered at the site, but due to its radiocarbon age (tenth century) and burial treatment it is likely to be associated with Kelvin (e.g., terminal or waning Swift Creek) (Ashley et al. 2007:11). Zooarchaeological data from the Swift Creek component indicate that the site may have been occupied on a year-round basis (Reitz and Quitmyer 1988).

Located 3 kilometers to the northwest of Cathead Creek, the Sidon Plantation site (9MC372) was excavated by Fred Cook (1995) during construction of a shopping mall. His salvage work documented a series of Swift Creek pit features, including a "shallow Swift Creek phase house pit" that contained a flexed human interment (Cook 1995:8–10). Another burial was located nearby, consisting of disarticulated and cremated remains from several individuals. These interments that seem to be associated with houses rather than mounds may be the best evidence for an entirely different mortuary tradition in Swift Creek contexts. One AMS date from human bone indicates that occupation of the site was in the seventh century.

Located less than 7 kilometers west of Sidon Plantation, along a tributary of the Altamaha River, the Lewis Creek site (9MC16) consists of a shell midden along the water's edge and five burial mounds further inland. Only one of the mounds has been investigated and dates to the Savannah II phase; however, the cultural affiliation of the other four mounds remains unclear (Cook 1966). The shell midden itself has never been excavated but has been extensively surface collected over the years as Swift Creek pottery continually eroded onto the bluff facing the creek (Ashley et al. 2007:11). Little has been determined about the spatial structure of the site, but a recent visit to the site in 2008 confirmed that shell midden deposits are extensive.

## Mortuary Mounds

There are two or more Swift Creek mortuary traditions represented on the Atlantic coast. Along the Lower St. Johns River, low mounds mostly less than a meter in height were raised over a period of centuries as human remains, artifacts, and earth were repeatedly added. At least fifteen of these mortuary mounds have been recorded, and all but one appear to have been located some distance away from village sites (Ashley and Wallis 2006). In contrast, Swift Creek mounds are rare to the north of the St. Johns River along the Georgia coast, undoubtedly in part due to site destruction in the absence of recorded investigations. As mentioned previously, a mound probably once existed at Sadlers Landing (9CM233), and other Swift Creek mounds have been noted along Turtle River in Glynn County and on St. Simons Island (Ashley et al. 2007:24). While Swift Creek mortuary mounds certainly existed in southeastern Georgia, another mode of burial, such as underneath houses, like at Sidon (9MC372), may also have been more common than current evidence suggests.

The mounds at Evelyn (9GN6) near the southern bank of the Altamaha River may represent still another form of mortuary ceremonialism. The Evelyn site itself is anomalous for several reasons. First, it is the only site along the coast that contains multiple Swift Creek mounds, with at least two and possibly more presumably dating to the Late Swift Creek phase (Ashley et al. 2007:13). Second, the site contains the only possible Swift Creek platform mound (Mound B) along the coast, consisting of several distinct layers of cultural strata with Swift Creek sherds and intermittent burials (Waring and Holder 1968). If Mound B does indeed have a Swift Creek affiliation, its construction and use may have been similar to other Woodland period platform mounds in the Southeast (Ashley et al. 2007:13; Jefferies 1994). Third, the Evelyn site provides convincing evidence of a substantial village site adjacent to the two Swift Creek mounds, a close proximity between mound and village that is not common to the south on the Lower St. Johns River. Fourth, Mound C, at 3 meters high in recent records of elevation (Ashley et al. 2007), is considerably taller than the majority of Swift Creek mounds on the Lower St. Johns River. Stratigraphy in the mound revealed that it was built in four or five stages (Chance 1974; Waring and Holder 1968:140), which stands in contrast to the low mounds of the St. Johns that mostly lack discrete internal stratigraphy that would be formed by major earthmoving events. Finally, Mound C contained artifacts such as quartz crystal and small bar gorgets that are uncommon on the coast but have been recovered at Swift Creek mounds much further inland (Ashley et al. 2007:14). In fact, David Anderson (1998) suggests that sites such as Evelyn were located along important exchange routes to the interior and were places of public consumption and competitive display of wealth between individuals and lineages. In all, the ceremonialism evidenced at Evelyn may have been more similar to that of central Georgia populations than to populations to the south along the St. Johns River.

Fifteen Woodland period mounds along the Lower St. Johns River have been attributed to the Swift Creek archaeological culture (Ashley and Wallis 2006:11). Twelve of these are known primarily through C. B. Moore's (1894, 1895, 1896) early work, with the remaining three excavated in later years, having somehow escaped Moore's detection (Ashley 1995; Johnson

1998; Wilson 1965). Most mounds along the river tended to be sited on bluff edges not directly on the water, although they very well may have commanded a view of the water. In general, the mounds yielded mainly complicated stamped and undecorated vessels, along with fewer St. Johns Plain, Dunns Creek Red, and Weeden Island series wares. Each of these minority wares appears to have been more common in mounds than in coeval middens. Other common items in the mounds included shell beads, modified and unmodified marine shell, pebble hammerstones, unmodified pebbles, hafted bifaces and chert flakes, celts, hematite (ocher), sandstone, mica sheets, and various copper artifacts (Ashley 1998:212). While some of these objects are similar to those exchanged throughout Hopewell interaction networks of the Eastern Woodlands (Seeman 1979), the majority of extralocal artifacts at Swift Creek mounds were acquired after the heyday of Hopewell interactions (Ashley and Wallis 2006:12). Based on the osteological populations and the context of mound artifacts, often placed throughout the mound rather than with particular individuals, Thunen and Ashley (1995) inferred an essentially egalitarian social structure. Certainly, the ostentatious burial treatments recorded in other Hopewell-related contexts in the Southeast and Midwest are mostly lacking on the Lower St. Johns (e.g., Brose and Greber 1979; Mainfort 1988).

Judging from Moore's (1894, 1895, 1896) descriptions, there appears to have been some variation in burial regimes and quantities of objects placed within mounds. While there is disparity in the height of mounds, ranging from 0.6 meters to 2.1 meters (Ashley 1998:209), the most notable disparity is in the quantities of human remains and objects (mostly pottery) that mounds contained. In some mounds, burials were abundant and objects were deposited by themselves or in caches, often with ochre. It is estimated that the Dent Mound contained more than 100 human interments, with males, females, and children represented (Ashley 1995). Excavation of approximately 30 percent to 40 percent of the Mayport Mound yielded more than 50 individuals, both adults and children (Wilson 1965:12–13). At these sites, pottery was ubiquitous, including many scores of whole vessels, intentionally broken or basally perforated vessels, and sherds numbering in the thousands. Moore (1894, 1895) seems to describe similar evidence at Arlington (8DU33), Point La Vista C (8DU40), Monroe (8DU13), Low Grant A (8DU15), and Low Grant E (8DU19) mounds. At most of these mounds Moore notes that human remains were encountered at "25 points," presumably indicating at least 25 interred individuals. These mounds also contained appreciable amounts of earthenware vessels and sherds. Moore describes Grant Mound E as "literally filled with earthenware—whole vessels, fragmentary ones, and sherds" (1895:

490). Grant Mound E actually contained few human burials, but this discrepancy may have been due to extremely poor preservation, which Moore (1895:489) himself acknowledges. All of the mounds rich in artifacts and human remains appear to be the continuous-use type of mound (cf. Sears 1958:277) in which the mound grew by accretion as artifacts and human remains were added over a period of centuries (Ashley 1998:213–214; Thunen and Ashley 1995:5).

I propose that among Moore's descriptions there may have been another type of mound that was constructed in fewer stages and over a much shorter period of time. At mounds such as South Jacksonville B (8DU36), Point La Vista A (8DU38) and B (8DU39), and Johnson (8DU10), human remains and pottery were comparatively limited. While human remains at these sites may have escaped detection due to poor preservation, the disparity in the abundance of pottery is striking. At these sites it appears there were no opportunities to incorporate new offerings over time, resulting in far fewer "fragments of [vessels that were] many feet apart, as though strewn upon the mound in course of construction" than at other mounds (Moore 1894:199). Instead, these mounds may have been erected quickly, and material was not continually added in subsequent years.

Among the clearly accretionary mounds there is some variation as well. At the Mayport Mound, extended burials predominated, while at the Dent Mound large aggregations of disarticulated remains were more common (Ashley 1995; Wilson 1965). These discrepancies may indicate very different patterns of group mobility or simply different mortuary regimes. As Jerald Milanich and Charles Fairbanks (1980:160) suggest, masses of bones of many individuals interred together may indicate that remains were processed in a charnel facility before interment. Both mounds contained Early and Late Swift Creek diagnostic pottery and appear to have been continuously used for centuries. In addition, no village site has been located in proximity to either of these mounds.

## Summary of the Cultural Landscape

The cultural landscape of the Atlantic coast can be divided into somewhat of a northern and southern dichotomy. Along the Lower St. Johns River, many accretionary mounds were initiated during the Early Swift Creek phase and continued to be used for centuries until the end of the Late Swift Creek phase. A few others, as noted, may have had shorter use lives. In all but one solitary case (Greenfield #8/9), villages on the Lower St. Johns River were situated some distance away from mounds. While Late Swift Creek populations continued to use many of the same mortuary mounds initiated by Early

Cultural History and Archaeological Overview / 77

Swift Creek groups, Late Swift Creek village sites rarely overlap with Early Swift Creek occupations. Early Swift Creek interactions seem to have been focused toward the Gulf Coast of Florida, whereas Late Swift Creek interactions were directed toward the Georgia coast as well.

On the Georgia coast there is little evidence of Swift Creek mounds, with Evelyn a confirmed exception and possibilities at the unexcavated mounds at Lewis Creek and in the mortuary components at Cathead Creek and Sadlers Landing that may have been razed prior to excavation (Ashley et al. 2007:22). While site destruction may partially explain regional differences, other modes of burial are also apparent, as demonstrated at the Sidon site (9MC372). At Evelyn (9GN6), the comparatively large conical burial mound and broad platform mound may show more cultural similarities to Swift Creek sites in central Georgia than Lower St. Johns mounds. In addition, the ostensible village midden at Evelyn is directly adjacent to the mortuary mound(s), a close proximity not recorded among the mounds and villages in northeastern Florida.

## Paddle Matches

Even in the midst of these apparent differences during the Late Swift Creek phase, there is definitive evidence of social interaction in the form of paddle matches identified from complicated stamped designs. Paddle matches confirmed by sherd-to-sherd comparison link sites in coastal Georgia to sites in south-central Georgia and northeastern Florida. Paddle matches link sites within these regions as well. There are presently 9 paddle matches linking 13 sites in northeastern Florida and southeastern Georgia (Figure 3.3) (Ashley et al. 2007; Ashley and Wallis 2006). This tally does not include several designs that link solitary coastal sites with inland sites (Ashley et al. 2007). Some of these paddle matches come from complete vessels or large portions of vessels and confirm variation in both the shape of matching vessels and orientation of paddle impressions.

There are three designs linking northeastern Florida and southeastern Georgia sites. Using Frankie Snow's numerical designations, design 34 connects the Dent (8DU68) and Grant (8DU14) mounds on the Lower St. Johns River with the Sidon site (9MC372) near the Altamaha River, about 115 kilometers away. Based on illustrations, this design is likely present at Kings Bay (9CM171) as well. Interestingly, at least two distinct vessel forms are represented, an open pot from Sidon and a collared jar from Grant (Figure 3.4). The orientation of the paddle stamping is identical, however.

Design 36 links the Dent Mound (8DU68) with three sites near the Al-

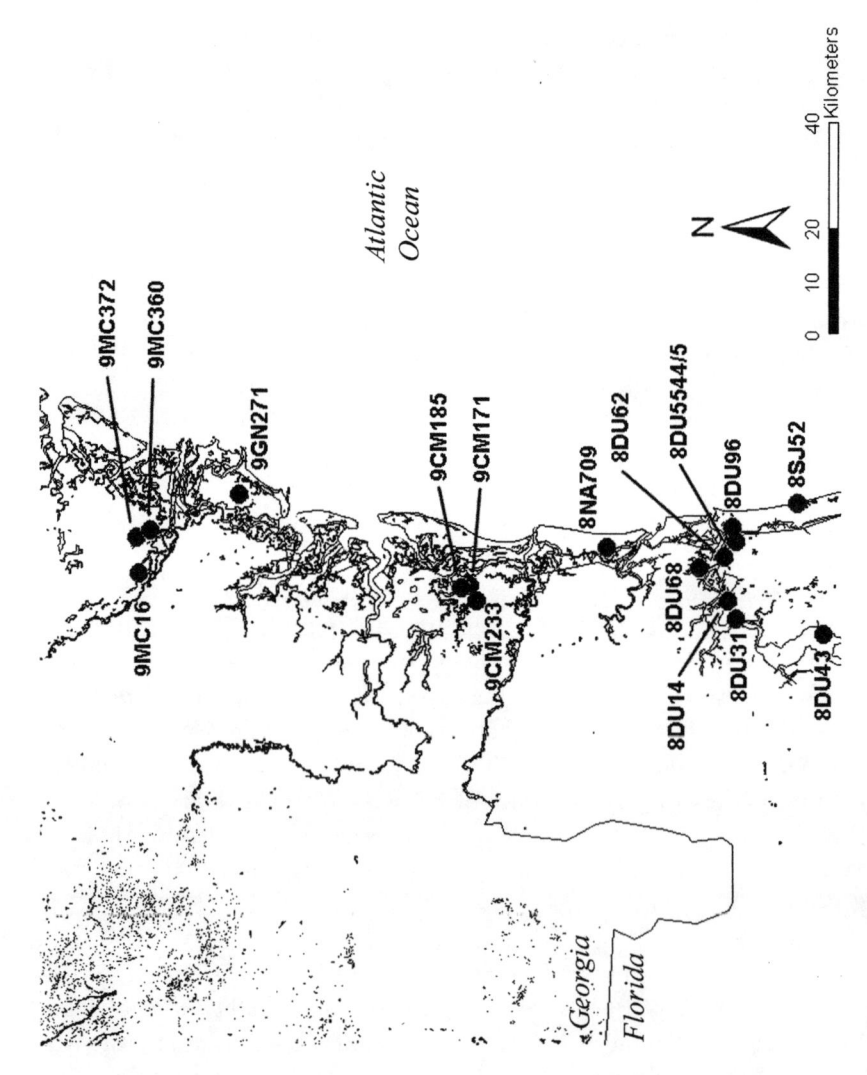

Figure 3.3. Swift Creek sites with paddle matches mentioned in the text.

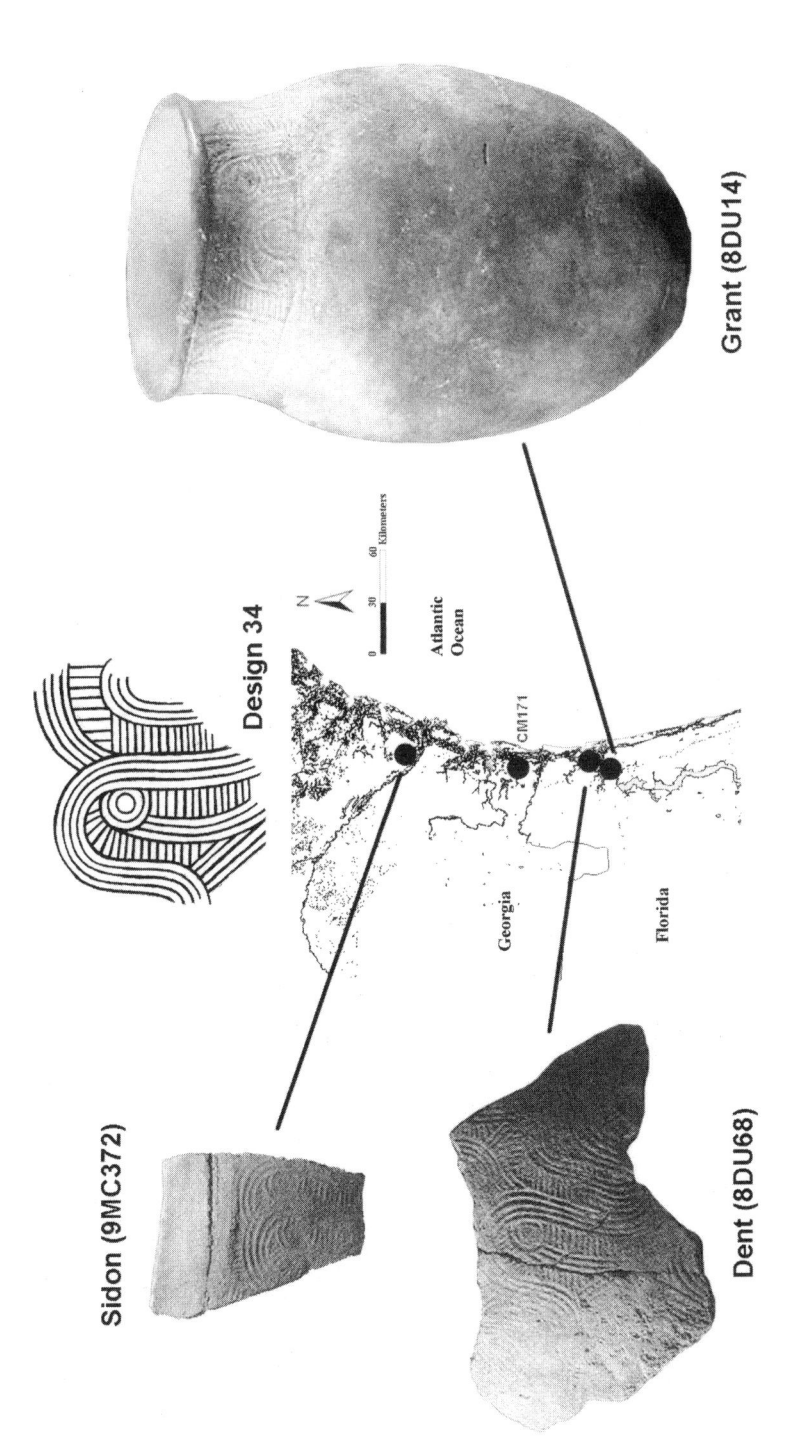

Figure 3.4. Reconstructed design 34 (by Frankie Snow) and select paddle matches. The Grant vessel is 18.5 centimeters tall. Artifacts held in the collections of National Museum of the American Indian, South Georgia College, and the Jacksonville Museum of Science and History (images by the author).

Figure 3.5. Reconstructed design 36 (by Frankie Snow) and select paddle matches. Artifacts held in the collections of the Jacksonville Museum of Science and History, South Georgia College, and the Antonio J. Waring Jr. Archaeological Laboratory, University of West Georgia (images by the author).

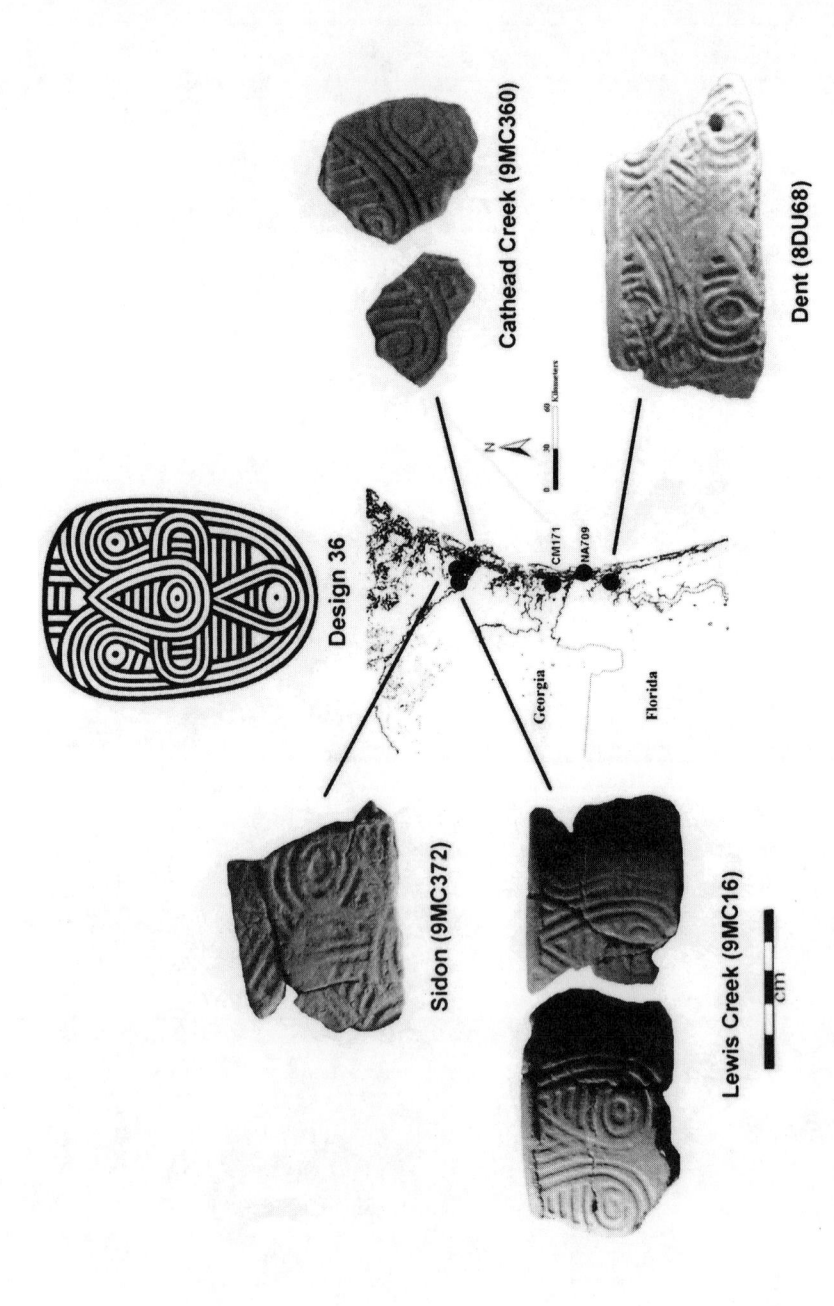

tamaha (9MC16, 9MC360, 9MC372) as well as Kings Bay (9CM171) and Crane Island (8NA709), just west of Amelia Island (Ashley and Wallis 2006). Vessel forms are very similar, consisting of restricted pots or bowls, but the size of the vessels vary dramatically with orifices ranging from 17 centimeters (9MC16) to 30 centimeters (8DU68). What is more, paddle orientation is unique on the Dent Mound vessel compared to the specimens from sites near the Altamaha River. While paddle impressions on most vessels were made with the long axis of the paddle perpendicular to the rim, the Dent Mound vessel has impressions nearly parallel to the rim (Figure 3.5).

Design 38 connects the Mayport Mound (8DU96) and the same three sites along the Altamaha River (9MC16, 9MC360, 9MC372) as well as the Shadman's Field (9GN271) site on St. Simons Island (Ashley and Wallis 2006). Two of these vessels, one from Mayport and the other from Lewis Creek, were partially reconstructed. These vessels are strikingly similar in terms of vessel form and rim treatment: both are sub-conoidal pots with thick, folded rims. However, their sizes are quite distinct, with orifice diameters of 26 centimeters (Mayport) and 36 centimeters (Lewis Creek). Also, paddle orientation is variable, oriented nearly perpendicular to the rim (Mayport) or nearly parallel to the rim (Lewis Creek) (Figure 3.6). Notably, the Mayport vessel exhibits crisp, clear impressions while the Lewis Creek vessel shows a crack in the wooden paddle, indicating that the Lewis Creek vessel was made sometime after the vessel from Mayport (Wallis 2004).

There are three designs that link sites within northeastern Florida. First, there is a match between the Dent (8DU68), Alicia B (8DU31), and Beauclerc mounds (8DU43). This is the sole Early Swift Creek paddle match in northeastern Florida, identified by charcoal temper and an AMS radiometric range for the Dent vessel between the fourth and fifth century (Ashley 1995). Notably, the Beauclerc specimen does not contain charcoal temper (Figure 3.7). Rim treatments among the Dent and Alicia B vessels, the latter illustrated by C. B. Moore (1895:plate 80), are identical. Second, I recently identified another match between the Dent Mound and a Greenfield peninsula (8DU5544/5) village site (Figure 3.8). AMS dating of soot from the rim of the village vessel yielded a calibrated 2-sigma range of AD 660 to 790 (Stephenson et al. 2002). A third match links two potentially quotidian contexts, comprised of one sherd that was included in the fill of the Browne Mound (8DU62), which may postdate Swift Creek occupation, and one from the Schmidt site (8SJ52) in St. Johns County to the south. A few sherds from the latter site show design wear and well-developed paddle cracks, indicating that this vessel was made later than other matching vessels at the site as well as the vessel from the Browne Mound (Ashley and Wallis 2006:12).

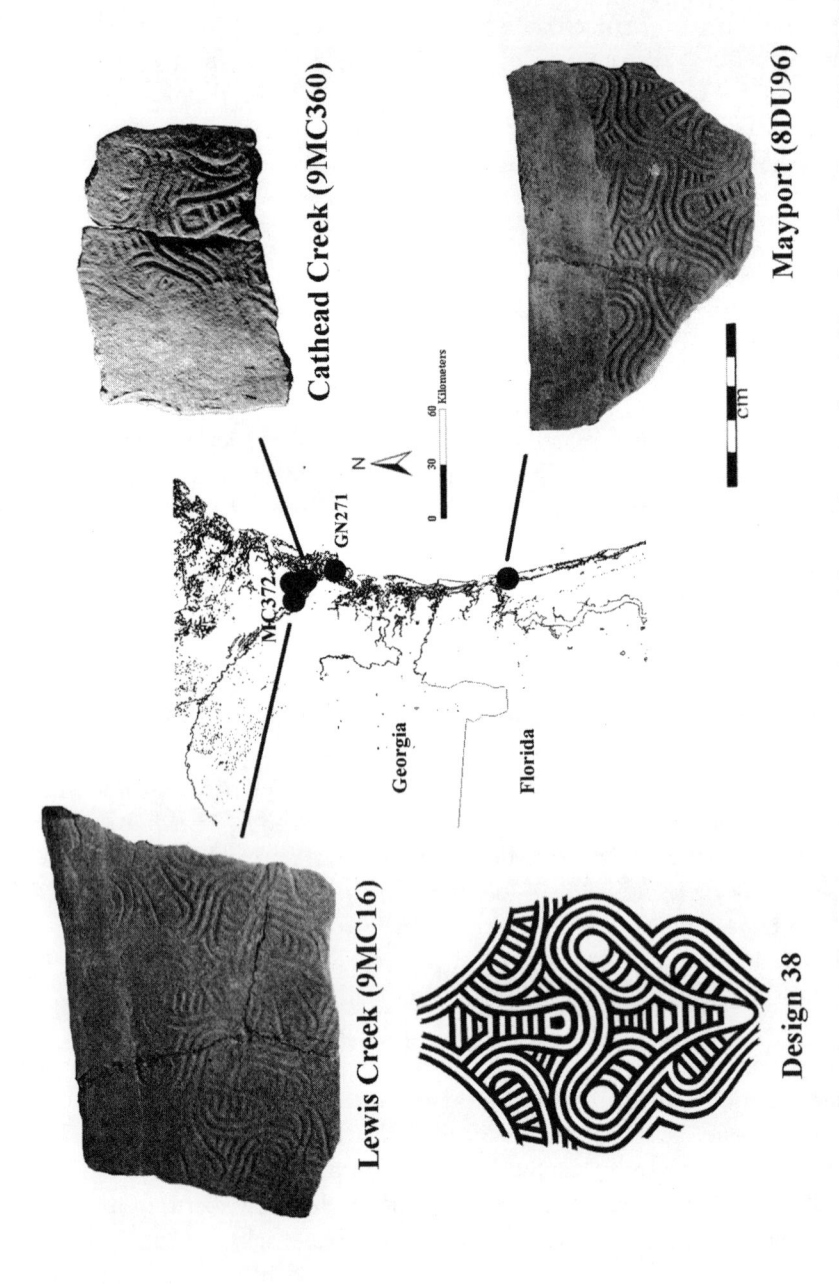

Figure 3.6. Reconstructed design 38 (by Frankie Snow) and select paddle matches. Artifacts held in the collections of the Florida Museum of Natural History, South Georgia College, and the Antonio J. Waring Jr. Archaeological Laboratory, University of West Georgia (images by the author).

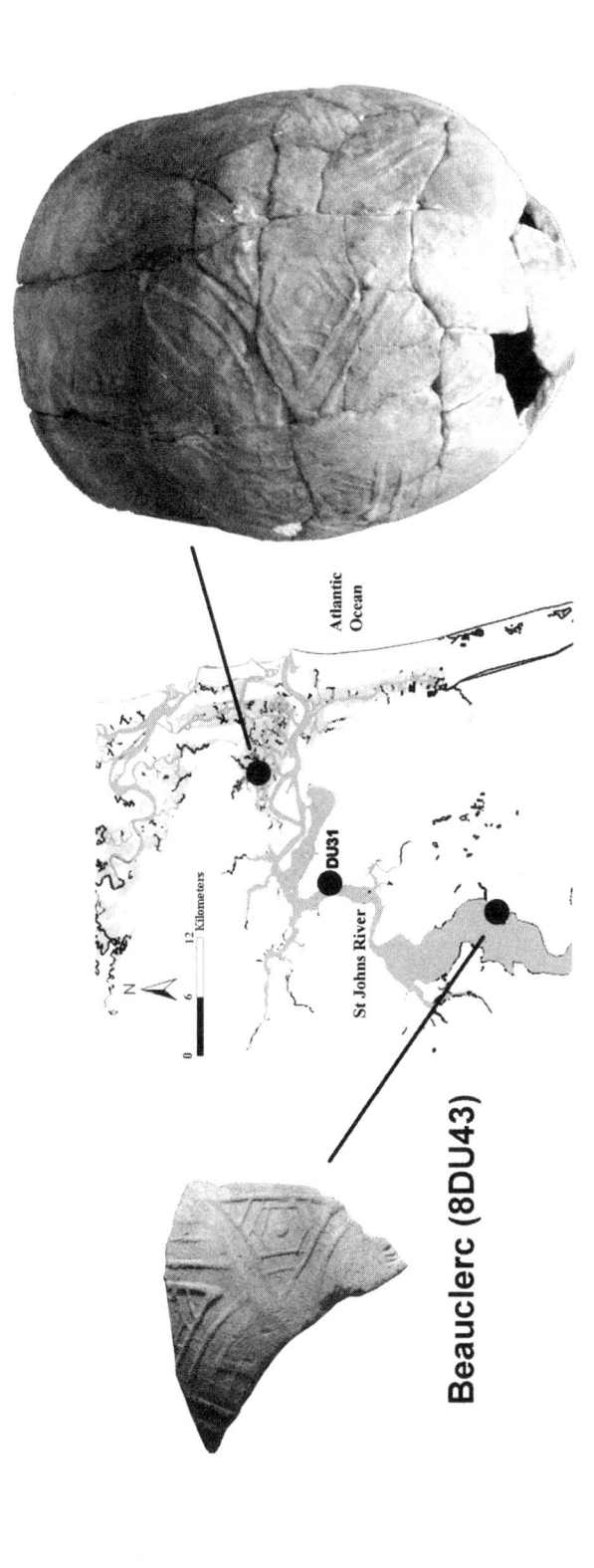

Figure 3.7. Unnumbered design and select paddle matches. The Dent vessel is 20 centimeters wide. Artifacts held in the collections of the Jacksonville Museum of Science and History and the National Museum of the American Indian (images by the author).

84 / Chapter 3

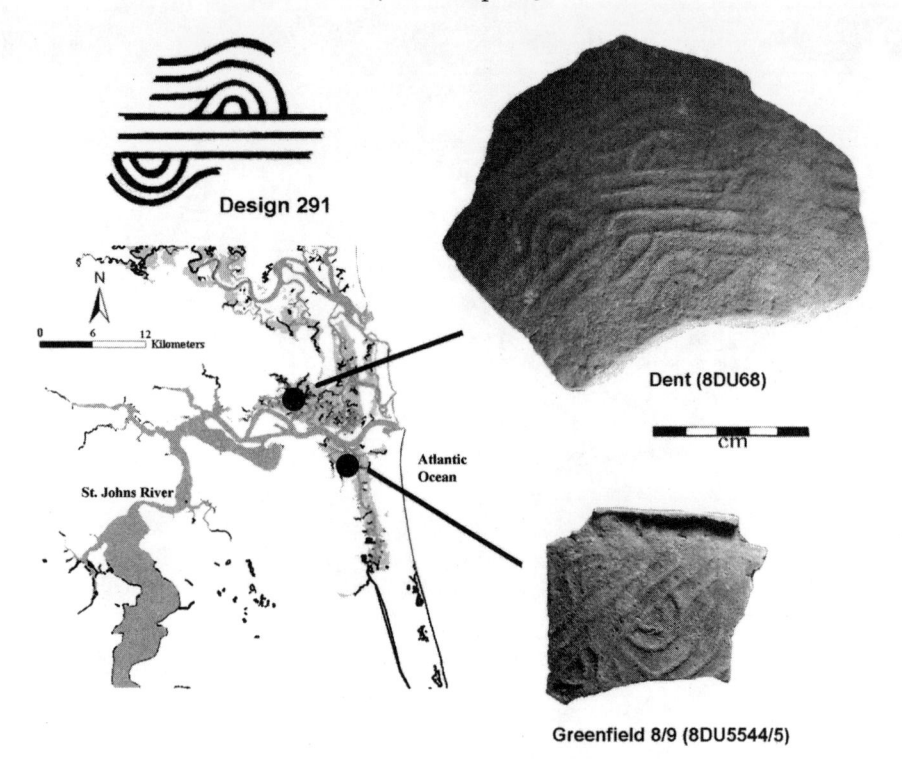

Figure 3.8. Reconstructed design 291 (by Frankie Snow) and paddle matches. Artifacts held in the collections of the Jacksonville Museum of Science and History and Environmental Services, Inc. (images by the author).

There are three designs that link sites in Camden County in southeastern Georgia. Designs 188 and 238 both link Kings Bay (9CM171) to Sadlers Landing (9CM233) along with several south-central Georgia sites. Design 142 links Sadlers Landing (9CM233) with Mallard Creek (9CM185) and several sites much further inland (Ashley et al. 2007:18). These Camden County sites are linked by eight designs with more than a dozen sites toward the interior coastal plain, mostly along the lower Ocmulgee River (Ashley et al. 2007:18–19).

To summarize, of the six paddle matches with sites on the Lower St. Johns River, all but one includes definitive mortuary mound assemblages. In contrast, none of the six matches with southeastern Georgia sites includes unambiguous mortuary contexts. This difference may reflect both sampling bias and different modes of burial along the coast. Among paddle matches, the diversity of vessel forms and variety of orientations of paddle impres-

Cultural History and Archaeological Overview / 85

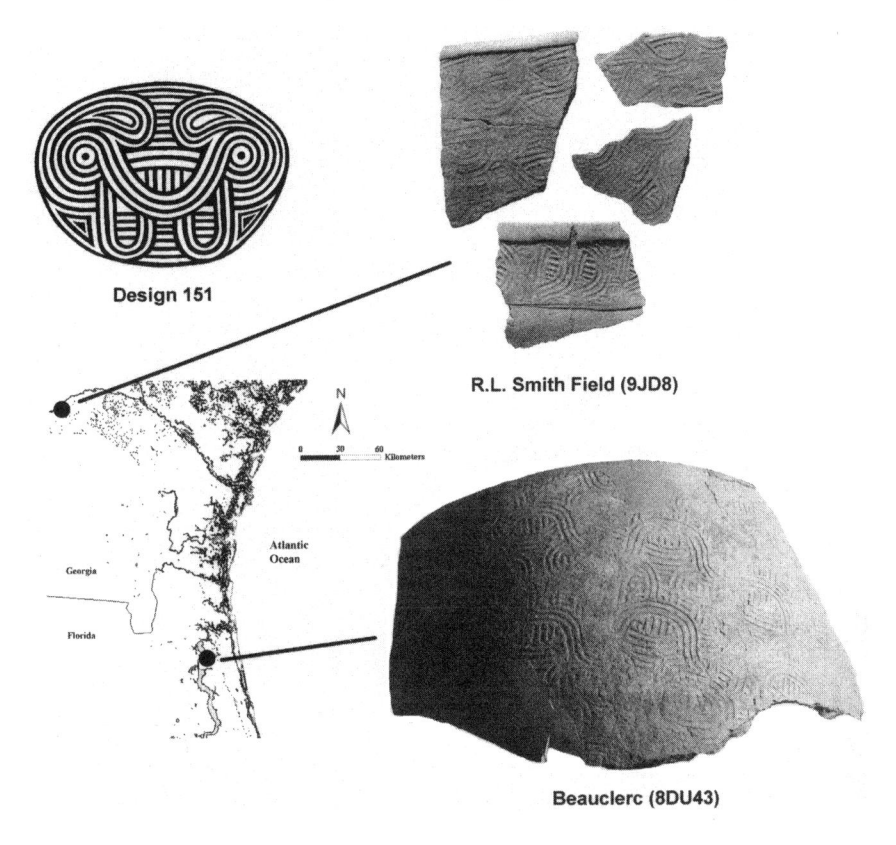

Figure 3.9. Reconstructed design 151 (by Frankie Snow), sherds bearing this design from 9JD8, and a nearly identical design from 8DU43. Artifacts held in the collections of South Georgia College (image courtesy of Frankie Snow) and the National Museum of the American Indian (image by the author).

sions among matching vessels separated by many kilometers may invalidate the idea that wooden paddles were personal property used by one individual (Wallis 2006a).

Georgia coastal assemblages include many paddle matches with the interior coastal plain, yet northeastern Florida assemblages contain no such matches. However, designs found on vessels from the Beauclerc Mounds (8DU43) on the Lower St. Johns River and the R. L. Smith Field site (9JD8) near the Ocmulgee River, though not a match, are similar enough to deserve mention (Figure 3.9). The size and number of elements in the designs are not identical, but they clearly represent the same fundamental theme. Rarely are two paddle designs so similar, except perhaps in the case of "sun" theme designs, characterized by a concentric circle element in the design center (Frankie Snow, personal communication, June 2008). While the similarities in these designs do not necessarily reflect direct social contact between south-central Georgia and northeastern Florida, they indicate some degree of mutual influence in specific forms of artistic representation.

## Summary

The Swift Creek archaeological culture was manifested on the Atlantic coast in regionally specific ways as populations with distinctive histories engaged larger-scale social and cultural developments. Variation in the rate at which complicated stamping was adopted, the size and number of mounds, the type of burial practices, and the layout of villages and mounds across the landscape show a spatial structure that mirrors deep historical differences of at least the previous millennium. It is probably no coincidence that the southern extent of sites with large amounts of Swift Creek pottery essentially mirrors the distribution of Deptford sites because the two archaeological cultures were clearly related (compare Figures 3.1 and 3.2). However, the closer proximity of the Lower St. Johns River to the St. Johns I cultures and Swift Creek cultures of the Gulf Coast led to a different cultural trajectory for each region.

On the Atlantic coast, Swift Creek Complicated Stamped pottery was first adopted on the Lower St. Johns River, presumably reflecting social interactions with populations on the Florida Gulf Coast. After about AD 500, populations living along the Atlantic coast from the Altamaha River to south of the mouth of the St. Johns River were making complicated stamped pottery. With the ubiquity of complicated stamping also came evidence of interaction along the coast in the form of paddle matches, which seem to have become more prevalent and conspicuous. While there are no Swift Creek paddle matches that link the Lower St. Johns and the Gulf Coast, social interaction between populations continued after AD 500 as evidenced by Weeden Island series vessels at Lower St. Johns sites. By detailing the contexts of pottery production, use, and deposition, the remaining chapters are devoted to deciphering the social interactions that have been only vaguely understood among Swift Creek populations on the Atlantic coast.

# 4

# Instrumental Neutron Activation Analysis

*Patterns of Swift Creek Interaction*

The complicated stamped designs on Swift Creek pottery often provide compelling evidence for social interaction across the landscape, but the potential of these serendipitous data is only beginning to come to fruition as they are combined with detailed considerations of context. Depositional context is routinely recorded by archaeologists—it is the identification of contexts of manufacture that holds new potential for understanding interaction. Identifying where vessels were made compared to where they were deposited is a significant step toward outlining object biographies and is crucial for understanding patterns of interaction in the past. Instrumental Neutron Activation Analysis (INAA) is an exceptionally powerful analytical technique for determining provenance, and it was not often used in the southeastern United States until recent years (but for discussion of earlier work see Rice 1980 and Smith 1998). However, as the INAA chemical database for the region grows, so too does the potential to decipher the provenance of vessels and thereby construct more robust models of interaction. Particularly compelling is the combination of INAA chemical data and the social contacts evidenced by Swift Creek paddle matches. This chapter presents the results of Instrumental Neutron Activation Analysis (INAA) of a sample of earthenware vessels from Swift Creek contexts and raw clays from the Atlantic coast, as recently reported (Wallis et al. 2010). These data indicate that nonlocal vessels, particularly complicated stamped ones, were deposited almost exclusively at mortuary mounds on the Lower St. Johns River. This pattern requires new explanations for paddle matches and forms of interaction that seem to have been bound up in mortuary ceremony.

## The Sample

The sampling strategy for the INAA portion of this study was informed by two related goals. First, the project was designed to estimate the range of compositional variation in presumably local pottery for the various locations sampled. Based on achievement of this first goal, the second objective was to evaluate the frequency of nonlocal pottery at sites. The spatial scale by which "local" and "nonlocal" pottery can be defined, of course, ultimately depends on the amount of chemical variation in the constituent materials distributed across the landscape. Thus, a large number of samples from each site was desirable for understanding intrasite variation while a large number of sampling locations of both raw materials and sherds from throughout the region would be advantageous for understanding chemical variation across the landscape. With a limited time and funding budget for INAA, these parameters were combined with a delicate balance.

Samples were taken from 313 vessels from 17 sites across northeastern Florida and southeastern Georgia (Table 4.1; Figure 4.1). These samples were divided fairly equitably by region: 173 derived from 8 sites in northeastern Florida and 140 came from 9 sites in southeastern Georgia. There were three criteria that were employed in choosing samples from each site. When assemblages were large and came from discrete contexts from well-documented sites, samples were chosen at random, resulting in a diversity of sampled pottery types. Alternatively, samples from surface collections or poorly documented excavations presented a unique challenge. In these cases, Swift Creek Complicated Stamped sherds were chosen in order to ensure contemporaneity and archaeological culture affiliation among samples. Finally, in some cases samples were limited to the preferences of curators who bristled at the suggestion of taking samples from reconstructed or whole vessels. Other than this last restriction, which may have introduced bias that I discuss in more detail with the analysis results, the sherds chosen from each site represent a random sample.

Twenty clay samples from around the region were also subjected to INAA, with data from an additional three samples appropriated from the MURR database from Keith Ashley's (2003) research (Figure 4.2; Table 4.2). These clay samples were drawn mostly from areas near the sherd sample sites, although a few from further south and west were tested in an attempt at evaluating larger spatial trends in chemical composition. The natural clay samples that derived from locations near archaeological sites chosen for the study were deemed to provide reasonable approximations of the range of chemical variation in the actual clay sources used by prehistoric potters. Identifying

Table 4.1. Site and type distribution of INAA pottery samples

| | CCS | CP | SWCRCS | STP | DEPT | STJP | DCR | MDS | GROG | WII | WIR | CAR | Incised | NI | Total |
|---|---|---|---|---|---|---|---|---|---|---|---|---|---|---|---|
| *Northeastern Florida* | | | | | | | | | | | | | | | |
| Dent Mound (8DU68) | 3 | 7 | 10 | 8 | | | | | | | | | | | 28 |
| Mayport Mound (8DU96) | 2 | 2 | 4 | 6 | 1 | 2 | | 2 | 1 | | | | | | 20 |
| McArthur Estates (8NA32) | | 2 | 19 | 4 | | | | | | 1 | | | | | 26 |
| Greenfield #7 (8DU5543) | 9 | 3 | 9 | 5 | | | | | | | | | | | 26 |
| Tillie Fowler (8DU17245) | 7 | 9 | 4 | 4 | | 1 | 1 | | | | 1 | 1 | | | 28 |
| JU Temp sites | | | 5 | 12 | | 1 | | | | | | | | | 18 |
| Greenfield #8/9 (8DU5544/5) | 1 | 1 | 11 | 10 | | 1 | | | | | | | | | 24 |
| Grant (8DU14) | | | 3 | | | | | | | | | | | | 3 |
| *Southeastern Georgia* | | | | | | | | | | | | | | | |
| Sidon (9MC372) | | | 11 | 10 | | | | | | | | | 1 | | 22 |
| Cathead Creek (9MC360) | | | 17 | 6 | | | | | | | | | | | 23 |
| Evelyn (9GN6) | | | 20 | 3 | | | | | | | | | | | 23 |
| Lewis Creek (9MC16) | | | 22 | 1 | | | | | | | | | | | 23 |

*Continued on the next page*

Table 4.1. Continued

| | CCS | CP | SWCRCS | STP | DEPT | STJP | DCR | MDS | GROG | WII | WIR | CAR | Incised | NI | Total |
|---|---|---|---|---|---|---|---|---|---|---|---|---|---|---|---|
| Kings Bay (9CM171) | | | 4 | | | | | | | | | | | | 4 |
| Kings Lake | | | 18 | | | | | | | | | | | 1 | 19 |
| Paradise Park (9WY8) | | | 6 | 2 | | | | | | | | | | | 8 |
| Oak Landing | | | 2 | 1 | | | | | | | | | | | 3 |
| Hallows Field (9CM25) | | | 15 | | | | | | | | | | | | 15 |
| Total pottery samples | | | | | | | | | | | | | | | 313 |

*Note:* Column headings are as follows: CCS, charcoal-tempered Swift Creek Complicated Stamped; CP, charcoal-tempered plain; SWCRCS, Swift Creek Complicated Stamped; STP, sand-tempered plain; DEPT, Deptford Check Stamped; STJP, St. Johns Plain; DCR, Dunns Creek Red; MDS, Mayport Dentate Stamped; GROG, grog-tempered plain; WII, Weeden Island Incised; WIR, Weeden Island Red; CAR, Carrabelle Punctated; Incised, incised (nondiagnostic); NI, net impressed (sand tempered).

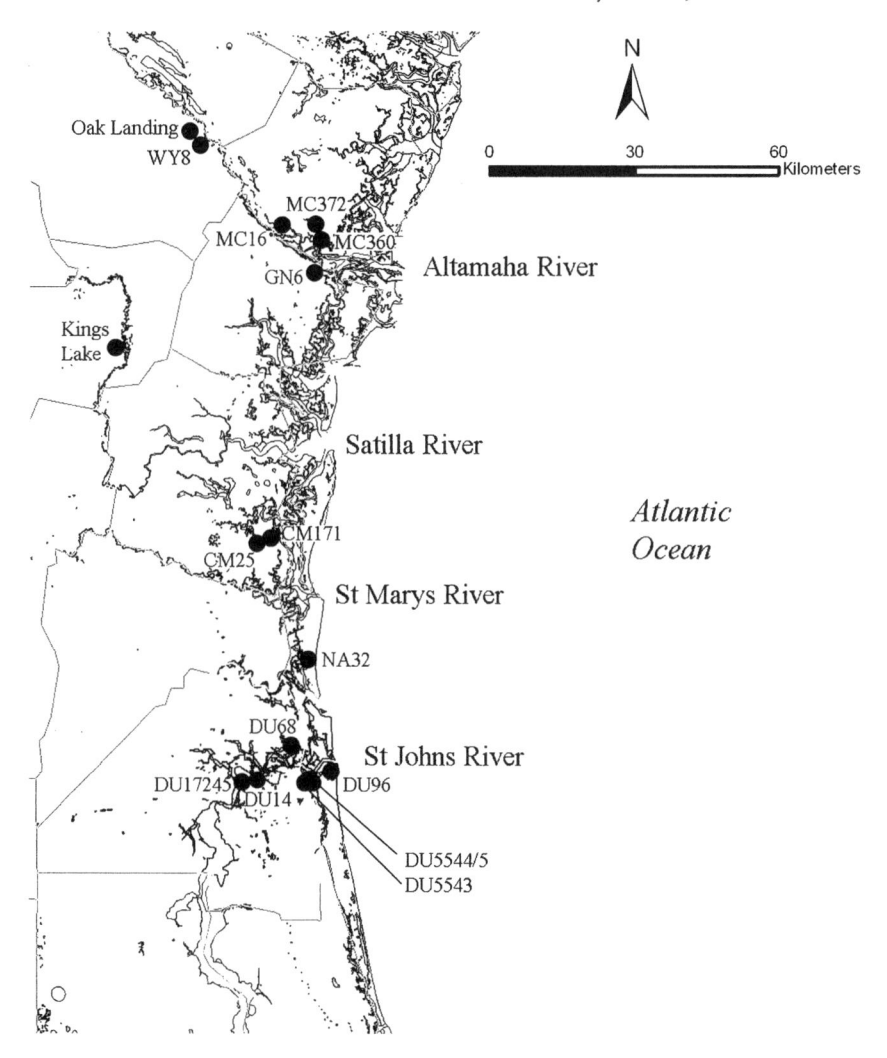

Figure 4.1. Distribution of sites with assemblages used in the INAA study.

the specific clay deposits exploited by potters thousands of years ago is both highly unlikely and impractical for most research programs due to the limitations of the archaeological record and the character of clay body constituents. Indeed, clay quarrying in the southeastern United States is a practice that leaves little identifiable material evidence, much less evidence that is temporally or culturally diagnostic. In addition, degrees of variation within natural clay bodies and the manipulation of clay constituents by potters make

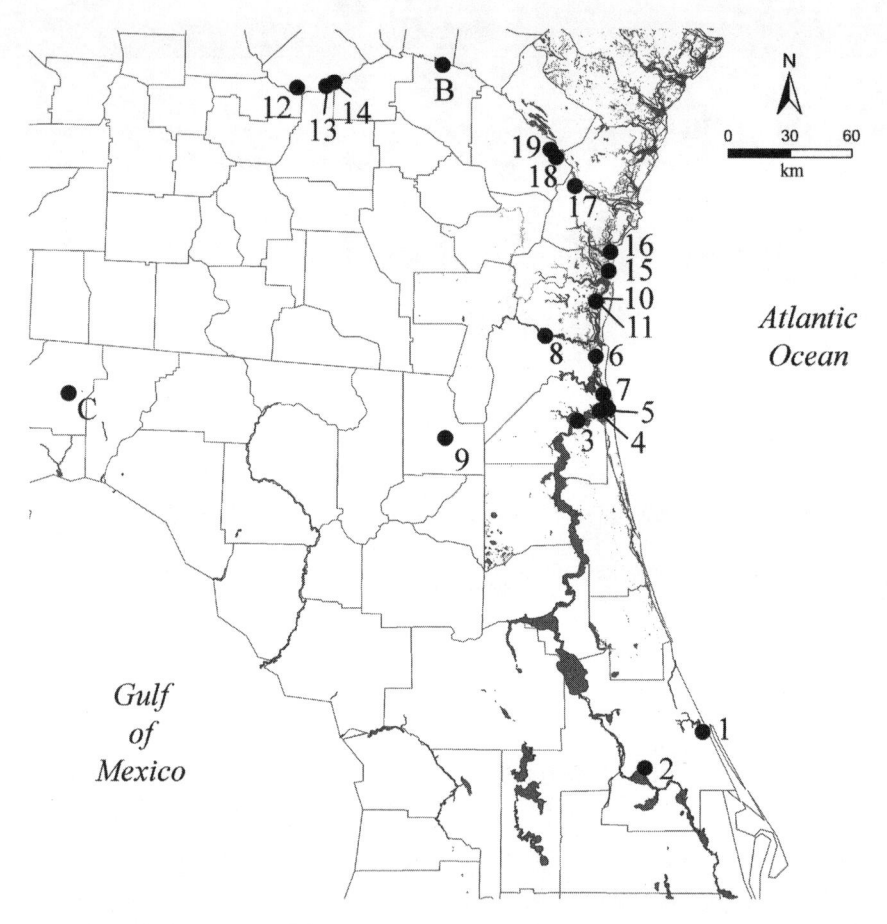

Figure 4.2. Distribution of clay samples in the INAA study. The location of clay sample A from South Carolina is not shown.

chemical and mineralogical identification of *specific* clay deposits used for particular earthenware vessels virtually impossible. Instead, a series of natural clay samples can be used to understand the range of chemical and mineralogical variation in an area; and, given demonstrable patterning in the results, these data can be used as proxies for the actual clay deposits that were used to make pottery.

## Instrumental Neutron Activation Analysis: Methods

Instrumental Neutron Activation Analysis (INAA) is an analytical technique used to characterize the chemical constituents of a material. The analysis is

Table 4.2. Clay samples in the INAA study

| Sample # | ANID | Provenience |
|---|---|---|
| 1 | NJW-315 | New Smyrna, South Riverside Drive |
| 2 | NJW-316 | Green Spring, creek bank |
| 3 | NJW-317 | Grant Mound, Feature 1 |
| 4 | NJW-318 | Oxeye Island, NE Jacksonville |
| 5 | NJW-319 | Grand Shell Ring, TU-4, L-13, Area U |
| 6 | NJW-320 | Amelia Island Airport, Fernandina Beach |
| 7 | NJW-321 | Little Talbot Island, Black Rock, Nassau Sound |
| 8 | NJW-322 | White Oak Plantation, St. Marys Riverbank |
| 9 | NJW-323 | Osceola Forest, Comp. 2, St. 13W, Tr. 2, St. 2 |
| 10 | NJW-324 | Cabin Bluff Shell Ring, TU-201, 95 cmbs |
| 11 | NJW-325 | Cabin Bluff Shell Ring TU-201, Level 8 |
| 12 | NJW-326 | China Hill, Telfair County, Georgia |
| 13 | NJW-327 | Coffee Bluff, Ocmulgee River |
| 14 | NJW-328 | "Hog Wallow" near Coffee Bluff, Ocmulgee River |
| 15 | NJW-329 | Jekyll Island (south) |
| 16 | NJW-330 | Jekyll Island (north) |
| 17 | NJW-331 | "Clay-hole Island", Altamaha River bank |
| 18 | NJW-332 | Lower Sansavilla, Altamaha River bank |
| 19 | NJW-333 | Lower Sansavilla, upland road cut |
| A | KHA089 | 38CH42 |
| B | KHA033 | Deen's Landing, upper Altamaha |
| C | KHA088 | 8LE151 |

*Note:* Samples 3, 5, 10, and 11 are derived from archaeological contexts. All others are natural clay deposits. Samples A, B, and C are from Ashley (2003).

based on the physical properties of the atomic nucleus, whereby gamma rays are released from a sample that has been bombarded with neutrons (i.e., irradiated) within a nuclear reactor (Glascock 1992:11–12). Specifically, the bombardment of a sample with neutrons results in unstable radioactive isotopes that decay with characteristic half-lives and emit gamma radiation characteristic of each of the elements. As these isotopes decay, the gamma rays can be measured to determine the quantities of various elements within a sample. As an especially sensitive and increasingly standardized chemical characterization technique, INAA continues to be a powerful analytical tool for the study of pottery in the context of exchange and interaction (Glascock 2002; Neff 1992, 2000; Steponaitis et al. 1996).

INAA of pottery results in the characterization of the bulk chemical composition of a sample. Because pottery samples are powdered and homogenized before irradiation, no attempt is made to differentiate the chemical profiles of clays and aplastic materials that make up a ceramic paste. Therefore, the aboriginal practice of removing materials from natural clay bodies or adding temper in the process of vessel manufacture can certainly affect the bulk chemical composition of earthenwares. However, experimental and statistical studies confirm that inordinate amounts of temper would usually need to be added to the paste of vessels in order to completely obscure the chemical profiles of different clays (Neff et al. 1988, 1989). There are several techniques that have been successfully used for evaluating the effects of temper in archaeological samples. One powerful technique employs a ceramic ecology approach: sampling a range of possible raw clay sources and tempering agents to tie chemical variation in pottery to different paste recipes (e.g., Neff and Bove 1999). Also, statistical procedures have been developed to remove the chemical effects of some tempers such as shell (Cogswell et al. 1998:64; Steponaitis et al. 1988). Shell tempering adds large amounts of calcium and strontium so that other elements are diluted. However, the diluting effects of shell can be mathematically corrected using the recorded proportions of calcium and strontium measured for each sample.

INAA methods of chemical characterization and multivariate statistical techniques for the interpretation of elemental concentrations have been extensively described elsewhere and will be described here only briefly (Glascock 1992; Neff 1994; Neff et al. 1989). Pottery samples were prepared by the author according to standard procedures at MURR and under the direction of MURR staff (Glascock 1992). A small fragment was removed from each sample and abraded using a silicon carbide burr. This burring procedure removes any adhering soil, glazes, slips, paints, or other potential contaminates on sample surfaces. The samples were then washed in deionized water and allowed to dry. Once completely dry, the samples were ground into a fine powder with an agate mortar and pestle, thus homogenizing each sample. The powder samples were then placed in an oven at 100 degrees C for 24 hours to remove excess moisture. Two analytical samples were prepared from the resulting powders. Approximately 150 milligrams of powder were weighed into high-density polyethylene vials used for short irradiations while 200 milligrams of each sample were weighed into high-purity quartz vials used for long irradiations. Each sample weight was recorded to the nearest 0.01 milligrams using an analytical balance, and the vials were sealed prior to irradiation.

As standard at MURR, INAA consisted of two irradiations and a total of three gamma counts on high-purity germanium detectors for each sample (Glascock 1992; Neff 1992, 2000). The short irradiation was performed through a pneumatic tube irradiation system, in which samples were each irradiated for 5 seconds in the reactor and then subjected to a 720-second gamma count. The second irradiation consisted of 24 hours within the nuclear reactor, with two counts subsequently performed, one after seven days of decay for 1,800 seconds (i.e., the "middle" count) and the other after three weeks of decay for 8,500 seconds (i.e., the "long" count). Combined, the two irradiations and three gamma counts allow detection of 33 elements. Based on the gamma counts, element concentration data were tabulated in parts per million.

The goal of the quantitative analysis was to identify groups among the samples that shared a consistent chemical composition presumed to correspond with geographically restricted sources or source areas (e.g., Weigand et al. 1977). The locations of sources can be deduced by comparing specimens with unknown provenance (e.g., earthenware vessels) to substances with known provenance (e.g., clay samples). Provenance can also be inferred by indirect methods such as the "criterion of abundance" (Bishop et al. 1982), whereby the chemical group with the most samples at a site is presumed to be local. Compositional groups can be viewed as "centers of mass" in the hyperspace defined by the measured elemental data (Glascock 1992:16). Each group is characterized by the location of its centroid in compositional hyperspace and unique correlations between the elements. Group assignment for each specimen is determined by the overall probability that the measured concentrations of a sample could have been obtained from a particular group. The elemental data were reduced to principal components (PCs), and group affiliation was evaluated according to Mahalanobis distances (see Baxter 1992; Baxter and Buck 2000; Bieber et al. 1976; Bishop and Neff 1989; Glascock 1992; Neff 1994, 2002).

## INAA Results

The standard procedures at MURR resulted in the measurement of 33 elements. However, 3 of these were ultimately removed from the quantitative data analysis. As is often the case with New World pottery, nickel (Ni) was below detection levels in the majority of samples and was therefore omitted during the analysis. After careful review of the distribution of calcium (Ca) and strontium (Sr) in the samples, these too were ultimately removed. These elements were present in measurable amounts in most samples, but upon viewing their spatial distribution, I became suspicious that calcium and strontium levels reflected the chemistry of the samples' depositional environment rather than the original constituent materials of pottery. Indeed,

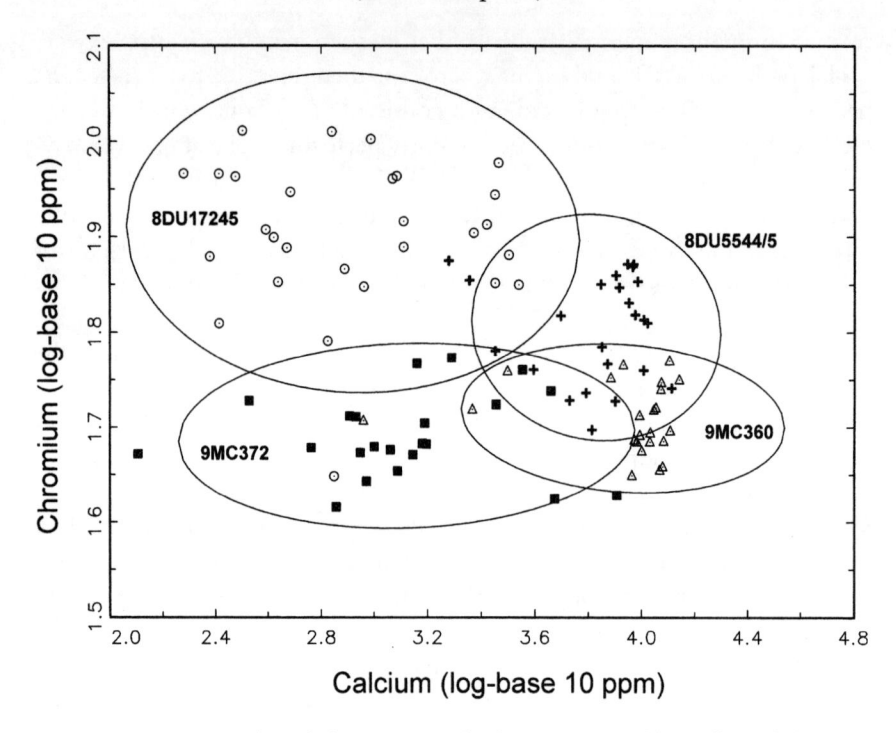

Figure 4.3. Bivariate plot of chromium and calcium in assemblages from shell-bearing (8DU5544/5 [crosses] and 9MC360 [triangles]) and shell-devoid (8DU17245 [circles] and 9MC372 [squares]) sites.

calcium and strontium levels were most elevated among assemblages from shell middens and typically diminished in samples from non-shell contexts. For example, samples from sandy sites like Tillie Fowler (8DU17245) and Sidon (9MC372) had consistently low levels of calcium while samples from shell midden sites such as Greenfield #8/9 (8DU5544/5) and Cathead Creek (9MC360) had dependably high calcium levels (Figure 4.3). Thus, there is some support for the possibility that calcium and strontium, as highly water soluble elements, could have been deposited in the pores of the permeable, low fired pottery, especially in wet environments.

The calcium data from clay samples provided little consolation. Calcium levels are generally highest among coastal clay deposits; however, some clay samples from very near the coast are conspicuously low in calcium (Figure 4.4). Furthermore, many of the clay samples with the highest calcium levels are from archaeological contexts in shell midden and thus were presumably subjected to the same processes that might have caused calcium and strontium enrichment in sherds. Given the isomorphic relationship between shell mid-

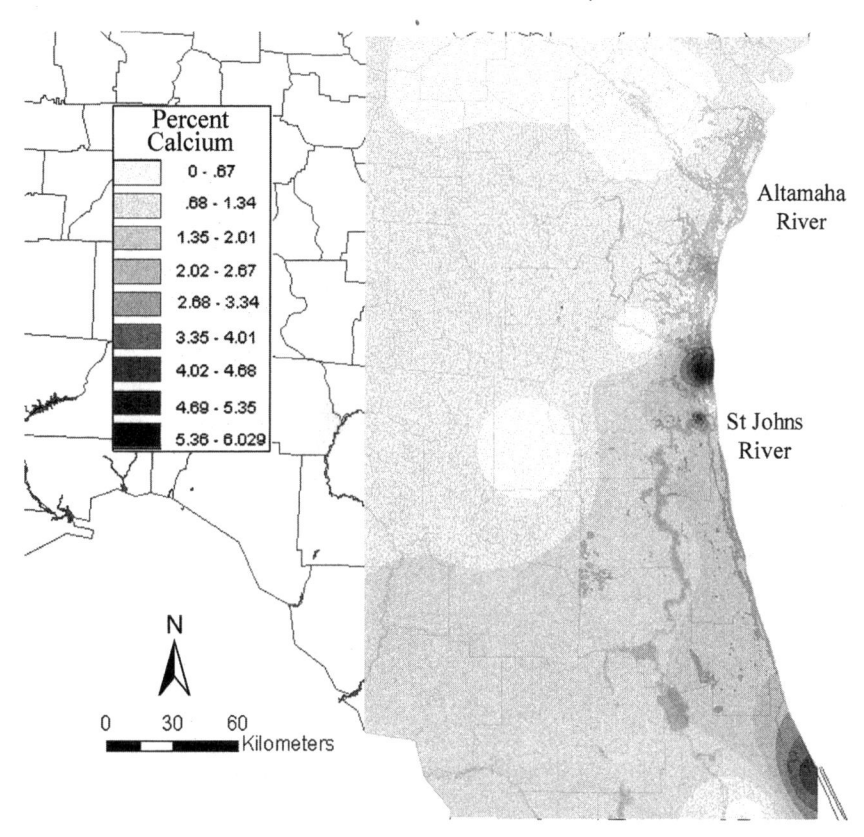

Figure 4.4. Inverse distance weighted (IDW) interpolation of calcium concentrations in both natural and archaeological clay samples. The highest concentrations come from archaeological deposits in shell middens.

dens and calcium and strontium levels in samples, diagenesis in shell midden contexts, or, alternatively, leaching (chemical loss) in non-shell contexts, may be the ultimate sources of variation. In-situ alteration of calcium levels was a potentially serious problem because variation in calcium explained a large percentage of variance within the sample in the first two PCs during preliminary quantitative analysis. As a precaution, a correction procedure was used to mathematically remove calcium and strontium from the samples and compensate for the diluting effect on the remaining 30 elements. As defined in James Cogswell et al. (1998:64) and Vincas Steponaitis et al. (1988), the following mathematical correction was used:

$$e' = \frac{10^6 e}{10^6 - 2.5c}$$

where $e'$ is the corrected concentration of a given element in ppm (parts per million), $e$ is the measured concentration of that element in ppm, and $c$ is the concentration of elemental calcium in ppm. After the calcium correction, statistical analysis was subsequently carried out on base-10 logarithms of concentrations on the remaining 30 elements.

## Composition Groups

Two distinct composition groups are recognized within the chemical data from pottery samples. Among the clay samples there are three additional provisional groups that are apparent in bivariate plots, but small sample sizes currently preclude statistical support for these partitions. Among pottery samples, Group 1 is comprised of 129 samples and is dominated by assemblages from sites near the Lower St. Johns River. Group 2 is made up of 98 samples and contains a majority of specimens from sites near the Lower Altamaha River. There were 86 pottery samples left unassigned to any group defined in the analysis.

PC plots do not reveal convincing separation of the groups, but they were instructive in identifying the elements that most contributed to compositional variation among samples. The first five PCs account for 77.5 percent of the variance in the data set. PC1 has many equally contributing elements, primarily potassium (K), sodium (Na), rubidium (Rb), cobalt (Co), manganese (Mn), and many of the rare earth elements: terbium (Tb), europium (Eu), cerium (Ce), samarium (Sm), neodymium (Nd), lanthanum (La). PC2 has a very strong contribution from arsenic (As). Contributions to PC3 are widely distributed, coming mostly from cesium (Cs), barium (Ba), potassium (K), and many rare earth elements. PC4 shows a strong contribution from sodium and somewhat less from manganese, while PC5 is dominated by cobalt.

The bivariate plots of the PCs show considerable overlap in the two groups. In general, the PCs demonstrate that Group 1 members have higher levels of each element on average while Group 2 members are comparatively deficient in most elements (Figure 4.5). Furthermore, Group 1 has more compositional variability among samples compared to Group 2, which has far less variation. These conclusions are borne out in the arithmetic means and standard deviations for each element among groups (Table 4.3). The only exception to lesser amounts of each element in Group 2 is cobalt, which is more abundant in Group 2 than Group 1. Thus, while Group 1 can be described as having comparatively high levels of every element and Group 2 contains comparatively low levels, cobalt demonstrates the opposite distribution among groups.

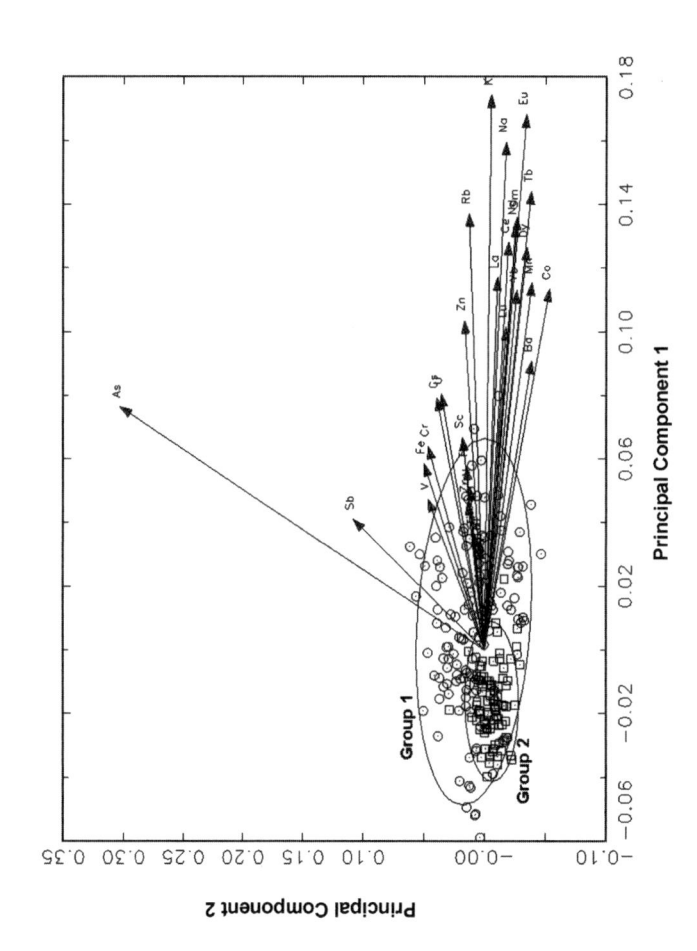

Figure 4.5. Biplot of the first two principal components along with the relative influence of each of the elemental variables. Ellipses represent 90 percent confidence level for Group 1 (circles) and Group 2 (squares) membership.

Table 4.3. Mean and standard deviation of elemental concentrations in each composition group

|  | Group 1 |  | Group 2 |  |
| --- | --- | --- | --- | --- |
| Element | Mean (ppm) | Standard deviation | Mean (ppm) | Standard deviation |
| As | 7.17 | 7.39 | 3.24 | 1.74 |
| La | 35.11 | 9.50 | 26.18 | 3.96 |
| Lu | 0.41 | 0.13 | 0.32 | 0.05 |
| Nd | 29.99 | 11.00 | 21.26 | 3.51 |
| Sm | 5.87 | 2.18 | 4.18 | 0.62 |
| U | 3.87 | 1.38 | 2.60 | 0.51 |
| Yb | 2.78 | 1.03 | 2.07 | 0.29 |
| Ce | 72.17 | 21.91 | 53.15 | 7.79 |
| Co | 4.65 | 1.76 | 6.59 | 1.10 |
| Cr | 75.19 | 12.78 | 51.87 | 5.19 |
| Cs | 3.40 | 1.10 | 2.92 | 0.73 |
| Eu | 1.02 | 0.51 | 0.68 | 0.12 |
| Fe (%) | 3.11 | .007 | 2.69 | .004 |
| Hf | 13.20 | 3.03 | 9.72 | 2.14 |
| Rb | 33.36 | 10.83 | 27.50 | 6.92 |
| Sb | 0.32 | 0.11 | 0.22 | 0.04 |
| Sc | 12.29 | 2.25 | 11.00 | 1.38 |
| Ta | 1.10 | 0.20 | 1.15 | 0.14 |
| Tb | 0.74 | 0.33 | 0.53 | 0.10 |
| Th | 12.41 | 1.90 | 10.76 | 1.34 |
| Zn | 41.53 | 10.95 | 36.81 | 7.12 |
| Zr | 334.07 | 84.43 | 232.64 | 54.39 |
| Al (%) | 7.12 | .012 | 6.88 | .009 |
| Ba | 272.02 | 100.23 | 319.92 | 150.46 |
| Dy | 4.46 | 1.85 | 3.38 | 0.59 |
| K | 6506.06 | 2552.45 | 3884.72 | 1192.57 |
| Mn | 126.56 | 56.75 | 118.54 | 58.84 |
| Na | 1870.48 | 859.34 | 1337.29 | 425.15 |
| Ti | 5008.90 | 690.66 | 4805.10 | 488.35 |
| V | 92.30 | 18.46 | 76.53 | 9.50 |

The overlapping bivariate plots of principal components show that the large degree of compositional variation in Group 1 generally subsumes the smaller range of variation in Group 2. However, the groups are confirmed by Mahalanobis distance to be statistically distinct. For Group 1, no specimen has greater than 0.25 percent chance of being in Group 2. By comparison, Group 2 members show an increased probability of membership in Group 1 because the more heterogeneous Group 1 subsumes much of the variation in the smaller group and causes more probability of inclusion. Still, no sample in Group 2 has greater than 4.80 percent probability of being in Group 1.

The chemical composition of clay samples is instructive in defining the compositional differences between pottery groups. While the number of clay samples is too small to create statistically meaningful groups that can be tested by Mahalanobis distance, there are recognizable geographical trends in the chemical data that conform to differences observed among pottery samples. Clays taken from three general regions tend to cluster together into three distinct chemical profiles: the Lower St. Johns River, Lower Altamaha River, and Lower Ocmulgee/Upper Altamaha River (Figure 4.6). Five clays from near the Lower St. Johns River (Group 3) are characterized by comparatively high levels of arsenic and chromium and low levels of cobalt, just like the pottery presumed to be locally made. In comparison, two Lower Altamaha River clays (Group 4) have low levels of arsenic and chromium and high levels of cobalt. A third clay (NJW333) from near the Lower Altamaha River appears to have an anomalous chemical profile. Taken from a dirt road along the high uplands several hundred meters south of the river in Wayne County, this sample may suffer from contamination or, more likely, simply reflect a different chemical composition compared to clays formed along the river banks. Four Upper Altamaha/Lower Ocmulgee clays (Group 5) are characterized by high levels of all elements except arsenic, which is consistently low. In essence, along the Ocmulgee/Altamaha drainage the clay deposits closest to the piedmont and mountains contain the highest concentrations of most elements (except arsenic); and these gradually diminish along the course of the river toward the coast, as is expected in comparisons of mountain, piedmont, and coastal plain regions of Georgia (Crocker 1999). Relatively high levels of cobalt and low levels of arsenic are attributes that are retained in the Lower Altamaha clays and consequently enable their differentiation from Lower St. Johns clays. Although there is much overlap, the orientation of the two pottery groups in bivariate plots of PCs generally conform to the differences observed among their presumed parent clays (Figure 4.7).

Clay samples taken from areas along the coast between the St. Johns and Altamaha rivers are quite variable in chemical composition. However, among

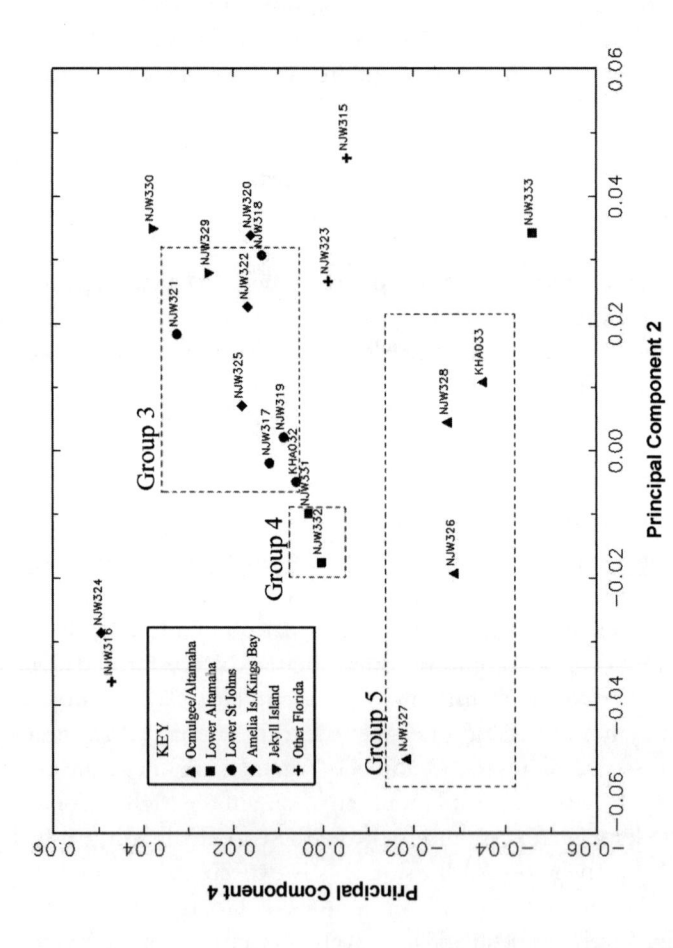

Figure 4.6. Bivariate plot of principal component 2 and principal component 4 for clay samples taken from the Lower St. Johns River, Lower Altamaha River, and Lower Ocmulgee/Upper Altamaha River. Tentative chemical groups are outlined.

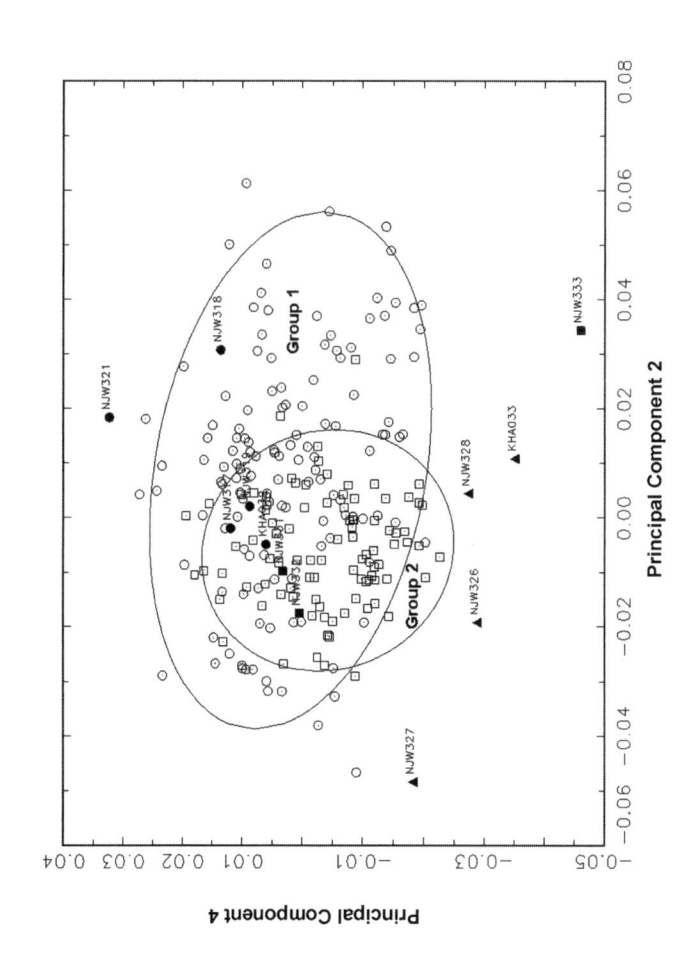

Figure 4.7. Same bivariate plot of principal component 2 and principal component 4 as Figure 4.6 but with pottery group members (Group 1 [white circles] and Group 2 [white squares]) and clay samples (Group 3 [black circles], Group 4 [black squares], and Group 5 [black triangles]) plotted. Ellipses represent 90 percent confidence of group membership.

six samples some generally shared characteristics include high levels of arsenic, cobalt, and chromium. With characteristic levels of arsenic and chromium similar to Lower St. Johns clays and levels of cobalt similar to Lower Altamaha samples, there is not a clear geographic trend in chemical composition from north to south. More clay samples are needed to outline the nuances of local chemical variation across the clay deposits of this region.

The partition in the pottery sample data is most easily viewed in a bivariate plot of chromium and cobalt because the distribution of these elements shows little overlap between groups (Figure 4.8). While Mahalanobis distance was used as the primary test for group membership, chromium and cobalt levels provided an extremely reliable comparison of group distinctions, with high levels of chromium and low levels of cobalt for Group 1, and low levels of chromium and high levels of cobalt for Group 2. The differences in cobalt levels are likely to be the result of differences in the origins of sedimentary materials along the two rivers, with the Altamaha River ultimately draining the piedmont and mountains, where cobalt levels are higher, and the St. Johns River running through the coastal plain, where cobalt levels are low (Figure 4.9A). The chromium levels among groups also correspond with differences in clay sources, with Lower Altamaha clays exhibiting slightly less chromium than their Lower St. Johns River counterparts (Figure 4.9B).

The pottery samples left unassigned to any group fall into three categories (Figure 4.10). Some of the samples (n = 28) are likely members to one of the two defined groups, but each varies enough to preclude official inclusion based on statistical probability. The remaining unassigned samples (n = 58) are either representative of various local manufacturing materials whose range of variation is poorly understood or nonlocal pottery from source locations poorly represented in the study (e.g., Middle St. Johns, Gulf Coast, central Georgia).

Sites near the Lower St. Johns River are dominated by Group 1 samples (Table 4.4). Diagnostic Early Swift Creek samples (charcoal tempered) have especially high frequencies of Group 1 membership, reflecting the unwavering prevalence of local production before AD 500. Among charcoal-tempered samples, 89 percent (n = 42) are Group 1 members and the remainder (n = 5) are unassigned. Limited Deptford (n = 1), Mayport Dentate Stamped (n = 2), and grog-tempered plain (n= 1) samples are all included in Group 1. As should be expected, only samples from Late Swift Creek contexts show any evidence of potential manufacturing origins in coastal Georgia. Among sand-tempered plain and Late Swift Creek samples, 65 are Group 1 members, 10 are confirmed Group 2 members, and 1 more is a very likely member of Group 2 but contains too great of a probability of Group 1 membership to

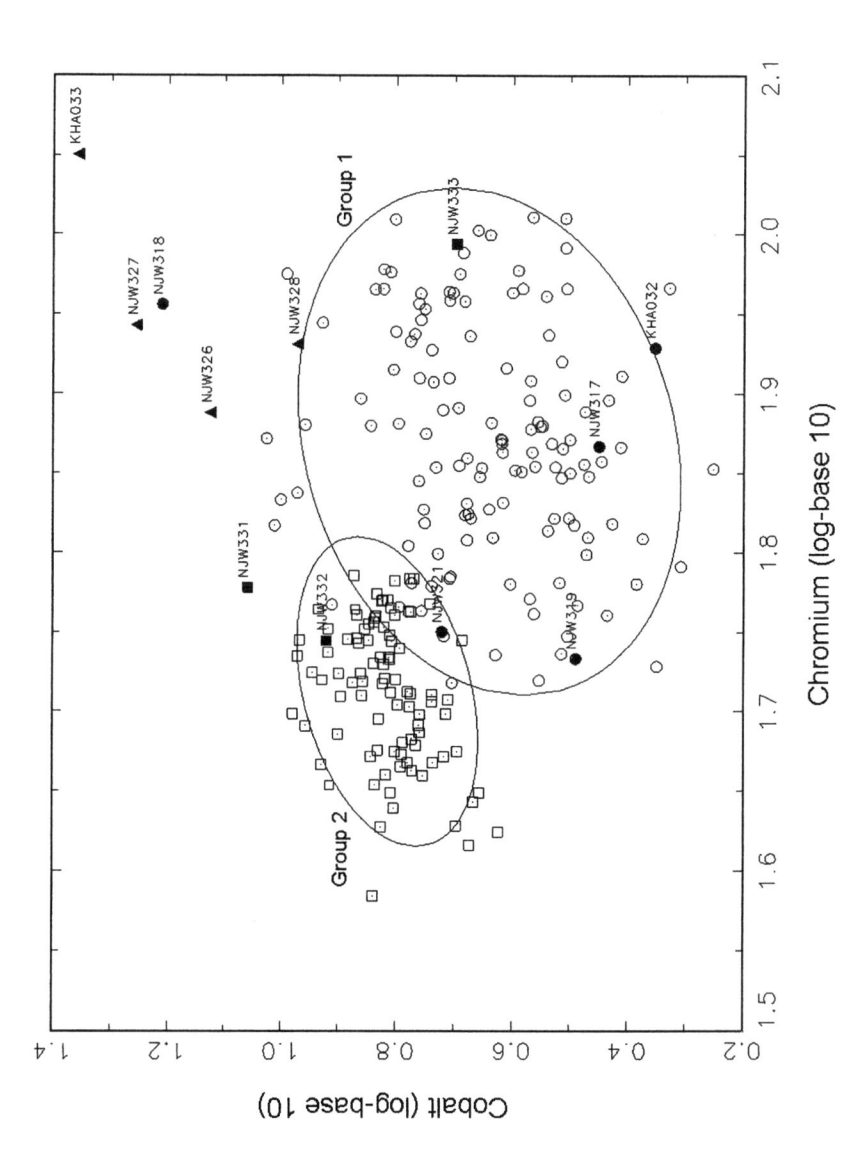

Figure 4.8. Bivariate plot of chromium and cobalt showing separation of pottery groups (Group 1 [white circles] and Group 2 [white squares]) and tentative clay groups (Group 3 [black circles], Group 4 [black squares], and Group 5 ([black triangles]).

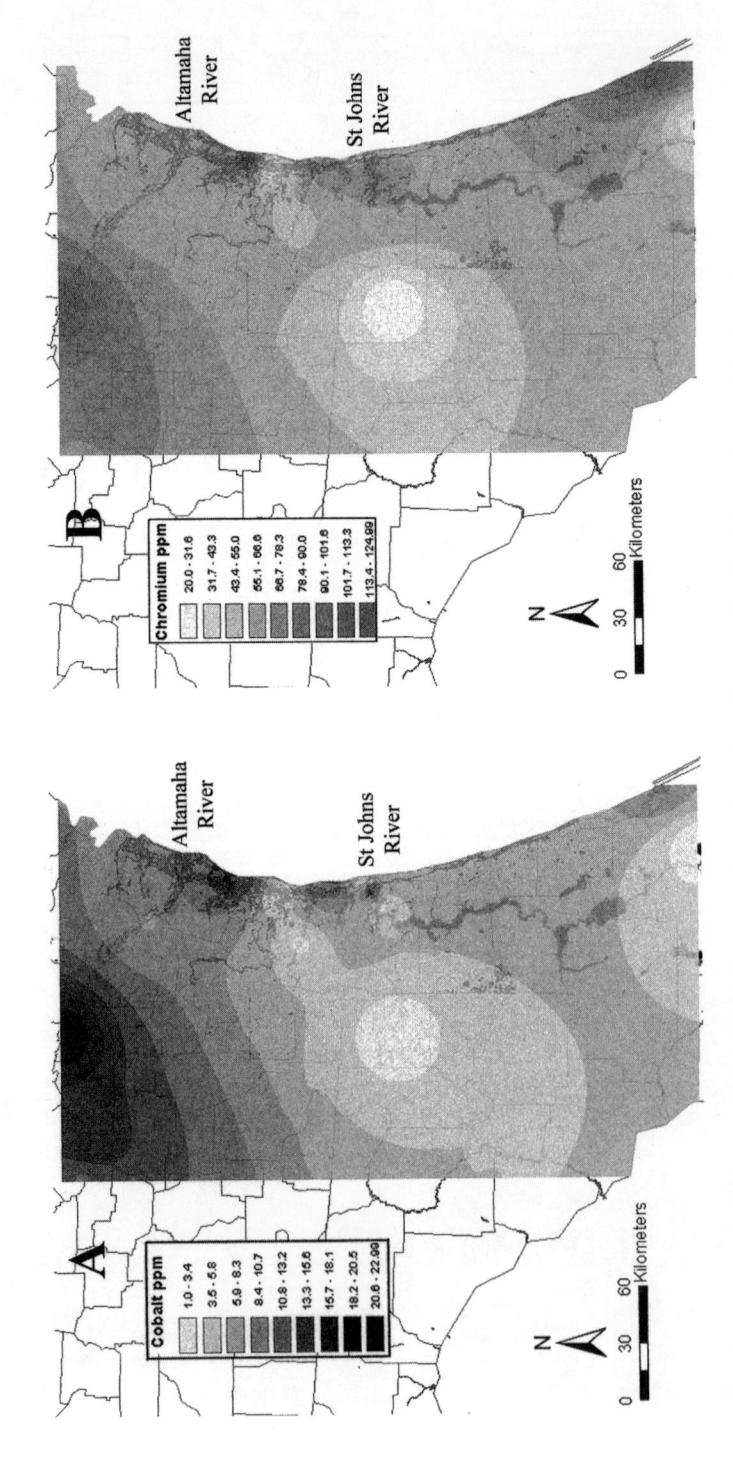

Figure 4.9. Inverse distance weighted (IDW) interpolation based on clay samples for (*A*) cobalt and (*B*) chromium.

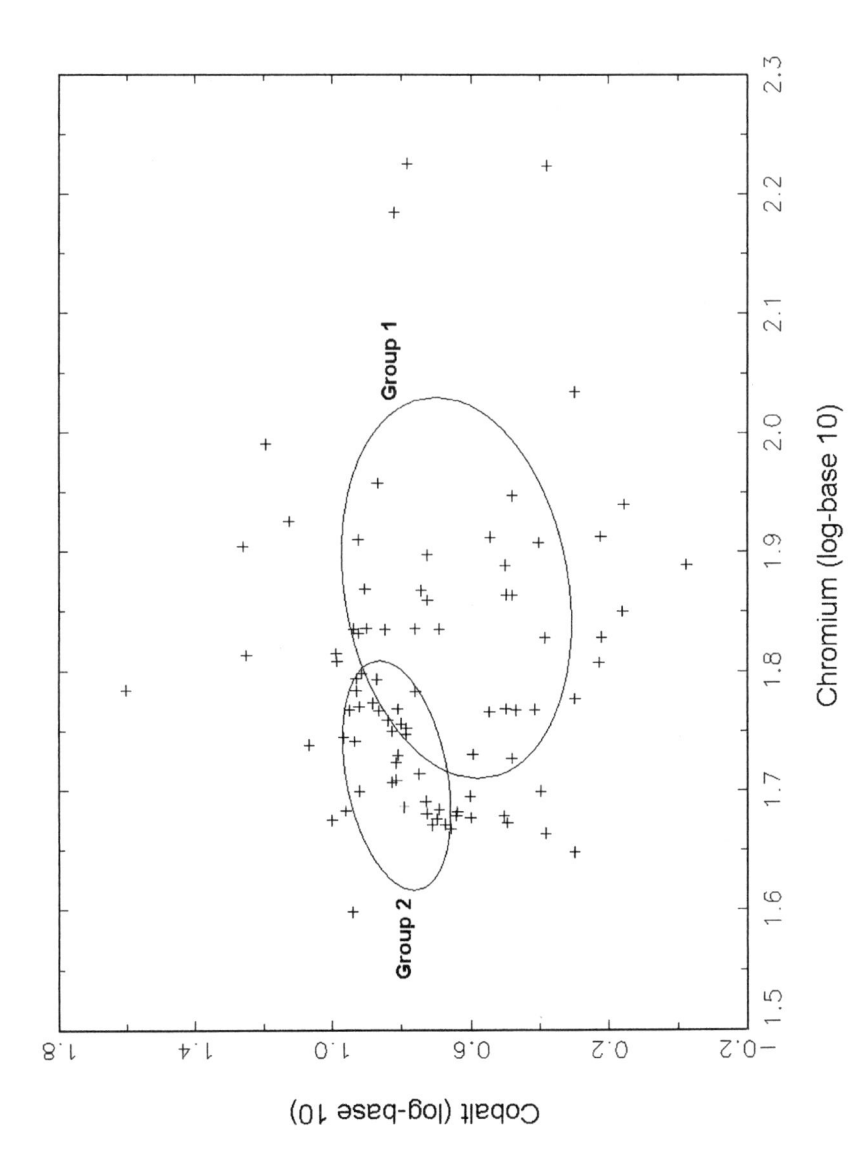

Figure 4.10. Bivariate plot of chromium and cobalt with unassigned samples represented by crosses. Ellipses represent 90 percent confidence of group membership.

Table 4.4. Pottery chemical group assignments by site

|  | Group 1 | Group 2 | Probable 1 | Probable 2 | Unassigned | Total |
|---|---|---|---|---|---|---|
| *Lower St. Johns* | | | | | | |
| Dent Mound (8DU68) | 20 | 5 | | | 3 | 28 |
| Mayport Mound (8DU96) | 11 | 3 | 2 | 1 | 4 | 21 |
| Greenfield #7 (8DU5543) | 24 | | | | 2 | 26 |
| Tillie Fowler (8DU17245) | 23 | | | | 5 | 28 |
| JU Temp Sites | 10 | | | | 7 | 17 |
| Greenfield #8/9 (8DU5544/5) | 20 | 2 | | | 2 | 24 |
| Grant (8DU14) | 2 | | | | 1 | 3 |
| Total | *110* | *10* | *2* | *1* | *24* | *147* |
| *Nassau, Camden, Charlton Co.* | | | | | | |
| McArthur Estates (8NA32) | 7 | 13 | 1 | | 5 | 26 |
| Kings Bay (9CM171) | 4 | | | | | 4 |
| Hallows Field (9CM25) | 5 | 4 | 3 | | 3 | 15 |
| Kings Lake | | 4 | 3 | | 12 | 19 |
| Total | *16* | *21* | *7* | | *20* | *64* |
| *Lower Altamaha* | | | | | | |
| Sidon (9MC372) | | 12 | 3 | 4 | 3 | 22 |
| Cathead Creek (9MC360) | | 17 | | 3 | 3 | 23 |
| Evelyn (9GN6) | 2 | 15 | 1 | 2 | 3 | 23 |
| Lewis Creek (9MC16) | | 19 | 2 | 1 | 1 | 23 |
| Paradise Park (9WY8) | 1 | 3 | 1 | | 3 | 8 |
| Oak Landing | | 1 | 1 | | 1 | 3 |
| Total | *3* | *67* | *8* | *10* | *14* | *102* |
| Total pottery samples | 129 | 98 | 17 | 11 | 58 | 313 |

be officially included. However, this last sample has greater than seven times the probability of belonging to Group 2 than Group 1.

Several unassigned samples from Lower St. Johns River sites are statistical outliers that may derive from nonlocal sources undefined in this study. All St. Johns Plain (n = 5) and Dunns Creek Red (n = 1) samples remain unassigned. These samples tend to have diminished levels of all elements, which may be the result of a paste recipe characterized by high levels of sponge spicule temper. Addition of this silica-based temper would be expected to have a diluting effect on the chemical constituents of spiculate pastes, similar to the effect of quartz sand temper (Michael Glascock, personal communications, 2008). Thus, the chemical differences in St. Johns Plain specimens may merely result from a different paste recipe, perhaps simply more temper by volume compared to sand-tempered samples. However, comparative pottery and clay specimens from the Middle St. Johns River area are needed to evaluate the possibility that these vessels were made using materials from much further upriver (south). Carrabelle Punctated (n = 1) and Weeden Island Red (n = 1) samples from the Lower St. Johns River area and a Weeden Island Incised (n = 1) sample from a site on Amelia Island (8NA32) are also unassigned and may have come from somewhere along the Gulf Coast of Florida, where these pottery types are more common. Comparative chemical data from specimens along the Gulf Coast and elsewhere are required to convincingly link the manufacture of these vessels to a particular nonlocal region.

Samples derived from sites in the areas between the mouth of the St. Johns River and the Altamaha River show a nearly even split between Group 1 (25 percent, n = 15), Group 2 (34 percent, n = 21), and unassigned (30 percent, n = 18) members. The remainder of the sample is comprised of probable Group 1 members (11 percent, n = 7). This broad distribution of samples among groups may result from the presumably variable chemical profiles of local clay sources in the coastal plain between the major drainages. Perhaps some clay deposits in this region are chemically similar to Lower St. Johns River clays while others are more similar to Lower Altamaha River clays. This possibility is supported by the high degree of chemical variation among six clay samples tested in the present study. However, given their proximity to both the St. Johns and Altamaha rivers, sites along this central region of the coast may also simply contain nonlocal pottery that was manufactured in areas to the north and south. Indeed, there is a correlation between group assignment and the size of quartz temper in a sample. The majority (n = 11) of Group 1 members from these central sites are tempered with fine sand, much more common at sites on the Lower St. Johns River. In contrast, all

21 Group 2 members are tempered with coarse sand, the nearly exclusive tempering material of the Lower Altamaha River region. Of the many unassigned samples, more than two-thirds contain medium and coarse sand temper and the remaining one-third contain fine sand temper. With traditional tempers from their respective regions, the Group 1 and Group 2 members may be vessels derived from the St. Johns and Altamaha river regions, respectively. Alternatively, perhaps the unassigned samples represent locally manufactured vessels from constituent materials poorly represented in the chemical study.

Samples from Altamaha River sites are mainly Group 2 members (67 percent, n = 68) or probable Group 2 members (9 percent, n = 9). A mere 3 percent (n = 3) are Group 1 members and 7 percent (n = 7) are likely Group 1 members. The remaining 14 samples are unassigned to any group defined in the analysis. Some of these samples, with comparatively elevated levels of most elements, may derive from the Ocmulgee River area, where clay samples exhibit these chemical characteristics. In bivariate plots of some elements, these Lower Altamaha River samples show similarities to 2 samples from the Hartford site (9PU1) near the Ocmulgee River (Mainfort et al. 1997). However, many more comparative samples are needed to link manufacturing origins of these vessels to the Ocmulgee River region.

## Discussion

The potential variation in the chemical composition of clays in the areas between the St. Johns and Altamaha rivers impedes the identification of foreign vessels at sites in Nassau, Camden, and Charlton counties. However, this is not a problem among samples drawn from sites along the Lower St. Johns and Lower Altamaha rivers, where clay samples establish consistent chemical profiles. I therefore restrict the identification of foreign vessels to sites along the two major drainages.

From the Lower St. Johns River sites there are ten samples that are Group 2 members and one other that is a *very* likely Group 2 member. Including this likely member, nine of the Group 2 vessels are Swift Creek Complicated Stamped and two are sand-tempered plain. Three of these Group 2 members have paddle matches with Altamaha River sites (Figure 4.11). First, both vessels that make up the design 34 match between the Dent Mound and the Sidon site belong to Group 2. Second, the Dent Mound vessel with design 36 belongs to Group 2 along with matching vessels from Cathead Creek and Lewis Creek. Another paddle-matching vessel with design 36 from Sidon is an unassigned outlier that is more likely to be a Group 1 member. Finally,

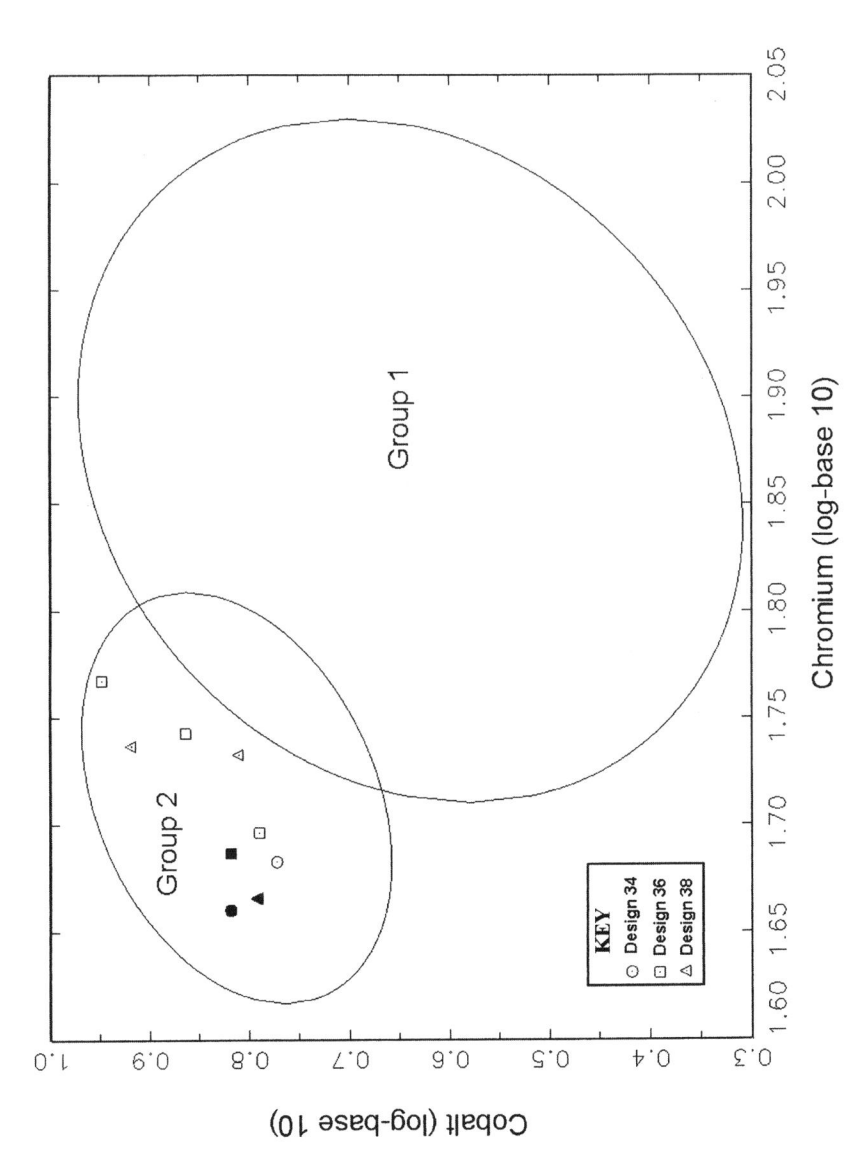

Figure 4.11. Bivariate plot of chromium and cobalt with paddle-matching samples plotted. Solid symbols represent samples from St. Johns River sites. Ellipses represent 90 percent confidence of group membership.

the Mayport Mound, Cathead Creek, and Lewis Creek samples that share design 38 are all Group 2 members. In sum, the three vessels from the Lower St. Johns that bear paddle matches that link them to Altamaha sites were all apparently made on the Altamaha River based on the chemical evidence. Thus, in all of these cases the vessels themselves, not the carved wooden paddles, were moved considerable distances.

In comparison, three vessels that share a paddle match (design 291) between two sites on the Lower St. Johns were all placed in Group 1, indicating that they were all made locally, defined broadly as the Lower St. Johns region. In the case of paddle matches in such close proximity that share the same chemical group, the data cannot be used to identify whether the earthenware vessels or the wooden paddle was moved.

The distribution of foreign-made vessels among Lower St. Johns sites is significant. Including the probable Group 2 member, 9 of 48 vessels from mounds are nonlocal, comprising 19 percent of the mound samples. Two of 96 vessels from middens were nonlocal, making up 2 percent of these assemblages. If we remove from the calculations the charcoal-tempered samples, which we know come from early contexts that pre-date Late Swift Creek interactions with coastal Georgia, the difference is more dramatic. At mounds, 9 of 34 vessels (nearly 27 percent) were made on the Altamaha, compared to only 2 of 69 vessels (3 percent) from middens (Figure 4.12). Notably, the Group 2 members found on Lower St. Johns sites are all tempered with coarse or medium grit, the predominant temper size in coastal Georgia. In fact, grit temper in a Lower St. Johns vessel appears to be a fairly reliable indicator that it was made in the coastal sector of Georgia, a point that will be returned to in the next chapter.

The identification of nonlocal vessels in northeastern Florida is limited to those that, based on chemical composition, were probably made somewhere near the Altamaha River. Unfortunately, this limitation may result from a severe sampling bias introduced through institutional restrictions that constrained the types of vessels that could be analyzed by destructive analysis. Specifically, the avoidance of many whole vessels from mounds resulted in no INAA samples of types that indicate Florida Gulf Coast affiliations, especially Weeden Island Incised, Weeden Island Red, and Crystal River Incised. Based on the limited INAA samples of these types from midden contexts, which were all unassigned outliers, I believe that many of these vessels from mounds may have derived from the Gulf Coast of Florida. If foreign-made, the prevalence of these Gulf Coast vessels at mortuary mounds compared to habitation sites on the Lower St. Johns River conforms to the same pattern

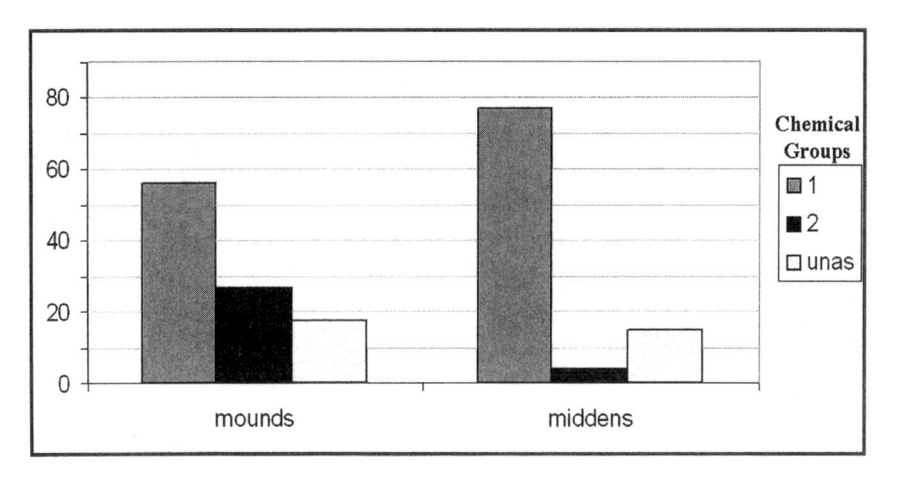

Figure 4.12. Percentage of chemical group assignments, excluding charcoal-tempered vessels, from mound (n = 34) and midden (n = 69) sites on the Lower St. Johns River.

as the rest of the assemblage: foreign pottery was overwhelmingly deposited in mounds.

The assemblages from sites along the Altamaha River are comprised of comparably fewer foreign-made vessels. Among 102 vessels from six sites, only 2 vessels from the Evelyn site and one from Paradise Park are Group 1 members and may have been made along the Lower St. Johns River. Two of these vessels are Swift Creek Complicated Stamped and the third is sand-tempered plain. There does not appear to be any correlation between temper and group membership, with fine sand, grit, and grog tempers all represented. The paucity of foreign-made vessels at Altamaha River sites compared to Lower St. Johns sites may be due to sampling bias, specifically, a lack of analyzed mortuary assemblages. In fact, the proportion of vessels identified in the middens of each region as being made in the other river valley is nearly identical, at roughly 3 percent. Future INAA of samples from mortuary mound contexts, such as Evelyn Mound C, might very well identify a much higher proportion of pottery made on the Lower St. Johns River. Whatever the case of mound pottery in Georgia, the chemical data indicate that vessels made nearly one hundred kilometers distant were not a major part of assemblages that were used for routine domestic tasks and that ultimately became part of domestic midden assemblages. Therefore, Swift Creek interactions, at least at the scale of contact between populations on the Lower St. Johns and Altamaha rivers, did not often involve the exchange of pots and/or their contents that were intended for normal use at villages.

## Summary

To summarize the basic findings of the INAA study, evidence for Early Swift Creek influence from the Gulf Coast remains fairly intractable in terms of foreign-made vessels. As we might expect, almost all charcoal-tempered vessels were made locally. Some of the outlier samples that could not be assigned to either of the two chemical groups are likely from the Gulf Coast, especially the Carrabelle Punctated, Weeden Island Incised, and Weeden Island Red vessels. Alternatively, St. Johns Plain and Dunns Creek Red vessels may be from the Middle St. Johns River area or simply have a different paste recipe. In all cases, comparative chemical data will be necessary to confidently assign a regional provenance.

We can much more definitively see some form of exchange in Late Swift Creek contexts along the Atlantic coast. According to the chemical data, Late Swift Creek "interaction" on the Lower St. Johns River seems to have been primarily centered on mortuary ceremony. The two analyzed mound assemblages from the Lower St. Johns River have a proportionally much greater number of vessels identified as made on the Altamaha River compared to village sites. The limited number of vessels at Altamaha River village sites that were identified as having been made somewhere near the Lower St. Johns River indicate that the same pattern may have pertained here as well, with mounds being the primary locus for the deposit of foreign pottery. What seems fairly certain with these data is that the foreign vessel assemblages found in each region are probably dominated not by the de facto refuse of moving people (from either marriage alliances or migration), or the containers for exchanged subsistence goods, but rather by gifts intentionally emplaced at locations of heightened ritual importance. The final offering of these gifts seems to have been in mortuary contexts, perhaps given in the context of deaths that obligated recognition of social connections and repayment of debts. Before exploring the implications of this conclusion further, in the next chapter I outline mineralogical data derived from petrographic analysis that complements the chemical groups to give a more nuanced view of production origins and patterns of exchange.

# 5
# Petrographic Analysis
*Patterns of Swift Creek Interaction*

The effectiveness of Instrumental Neutron Activation Analysis (INAA) in differentiating local and nonlocal pottery has been questioned (Shrarer et al. 2006; Stoltman et al. 2005; Stoltman and Mainfort 2002). Specifically, James Stoltman and colleagues (2005:11214) argue that petrographic point-count data are superior to chemical data because the identification of the mineral constituents in ceramic pastes allows for nuanced understandings of both added tempers and the parent rock of constituent clays. However, this is not always the case, as sometimes the chemical variation in constituents (especially clays) is not attributable to microscopically visible mineralogical variation (Stoner et al. 2008). I follow a more moderate approach that recognizes the complementary nature of chemical and mineralogical data (e.g., Bishop et al. 1982; Neff et al. 2006; Stoner et al. 2008). Indeed, the most problematic aspect of attempting to source clays using bulk chemical composition analyses of pottery is that variation in composition between samples may reflect a suite of materials added to clay. As repeatedly cautioned by researchers using INAA, ceramics are composite materials that require careful considerations of life histories that may have contributed to distinct chemical compositions through processes like the addition of temper and diagenesis (Glascock 2002:3; Neff et al. 2006). Given these potentially complicating factors, studies of pottery distribution benefit from multiple sourcing methods that can be used to test the results derived from different data. With this goal in mind, a sample of the INAA assemblage was selected for petrographic analysis.

## The Sample

Petrographic analysis was performed on thin sections from a total of 69 vessels from 14 sites and 10 unique clay samples (Table 5.1; Table 5.2). Of these, 57 of the pottery samples and all of the clays were analyzed expressly for the current study while additional data from 12 pottery samples was incorporated from previous research (e.g., Wallis 2004; Wallis et al. 2005). All samples were selected with the goals of representing the range of variation in aplastic constituents, approximating the relative frequency of each paste recipe within the total assemblage, and being proportionate with the INAA samples from each site. Using characterizations of the paste from analysis with a binocular microscope as well as typological designations, 43 vessels from sites in northeastern Florida and 26 from sites in southeastern Georgia were selected (Table 5.1). These petrographic samples represent 25 percent and 19 percent of the INAA samples from each region, respectively. A comparatively greater proportion of the INAA sample from northeastern Florida was selected for petrographic analysis in order to accommodate the greater range of variation in aplastic constituents and typological diversity in this region compared to southeastern Georgia. Petrographic analysis of clays was limited to samples from the Atlantic coast near the archaeological sites represented in this study (Table 5.2).

## Methods

The methods of petrographic analysis employed in this study are explained by Ann Cordell (2008). In brief, the analysis was conducted to evaluate compositional and textural variability in the samples and to document potential matches between pottery samples and clays. Point counts were made for quantifying relative abundance of inclusions. This procedure involved using a petrographic microscope with a mechanical stage and generally followed recommendations by Stoltman (1989, 1991, 2001). A counting interval of 1.0 millimeter by 0.5 millimeter was used in most cases. A counting interval of 1 millimeter by 1 millimeter was used in the 12 cases that had been analyzed for a previous study (Wallis 2004; Wallis et al. 2005). Each point or stop of the stage was assigned to one of the following categories: clay matrix, void, silt particles, charcoal temper, grog temper, bone temper, biogenic silica (sponge spicules, phytoliths, diatoms), and very fine through very coarse quartz and other aplastics of varying compositions. For cases in which fewer than 200 points were counted (n = 8), the thin sections were rotated 180 degrees on the mechanical stage and counted a second time (after Stolt-

Table 5.1. Site and type distribution of petrographic analysis pottery samples

| | CCS | CP | SWCRCS | STP | GROG | WII | WIR | Total |
|---|---|---|---|---|---|---|---|---|
| *Northeastern Florida* | | | | | | | | |
| Dent Mound (8DU68) | 1 | 2 | 5 | 1 | | | | 9 |
| Mayport Mound (8DU96) | 1 | 3 | 1 | | 1 | | | 6 |
| McArthur Estates (8NA32) | | 2 | 5 | | | 1 | | 8 |
| Greenfield #7 (8DU5543) | 3 | | 2 | 1 | | | | 6 |
| Tillie Fowler (8DU17245) | 1 | 1 | 1 | 1 | | | 1 | 5 |
| JU Temp Sites | | | 2 | 2 | | | | 4 |
| Greenfield #8/9 (8DU5544/5) | | 1 | 2 | 2 | | | | 5 |
| *Total* | 6 | 9 | 18 | 7 | 1 | 1 | 1 | 43 |
| *Southeastern Georgia* | | | | | | | | |
| Sidon (9MC372) | | | 5 | 1 | | | | 6 |
| Cathead Creek (9MC360) | | | 5 | | | | | 5 |
| Evelyn (9GN6) | | | 3 | 2 | | | | 5 |
| Lewis Creek (9MC16) | | | 4 | | | | | 4 |
| Kings Lake | | | 3 | | | | | 3 |
| Paradise Park (9WY8) | | | 1 | | | | | 1 |
| Hallows Field (9CM25) | | | 2 | | | | | 2 |
| *Total* | | | 23 | 3 | | | | 26 |
| Total pottery samples | 6 | 9 | 41 | 10 | 1 | 1 | 1 | 69 |

*Note:* Column headings are as follows: CCS, charcoal-tempered Swift Creek Complicated Stamped; CP, charcoal-tempered plain; SWCRCS, Swift Creek Complicated Stamped; STP, sand-tempered plain; GROG, grog-tempered plain (non-diagnostic); WII, Weeden Island Incised; WIR, Weeden Island Red.

Table 5.2. Clay samples selected for petrographic analysis

| Sample # | ANID | Petrographic ID | Provenience |
|---|---|---|---|
| 3 | NJW-317 | C03-58c | Grant Mound, Feature 1 (Duval Co.) |
| 4 | NJW-318 | C04-59c | Oxeye Island, NE Jacksonville (Duval Co.) |
| 5 | NJW-319 | C05-60c | Grand Shell Ring, TU-4, L-13, Area U (Duval Co.) |
| 6 | NJW-320 | C06-61c | Amelia Island Airport, Fernandina Beach (Nassau Co.) |
| 7 | NJW-321 | C07-62c | Little Talbot Island, Black Rock, Nassau Sound (Nassau Co.) |
| 10 | NJW-324 | C10-63c | Cabin Bluff Shell Ring, TU-201, 95 cmbs (Camden Co.) |
| 13 | NJW-327 | C13-64c | Coffee Bluff, Ocmulgee River (Telfair Co.) |
| 15 | NJW-329 | C15-65c | Jekyll Island (south) (Glynn Co.) |
| 17 | NJW-331 | C17-66c | "Clay-hole Island", Altamaha River bank (Glynn Co.) |
| 18 | NJW-332 | C18-67c | Lower Sansavilla, Altamaha River bank (Wayne Co.) |

man 2001:306). Most of the point counts were made using the 10X objective, but the 25X objective (with plane-polarized light) was used to search for occurrence of siliceous microfossils such as sponge spicules, phytoliths, and diatoms. Size of aplastics was estimated with an eyepiece micrometer with reference to the Wentworth Scale (Rice 1987:38). A comparison chart of percentage of particle abundance (Rice 1987:349, figure 12.2) was also used for estimating relative abundance of constituents occurring in low frequency. All analyses were carried out by Ann S. Cordell in the Florida Museum of Natural History Ceramic Technology Laboratory (FLMNH-CTL).

In addition to the petrographic analyses, pottery samples of sufficient size were refired to standardize color comparisons between samples, to assess relative iron content of the clays represented by the samples, and for comparison to the clay samples. A lapidary saw was used to control the desired size of fragments for refiring, but not all sherds in the sample were large enough to spare removal of pieces for refiring. Sherds were refired in an electric furnace at a temperature of 800 degrees C for 30 minutes, conditions that probably exceeded those of the original firings. Raw clay samples were also fired under comparable conditions. The kiln temperature was initially set at 275 degrees

C and held for 10 minutes with the kiln door slightly open to allow for the escape of water vapor. The kiln door was then shut completely and the temperature was raised to 800 degrees C. After about 15 minutes, the 800 degrees C temperature was achieved and maintained for 30 minutes. The total firing time was approximately 75 minutes. Prior to refiring, original core color/degree of coring was recorded for each sherd (from a fresh break) with reference to five nominal categories ranging from "no coring" to "heavy dark coring." A fresh break was made after refiring to note color changes. Four nominal refired color categories were distinguished on the basis of gross visual differences and correspond with relative iron contents ranging from very low to high. The results of refiring are included in descriptions of the mineralogical groups in Tables 5.1 and 5.2. However, comparison of refired color designations and the more precise quantification of iron by INAA reveal only a very general correlation between color and iron (Fe) content. Therefore, the refired color of sherds was not considered to be a significant variable in distinguishing mineralogical groups.

## Results

Mica, sponge spicules, phytoliths, diatoms, silt grains, and very fine sand were considered significant for defining clay resource groupings among the 69 pottery samples. The first five constituents are considered naturally occurring in some clays. Quartz aplastics falling into silt and very fine Wentworth particle sizes are usually also considered as naturally occurring constituents of the clay source (Rice 1987:411; also see Stoltman 1989:149–150, 1991:109–111). Differences in fine through very coarse quartz particle sizes and other constituents are attributed to tempering practices, although some fine sand may be naturally present in some cases, based on variability in some of the clay samples. Based on these six naturally occurring constituents, six petrographic paste groupings were specified for pottery samples (Table 5.3). Each group represents a hypothetical resource group made up of one or more clay resources that are similar in terms of these six criteria. Based on the same criteria, some of the clays were assigned to one or more of the six pottery paste categories, while others formed their own categories.

Five predominant temper categories were observed in the sample: charcoal temper, quartz sand, quartz grit (particle size less than or equal to 0.5 millimeters; includes some quartzite), quartz sand and grit, and grog temper (Table 5.4). Bone temper was observed in some samples but was never the predominant constituent. Other constituents include mica (muscovite and biotite or some other slightly pleochroic mica), feldspars (mainly microcline and pla-

Table 5.3. Summary descriptions of variability in petrographic paste categories

| Petrographic paste group | Sample size | Estimated silt (%) | Very fine quartz (%) | Mica | Sponge spicules | Phytoliths | Diatoms | Refired color |
|---|---|---|---|---|---|---|---|---|
| A | 31 | 3–5 | 6 | Rare to occasional | Absent or rare | Absent or rare | | Moderate–high iron |
| A–clay | 4 | 1–5 | 5–10 | Rare to none, but might vary | None to rare | None to rare | | Moderate to high iron |
| B | 16 | 3–5 | 5 | Rare to occasional in most | Rare to occasional | Occasional to frequent | | Low to moderate–high iron |
| C | 4 | 3–5 | 2 | Rare to occasional in most | Occasional to frequent | Variable | | Low to moderate iron |
| D | 13 | 3–10 variable | 11 | Occasional to frequent | Absent to rare | Rare to absent | | Low to moderate–high iron |
| E | 4 | 3–10 variable | 5 | Occasional to frequent | Occasional to frequent | Variable | | 2 n = 1 |
| F | 1 | 3 | 19 | Occasional to frequent | Occasional to frequent | Rare to occasional | Occasional | |
| F/G clay | 3 | 1–3 | Variable | Rare to occasional | Rare | Absent to rare | Occasional to frequent | Moderate to high iron |
| H clay | 1 | 3–5 | 9 | Rare | 18% | Not observed | | Moderate iron |
| I clay | 2 | Variable | Variable | Frequent | Occasional to frequent | Variable | Extremely rare | Low to moderate |

Table 5.3. Continued

| Petrographic paste group | Temper group | INAA group | Relationship to clay samples |
|---|---|---|---|
| A | Charcoal = 10<br>sand = 7<br>grog = 1<br>grit & sand = 5<br>grit = 8 | 1 (most charcoal, grog, sand) and 2 (most grit, grit & sand) | Possible affinity to clays 4, 5, 6, and 17 |
| A-clay | Clay 4, 5, 6, 17 | 3, 4, UO | Most similar to paste A; possible affinity to pastes B and C if deposits vary in frequency of phytoliths and sponge spicules |
| B | Charcoal = 2<br>sand = 1<br>grog = 1<br>grit & sand = 3<br>grit = 9 | Mostly 2 | Possible affinity to clays 5 and 6 if deposits vary in frequency of phytoliths |
| C | Grit = 4 | 2 | Possible affinity to clays 5 and 6 if deposits vary in frequency of sponge spicules |
| D | Charcoal = 3<br>sand = 9<br>grog = 1 | 1 | Possible affinity to A clays 4, 6, and 17 if deposits vary in mica frequency |
| E | Grog = 1<br>grit & sand = 2<br>grit = 1 | Variable | Possible affinity with I clays 13 and 18 or A clays if deposits vary in mica, spicules, and phytoliths |
| F | Grog = 1 | 1 | Possible affinity to clay 18 in mica, spicule, and phytolith frequency, but diatom species difference precludes a match; might be more similar to F/G clays |
| F/G clay | Clay 7, 10, 15 | 3, UO | Possible affinity to paste F in diatom species |
| H clay | Clay 3 | 3 | No matches with any of the pottery samples |
| I clay | Clay 13, 18 | 4, 5 | Similar to paste F, but diatom species difference precludes a match |

Table 5.4. Summary descriptions of variability in gross temper categories

| Gross temper | Sample size | Tempers | Matrix (%) | Aplastics (%) | Sand (%) | SSI.5/1* | Silt e/p** | Very fine quartz (%) | Fine quartz (%) | Medium quartz (%) | Coarse quartz (%) | Very coarse quartz (%) |
|---|---|---|---|---|---|---|---|---|---|---|---|---|
| Charcoal | 15 | 9% charcoal temper (grog present in 7 cases; bone temper in 3 cases) | 60 | 40 | 26 | 0.96/1.10 | 4%/3% | 6 | 16 | 2 | <1 | |
| Grog | 5 | 2–4% crushed sherds (bone temper in one case) | 55 | 45 | 36 | 1.05/1.21 | 5%/3% | 9 | 17 | 5 | 1 | |
| Sand | 17 | Quartz sand (grog temper rare in 3 cases; charcoal temper rare in 1 case) | 58 | 42 | 36 | 0.94/1.10 | 4%/4% | 10 | 20 | 2 | <1 | <1 |
| Grit and sand | 10 | Quartz sand and grit (grog temper rare in 2 cases) | 56 | 44 | 39 | 1.52/1.62 | 4%/3% | 6 | 14 | 10 | 4 | <1 |
| Grit | 22 | Grit-sized quartz and quartzite (charcoal present in 1 case) | 60 | 40 | 38 | 1.97/2.02 | 4%/2% | 3 | 8 | 11 | 8 | 2 |

*Silt size index: with very fine grains counting as 0.5/with very fine counting as 1.
**Silt: estimated percentage of silt grains/actual percentage calculated from point count.

Table 5.4. Continued

| Gross temper | Mica, sponge spicules, phytoliths | Petrographic paste | Other constituents |
|---|---|---|---|
| Charcoal | Mica rare to occasional in most cases; sponge spicules and phytoliths present/rare in most cases | A = 67%<br>B = 13%<br>D = 20% | 2% polyxQ<br>1% feldspars<br><1% heavies |
| Grog | Variable mica, sponge spicules, and phytoliths | A, B, D, E, F | 2% polyxQ<br>2% feldspars<br>2% heavies |
| Sand | Variable mica; sponge spicules and phytoliths absent or rare in most cases | A = 41%<br>B = 6%<br>D = 53% | 2% polyxQ<br>2% feldspars<br>1–2% heavies |
| Grit and sand | Mica, sponge spicules rare to occasional in most cases; variable phytoliths | A = 50%<br>B = 30%<br>E = 20% | 2% polyxQ<br>1% feldspars<br>1–2% heavies |
| Grit | Mica rare to occasional in most cases; sponge spicules present/rare in all but 6 cases; phytoliths occasional to frequent in half the cases | A = 36%<br>B = 41%<br>C = 18%<br>E = 5% | 4% polyxQ<br>1% feldspars<br>1% heavies |

gioclase), granitic rock fragments (rarely), ferric concretions or nodules, birefringent grains (epidote, amphibole, UID minerals), and siliceous microfossils (sponge spicules, phytoliths, diatoms). Most of these other constituents that are probably naturally occurring in the potting clays were variously observed in the sample, especially mica, ferric concretions, and the siliceous microfossils. Feldspars and other birefringent minerals may be naturally present or introduced along with sand temper. The siliceous microfossils in the present sample are only detectable in thin section with magnifications ranging from 250X to 400X. Most of the sponge spicules and diatoms are fragmentary and are presumed to be natural constituents of the clay resources used for vessel manufacture.

The six petrographic groups can be described according to the relative abundance of aplastic constituents considered to be natural inclusions in the exploited clays. Of these, variation in the occurrence of mica, sponge spicules, phytoliths, and diatoms are most significant (Figure 5.1). Group A is comprised of the most samples (n = 31) and is characterized by rare to occasional mica, absent or rare sponge spicules, and, most conspicuously, absent or rare phytoliths. Based particularly on the absence or rarity of phytoliths, four clays are also assigned to Group A. However, the potential in each clay for variability in some constituents makes other group designations possible as well. Group B (n = 16) is similar to Group A but is differentiated by the occasional to frequent occurrence of phytoliths. Group C (n = 4) contains variable frequencies of phytoliths and mainly differs from Groups A and B in the occasional to frequent occurrence of sponge spicules. Group D (n = 13) is defined primarily by occasional to frequent mica. Group E (n = 4) is characterized by high frequencies of mica, like Group D, but with occasional to frequent sponge spicules. Group F is comprised of a single sample and is similar to Group E but with occasional diatoms. Group F/G clays (n = 3) are a potential match for the Group F sherd because of matching species of diatoms. However, these clays differ from Group F in having only rare sponge spicules and rare to occasional mica. The single clay that constitutes Group H, from a prepared clay stockpile from an archaeological context at the Grant site (8DU14), is defined by sponge spicules as the predominant aplastic inclusion and does not match any of the pottery samples in this study. Finally, Group I clays (n = 2) are defined by very high mica content, occasional to frequent sponge spicules, and rare diatoms.

The five gross temper groups defined in the analysis are not isomorphic with the six clay resource groups (Table 5.4). For example, Group A and B specimens are found in each of the five temper categories. Alternatively, the smaller Groups C, D, and E demonstrate some important correlations. Group

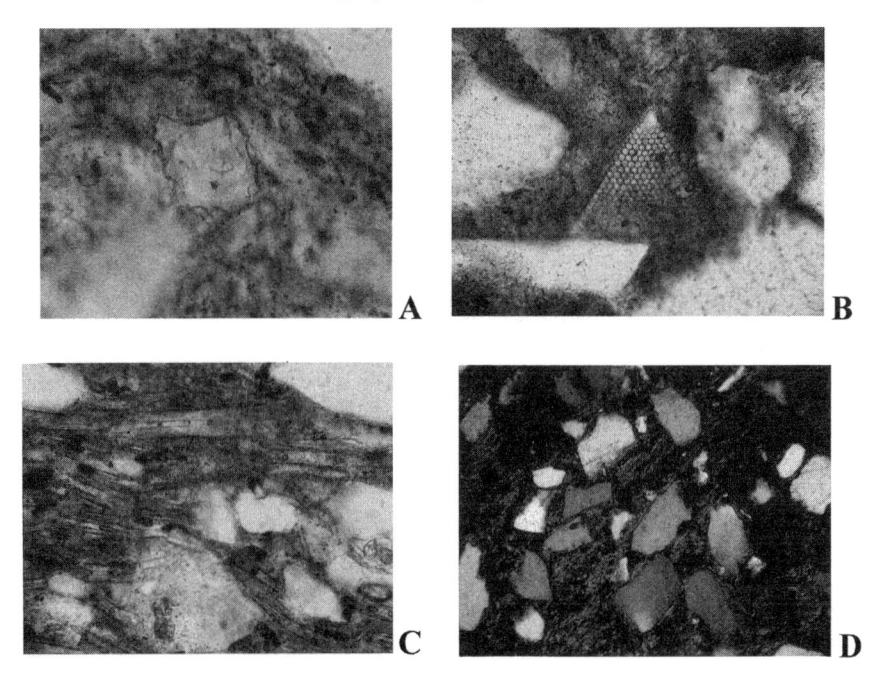

Figure 5.1. Mineral constituents useful for distinguishing clay resource groups: (*A*) phytolith, sample 2008-63; (*B*) diatom, sample 2008-62; (*C*) sponge spicules, sample 2008-58; (*D*) absence of these natural constituents (with fine sand temper), sample 2005-24. All images with plane-polarized light and 25X magnification; except *D* with cross-polarized light and 10X magnification (images courtesy of the Florida Museum of Natural History Ceramic Technological Laboratory).

C samples (n = 4) are comprised entirely of grit-tempered sherds. Group D (n = 13) consists primarily of sand-tempered sherds but also some charcoal-tempered samples. Group E (n = 4) samples are made up of grit-tempered or grit-and-sand-tempered sherds. These correlations reveal an intersection between mineralogically distinct clays and geographically circumscribed tempering traditions. To review, grit temper predominates in Swift Creek assemblages along the Altamaha River and as far south as Amelia Island while fine sand temper (often with charcoal before AD 500) dominates Lower St. Johns River assemblages (Ashley and Wallis 2006).

The petrographically defined resource groups correspond with geographical areas that can be usefully summarized by county (Table 5.5). Group A samples come primarily from the southernmost counties, Duval (58 percent) and Nassau (19 percent). Likewise, Group D samples are mostly from Lower St. Johns sites in Duval County (77 percent). Group E is made up exclusively

Table 5.5. Mineralogical paste categories by county and INAA group

| Paste category | County | INAA G1 | INAA G2 | INAA unassigned | Total |
|---|---|---|---|---|---|
| A | Duval | 13 | 3 | 3 | 19 |
|   | Nassau | 3 | 1 | 2 | 6 |
|   | Camden | 1 |   |   | 1 |
|   | Brantley |   |   | 1 | 1 |
|   | Glynn |   | 1 |   | 1 |
|   | McIntosh |   | 3 |   | 3 |
| Total |   | 17 | 8 | 6 | 31 |
| B | Duval | 2 | 2 |   | 4 |
|   | Nassau |   | 1 | 1 | 2 |
|   | Camden |   | 1 |   | 1 |
|   | Glynn |   | 2 |   | 2 |
|   | McIntosh |   | 5 | 2 | 7 |
| Total |   | 2 | 11 | 3 | 16 |
| C | Duval |   | 1 | 1 | 2 |
|   | Brantley |   | 1 |   | 1 |
|   | Wayne |   | 1 |   | 1 |
| Total |   |   | 3 | 1 | 4 |
| D | Duval | 9 |   | 1 | 10 |
|   | Glynn | 1 |   |   | 1 |
|   | McIntosh |   |   | 2 | 2 |
| Total |   | 10 |   | 3 | 13 |
| E | Brantley |   |   | 1 | 1 |
|   | Glynn | 1 |   |   | 1 |
|   | McIntosh |   | 1 | 1 | 2 |
| Total |   | 1 | 1 | 2 | 4 |
| F | Duval | 1 |   |   | 1 |

of samples from Brantley, Glynn, and McIntosh counties, all in Georgia. Group B and C samples are more evenly divided by county, but many of the Duval County specimens may be foreign imports based on INAA data. Specifically, the INAA results indicate that two of the Group B specimens from Duval County are foreign imports from the Altamaha region (e.g., chemical Group 2) while one from Nassau County is unassigned to either chemical group. This leaves only two (13 percent) of the Group B specimens as locally produced in northeastern Florida based on the INAA data. Similarly, both

Duval County specimens in petrographic Group C are likely imports based on chemical data, one a chemical Group 2 member and the other unassigned to any chemical group.

In sum, based on the geographical correlation with mineralogical groups, the petrographic analysis identified two resource groups presumed to be local to the Lower St. Johns River area and three resource groups local to the Altamaha River area. The two Lower St. Johns groups are Group A and Group D, which differ from each other mostly in terms of mica content. The three Altamaha groups are B, C, and E, the latter two groups sharing occasional to frequent sponge spicules. Without more samples, the single sherd containing diatoms and sponge spicules (Group F) cannot be confidently assigned a geographic origin.

In general, the mineralogical groups defined by the petrographic analysis are corroborated by the INAA chemical groups (Table 5.5). In mineralogical Group A, more than twice as many samples are chemical Group 1 members (local to the Lower St. Johns River) compared to chemical Group 2 members (local to the Altamaha River). Group B contains more than three times as many chemical Group 2 members as chemical Group 1 members. Group C includes only chemical Group 2 or unassigned samples while Group D contains only Group 1 or unassigned specimens. Group E is the most variable in terms of chemical composition but also suffers from small sample size, with only four members.

The data from petrographic analysis of limited clay samples help clarify some of the discrepancies between mineralogical group members, chemical group members, and their geographic distribution. Group A clays come from sites throughout the study region, from Glynn, Nassau, and Duval counties. Therefore, Group A clay resources, and by extension Group A pottery, are unlikely to be restricted exclusively to the Lower St. Johns River. In other words, the wide distribution of Group A clays sets up an expectation for multiple origins among Group A pottery members. There are no natural mineralogical differences between Group A clay resources distributed throughout the project area, but INAA was able to identify geographically significant chemical differences between them. However, based on the "criterion of abundance" (Bishop et al. 1982) among sherds, Group A mineralogical characteristics may at least be more prevalent, though not exclusive, in clay resources toward the south.

Group F/G clays are also widely distributed, derived from Glynn, Camden, and Nassau counties, although none come from Duval County. For the purposes of this study, the spatial distribution of these Group F/G clays has little bearing on the sourcing of sherds because only one sherd potentially matches this group. Group I seems to be the only clay group with a significant spatial correlation as the two clays comprising this group both come from the Ocmulgee/Altamaha river drainage. Group I clay is the only mineralogical group that contains moderate amounts of both sponge spicules and mica, firmly tying pottery Groups C and E to this drainage area. In fact, occasional to frequent naturally occurring sponge spicules only occur in these two Georgia clay samples and pottery samples in these two Georgia pottery groups. The lone member of Group F also contains occasional to frequent sponge spicules, but this vessel is tempered with spiculate paste grog that may have introduced them to the prepared paste.

## Complementing the Chemical Evidence

Through the similarity of mineral constituents in some clays across the region, the mineralogical Group A crosscuts the two chemical groups determined by INAA. The other mineralogical groups mostly conform to the two chemical groups but also parse them further into subdivisions based on mineralogical differences. This relationship is evident in comparisons of the mineralogical and chemical categories assigned to vessels with matching paddle designs (Table 5.6). With the exception of one unassigned sample, all vessels with paddle-matching designs 34, 36, and 38 share the same chemical Group 2 but are split among two different mineralogical groups, A and B. These vessels were all probably made near the Altamaha River, based on the chemical evidence, but with two or more mineralogically different clay sources. However, paddle-matching vessels belonging to the same chemical *and* mineralogical groups are more likely to have been made from the same clay source. This is the case among three of the paddle matches. Vessels with design 36 from the nearby sites of Cathead Creek (9MC360) and Lewis Creek (9MC16) are assigned to chemical Group 2 and mineralogical Group B. Vessels with design 38 from Lewis Creek and the quite distant Mayport Mound (8DU96) are members of chemical Group 2 and mineralogical Group A. In comparison, vessels sharing design 291 from two sites on the Lower St. Johns River, the Dent Mound (8DU68) and Greenfield #8/9 (8DU5544/5), belong to chemical Group 1 and mineralogical Group A. Alternatively, two paddle-matching vessels from the same site (8DU5544/5) have different mineralogical designations, Group A and Group D, distinct groups both local to the Lower St. Johns River area. Thus, the data from INAA and petrographic analysis complement one another, each providing data for further distinctions where the other indicates homogeneity.

Table 5.6. Paddle-matching samples by INAA and petrographic groups

| Petid | INAAid | Site | Temper | Petpaste | INAA | Paddle # |
|---|---|---|---|---|---|---|
| 2008-26 | NJW-174 | 9MC372 | Grit | A | 2 | 34 |
| 2008-32 | NJW-027 | 8DU68 | Grit | B | 2 | 34 |
| 2008-04 | NJW-010 | 8DU68 | Grit & sand | A | 2 | 36 |
| 2008-27 | NJW-177 | 9MC372 | Grit & sand | B | Unas* | 36 |
| 2008-39 | NJW-195 | 9MC360 | Grit & sand | B | 2 | 36 |
| 2008-49 | NJW-241 | 9MC16 | Grit & sand | B | 2 | 36 |
| 2004-01 | NJW-242 | 9MC16 | Grit | A | 2 | 38 |
| 2004-18 | NJW-038 | 8DU96 | Grit | A | 2 | 38 |
| 2008-40 | NJW-196 | 9MC360 | Grit | B | 2 | 38 |
| 2008-06 | NJW-021 | 8DU68 | Sand | A | 1 | 291 |
| 2008-21 | NJW-152 | 8DU5544/5 | Sand | D | 1 | 291 |
| 2008-25 | NJW-169 | 8DU5544/5 | Sand | A | 1 | 291 |

*Note:* Column headings are as follows: Petid, petrographic analysis indentification; INAAid, instrumental neutron activation analysis identification; Petpaste, petrographic (mineralogical) paste category; INAA, instrumental neutron activation analysis chemical group.
*Unassigned to any chemical group defined in the analysis.

The petrographic analysis was also useful in evaluating the potential sources of chemical variation in the INAA data. One potentially obfuscating factor in identifying chemical variation in the clay resources used to manufacture vessels was variation in the amount of temper used. As reviewed in the previous chapter, there is a strong correspondence between chemical group assignment and type of temper. Group 1 members are overwhelmingly tempered with fine sand and/or charcoal while Group 2 members are predominantly "grit-tempered" (medium or coarse sand). Quartz tempers are known to dilute the chemical constituents in bulk chemical profiles because, except for traces of hafnium and zirconium, the elements that comprise quartz itself are not detected by INAA (Neff et al. 1989:66; Steponaitis et al. 1996: 559). Because Group 2 contained, on average, lower concentrations of each measured element and larger quartz particles compared to Group 1, a record of the proportion of quartz tempers based on petrographic point counts was useful in understanding the chemical effects of this temper.

The point-count data revealed that chemical Group 2 contains slightly more quartz than Group 1 and would therefore be presumed to have a diluting effect on the chemical composition of members of this group (Table 5.7). However, the comparatively low quartz percentage in Group 1 also corre-

Table 5.7. Percentage of quartz among chemical groups

|  | Group 1 | Group 2 |
|---|---|---|
| Number | 29 | 25 |
| Mean | 27% | 35% |
| Standard deviation | .078 | .054 |
| Minimum | 9% | 21% |
| Maximum | 38% | 42% |

sponds with charcoal temper in many samples, a siliceous material that might also have a diluting effect. When charcoal temper percentages are added to the quartz percentages, the mean for Group 1 is 31 percent (with a standard deviation of .052), closer to the Group 2 mean of 35 percent.

Scatter plots and correlation coefficients show correlation between many elements and the amount of temper in a sample (Figure 5.2; Table 5.8). Among 31 measured elements, all but 2 show a negative correlation between element concentrations and proportion of quartz. However, the strength of this correlation varies dramatically among elements. For example, the elements scandium (Sc), aluminum (Al), chromium (Cr), and uranium (U) show fairly strong negative correlation with quartz while cobalt (Co), titanium (Ti), calcium (Ca), and manganese (Mn) have comparatively weak negative correlations. The majority of elements have correlations with quartz somewhere between these two extremes. Some of these correlations help explain the chemical differences between INAA groups. For example, chromium, which was a fairly reliable indicator of group membership in the chemical analysis, shows a strong negative correlation with quartz ($r = -.59$), indicating that chromium deficiency in many of the Group 2 samples is likely due to the diluting effect of quartz temper in high proportions. However, there is also a noticeable paucity of chromium in two of the three lower Altamaha clays, indicating that low chromium values in the clays used for Group 2 pottery may have contributed to this deficiency as well.

Among the elements that show weak correlation with quartz, some correspond with particularly small chemical differences between INAA groups. For instance, there is a 6 percent difference in manganese between Group 1 and Group 2 and an equally low correlation between this element and the percentage of quartz ($r = -.04$). In contrast, the distribution of cobalt between chemical groups does not correspond with the proportion of quartz. Cobalt shows relatively little correlation with quartz ($r = -.22$), yet all chemical Group 2 members contain comparatively high levels of cobalt,

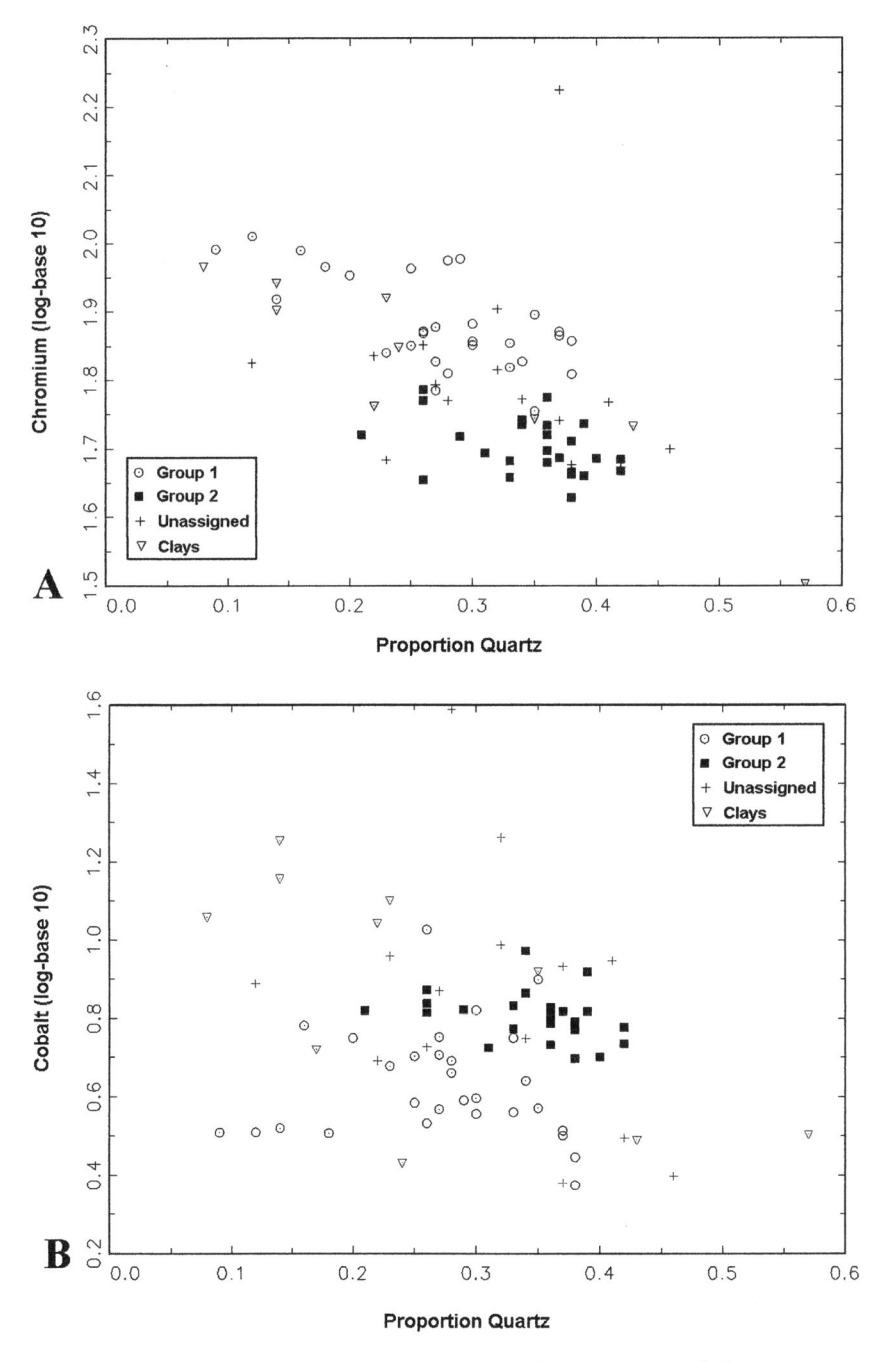

Figure 5.2. Group assignments by quartz and (*A*) chromium, (*B*) cobalt.

Table 5.8. R-squared value for the linear regression model and correlation between elements or principal components (PC) and quartz proportion

| Element or PC | R-squared | Correlation (r) |
| --- | --- | --- |
| As | 0.127 | −0.357 |
| La | 0.159 | −0.398 |
| Lu | 0.1551 | −0.3939 |
| Nd | 0.1278 | −0.3575 |
| Sm | 0.1445 | −0.3802 |
| U | 0.2903 | −0.5388 |
| Yb | 0.1339 | −0.3659 |
| Ce | 0.1435 | −0.3788 |
| Co | 0.0477 | −0.2184 |
| Cr | 0.34 | −0.587 |
| Cs | 0.1497 | −0.3869 |
| Eu | 0.2185 | −0.4674 |
| Fe | 0.1761 | −0.4196 |
| Hf | 0.0305 | 0.1746 |
| Ni | n/a | n/a |
| Rb | 0.2384 | −0.4883 |
| Sb | 0.217 | −0.4658 |
| Sc | 0.4627 | −0.6802 |
| Sr | n/a | n/a |
| Ta | 0.0631 | −0.2513 |
| Tb | 0.1574 | −0.3967 |
| Th | 0.0837 | −0.2894 |
| Zn | 0.2227 | −0.4719 |
| Zr | 0.0075 | 0.0867 |
| Al | 0.3588 | −0.599 |
| Ba | 0.063 | −0.251 |
| Ca | 0.0164 | −0.128 |
| Dy | 0.1827 | −0.4274 |
| K | 0.2449 | −0.4949 |
| Mn | 0.0014 | −0.038 |
| Na | 0.114 | −0.3376 |
| Ti | 0.0212 | −0.1456 |
| V | 0.0929 | −0.3048 |
| PC 1 | 0.1241 | −0.3523 |
| PC 2 | 0.0358 | −0.1892 |
| PC 3 | 0.1365 | −0.3695 |
| PC 4 | 0.004 | −0.0636 |
| PC 5 | 0.0026 | 0.0511 |

demonstrating that this chemical difference stems from differences in the constituent clays rather than the diluting effects of temper (Figure 5.2). Thus, although quartz temper seems to have had a diluting effect on cobalt levels, the differences in cobalt between the constituent clays used for each chemical group are significant enough to remain useful in partitioning the data.

Hafnium (Hf) and zirconium (Zr) are the only elements that demonstrate the opposite correlation with proportion of quartz, with each element increasing slightly in direct proportion to the amount of quartz. This relationship is expected because hafnium and zirconium are common trace elements in quartz. These elements were not fundamental to determining chemical group affiliations, but it is worth noting that Group 1 includes an average of roughly 30 percent more hafnium and zirconium than Group 2, yet Group 2 contains more quartz than Group 1. Therefore, although the hafnium and zirconium levels of pottery samples were inflated in relation to the amount of quartz temper added by ancient potters, Group 1 clay resources naturally contained more of these elements before temper was added.

Scatter plots and correlation coefficients of quartz and principal components, which can be conceptualized as linear combinations of the elements, show variable correlation that corresponds with the various contributions of each element (Figure 5.3; Table 5.8). Principal component 1 (PC1) and PC3 show the strongest correlations with quartz, reflecting strong contributions from elements subjected to the heaviest effects of dilution: potassium (K), rubidium (Rb), cesium (Cs), and many of the rare earth elements. In contrast, PC2, PC4, and PC5 show the weakest correlations due to significant contributions from elements apparently less susceptible to dilution through the addition of quartz, especially barium (Ba), manganese (Mn), cobalt (Co), hafnium (Hf), and zirconium (Zr). Consequently, bivariate plots of these principal components structured the partitions in the chemical data much better than PC1 and PC3, which may have been more heavily influenced by the diluting effects of quartz. Thus, as many researchers have recognized in their analyses of a variety of temper materials (Bishop et al. 1982; Neff et al. 1988, 1989), temper can affect the levels of each element differently, diluting some and augmenting others. In the case of this particular sample, quartz temper appears to have diluted some elements while having little effect on others. As might be expected for quartz, which is almost pure silicone dioxide ($SiO_2$), there is no evidence that the temper added measurable chemical constituents to the paste of vessels except for small amounts of hafnium and zirconium.

Notably, the same relationships between chemical concentrations and proportion of quartz pertain to clay samples, most of them raw clay samples from

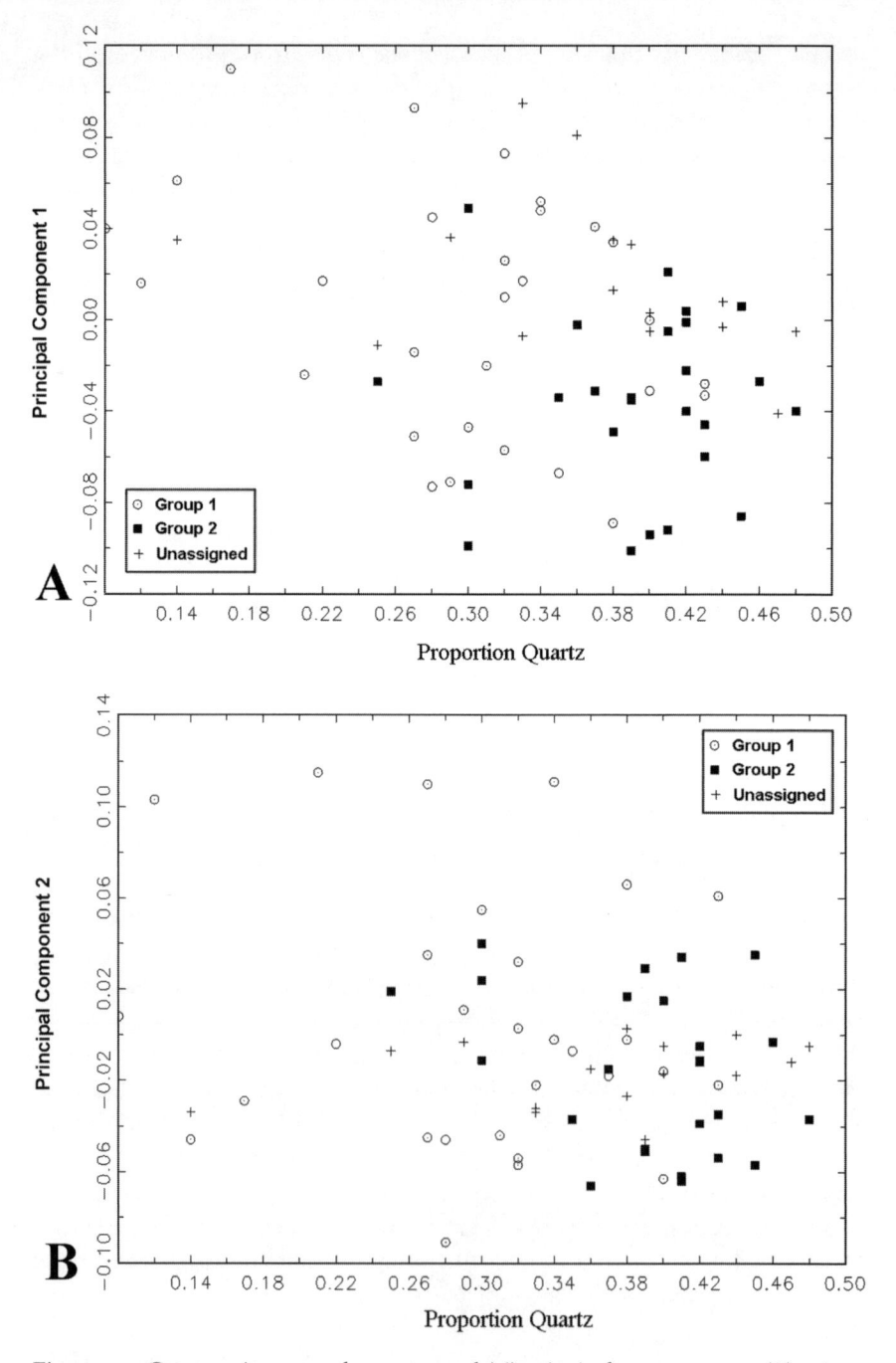

Figure 5.3. Group assignments by quartz and (*A*) principal component 1, (*B*) principal component 2.

natural deposits (i.e., not archaeological). The elements chromium (Cr), antimony (Sb), and zinc (Zn) are especially diluted in direct proportion to quartz, while other elements appear to be only weakly correlated. There is a very wide variation in the proportion of quartz in the clay samples, ranging from 8 percent to 57 percent in the natural deposits, and these proportions do not correspond with specific geographic areas but are distributed broadly across the landscape. Yet these disparities in quartz and their presumed diluting effect on some chemical constituents do not obfuscate the chemical partitions in the data that are geographically significant. In element and principal component plots, clays from the Lower St. Johns, Lower Altamaha, and Upper Altamaha/Lower Ocmulgee each generally cluster together in their respective geographic groups, regardless of the wide variation in quartz proportions. The same is true of pottery samples, in which some elements, particularly cobalt, were not diluted by quartz temper enough to conceal the chemical differences attributable to regionally distinct clays.

## Summary

The petrographic analysis resulted in six distinctive mineralogical groups among the pottery samples. Based on the geographic correlation of these pottery groups and comparisons with clay samples, three of the groups are comprised of Altamaha River–area resources (B, C, and E), one group is local to the Lower St. Johns River (D), and the remaining groups are either not geographically distinctive (A) or sample size is too small to designate a geographic affiliation (F). These mineralogical groups complement the chemical data obtained from INAA. Partitions in the chemical data usefully distinguish the regional origins of ubiquitous mineralogical Group A samples, while mineralogical differences were used to identify distinctive clay resources within the broadly defined chemical groups.

The combination of methods therefore provides an exceptionally nuanced view of pottery production and distribution. When combined with paddle-match data, the mineralogical group assignments show that some matching vessels were very likely to have been made from the same clay deposits, while others were made in the same region but with mineralogically distinct clays (perhaps, though not necessarily, at different villages). These conclusions bring us much closer to understanding the production origins of some vessels, especially those with paddle matches.

Petrographic point counts were also useful in evaluating the chemical differences between groups. Although the correlation between quartz and the chemical data indicates that most elements were diluted by the addition of quartz temper, not all elements were diminished equally. Fortunately, geographic differences in the concentration of some elements were pronounced enough to enable assignment of a regional provenance to most pottery samples regardless of dilution through temper.

# 6

# The Form, Technology, and Function of Swift Creek Pottery

Swift Creek pottery has already proven to be an excellent time marker for seriation and, through the reconstruction of designs, a useful database of social interaction. However, these data tell us little about the utilitarian functions of vessels, which are critical to understanding their roles in the social lives of people. Building on a respectable understanding of the temporality of the Swift Creek contexts in this study as well as the transport of vessels across the landscape, there were several questions that the analysis of the technological and functional aspects of pottery was designed to address: (1) How were vessels made? (2) What kinds of vessels (in a functional sense) were made? (3) Where and for what purpose were the various kinds of vessels used? These are basic questions about how pottery was employed in daily life; and, as James Skibo (1992:4) relates, I view them as foundational to the archaeological pursuit of culture reconstruction. Having knowledge of the transport of vessels, the formal, technological, and the functional variation of earthenware vessels provides clues to deciphering patterns of social interaction in Swift Creek contexts.

This chapter begins with a review of two concepts that are critical to comprehending the diversity of Swift Creek pottery assemblages. First, the idea of technofunction can be used to highlight the properties of materials and patterns of use, which in the case of pottery can be used to define fairly specific functional parameters for each individual vessel form defined from archaeological assemblages. Second, discussion of technofunction necessitates a review of style, defined simply as alternative ways of doing. Drawing on the idea of technological style, variations in the technological properties of pottery can reflect social identities in various ways and thereby be useful in delimiting patterns of interaction.

Technofunctional data are presented in four sections. First, vessel forms are defined based on the sizes and shapes of whole or substantially reconstructed vessels. The function of these vessels is inferred through their morphological suitability for particular tasks and corresponding frequencies of use alteration. These data help define functional categories for various vessel forms. Second, vessel size and use-alteration frequencies are discussed for all assemblages in order to identify vessel forms and potential functions even among small sherds. Third, rim thickness is compared across all assemblages, drawing particular attention to the temporal and geographical trends of this attribute. Fourth, the general paste characteristics of vessels are categorized and their distribution described. The chapter concludes with a synthesis and discussion of all technofunctional data and implications for understanding the social contexts of pottery production and use. Ultimately, the technofunctional data reflect conspicuous functional differences between mortuary mound and village midden pottery assemblages and stylistic differences between northern and southern site collections. In the midst of ceremonial and special-use vessels at Lower St. Johns mortuary mounds were buried nonlocal Swift Creek Complicated Stamped vessels with the technological style of Altamaha village wares. I argue that their use and deposition at mortuary mounds indicates a recontextualization of nonlocal cooking vessels in which indexical qualities could be enacted in ceremony.

## Technofunction

The analysis of pottery described in this chapter follows in the tradition of what Prudence Rice calls "technological ceramic analysis" (1987:310) or what others have called the analysis of "technofunction" (e.g., Skibo 1992; term taken from Binford 1962, 1965). Recent years have seen a dramatic increase in the number of analyses of ceramic function and use (Rice 1996:138), moving beyond the traditional culture-historical utility of potsherds as time markers. Instead, pots can be considered as tools (Braun 1983), and analysis is focused on the physical properties of materials and patterns of use. In this type of technological analysis an important analytical distinction must be made between data that can be used to infer vessel function and data that can be taken as direct evidence of use (Linton 1944; Rice 1996; Skibo 1992). To paraphrase Ralph Linton's (1944) oft-cited statement, we may not always be able to determine with certainty what a ceramic vessel was used for, but we may often identify the functions for which it would have been well suited.

# The Form, Technology, and Function of Swift Creek Pottery / 139

Vessel attributes such as morphology (size and shape), paste composition, wall thickness, and surface treatment can all be manipulated during manufacture so that the vessel is better suited for a particular function, but these data are not evidence of vessel use (Skibo 1992).

The size and shape of vessels, particularly the openness of vessel profile, rim diameter, and volume, have proven to be general predictors of patterns of use in ethnographic studies (Smith 1988). A common drawback to these useful data in archaeological research is that large portions of vessels are necessary, a situation not common in all archaeological contexts. This limitation can be somewhat ameliorated by using some of the many established techniques for estimating vessel shape and capacity from sherds (Rice 1987:222–224). In contrast to vessel morphology, the analysis of paste composition is not limited by the small portions of vessels commonly found in archaeological contexts. Paste constituents affect performance characteristics during manufacture and use, including clay workability, paste shrinkage, thermal shock resistance, impact and abrasion resistance, heating effectiveness, and evaporative-cooling effectiveness (Rice 1987:54–110, 226–232; Skibo 1992:36–37). A major focus of experimental studies has been the function of cooking pots as they relate to the physical properties of surface treatments and paste constituents (Schiffer 1990; Schiffer and Skibo 1987; Schiffer et al. 1994; Skibo et al. 1989). While knowledge of the physical properties of materials can help to infer the best function for vessels, two caveats should be noted. First, alterations in the physical properties of vessels can at once affect multiple performance characteristics, and the researcher cannot always be sure which (if any) were the impetus for adoption. For example, organic temper can be advantageous in the manufacturing process but results in a vessel that is less durable and less efficient in direct-heat cooking than a sand-tempered alternative (Skibo 1992:37). Yet the disadvantages of organic temper as a conductor of heat cannot be used to predict that vessels were not used to cook over fire, as demonstrated by use-alteration data that indicate that some fiber-tempered vessels were used for direct-heat cooking in the Southeast (Sassaman 1993:144–148; Waggoner 2006). Second, although the physical properties of vessels make them better suited for some tasks more than others, ethnographic research indicates that many vessels are multifunctional (Deal and Hagstrum 1994; DeBoer and Lathrap 1979; Skibo 1992). Even if an intended function can be inferred from the physical properties of vessels, impromptu or expedient uses cannot be determined by these methods.

In the strictest sense, *evidence* of use can be derived only from use alteration (Arthur 2002; Hally 1983, 1986; Skibo 1992). Use alteration comes in two basic forms: deposits on vessels such as soot or food residue and vessel attrition such as abrasion or pitting (Skibo 1992). Sooting on vessel surfaces is commonly used to show that a vessel was used for cooking and the orientation of soot can indicate the position of a pot on the fire (Hally 1983; Linton 1944; Mills 1986; Skibo 1992). The residue of vessel contents can be identified using a variety of chemical techniques (Rice 1996:144–147). A limitation of using deposits on vessels as evidence of use is that not all uses of a vessel result in accretions. Alternatively, Skibo (1992:40) argues that surface attrition has the potential to provide evidence for any type of pottery use. The most commonly used category of attrition is abrasion, which results from actions such as stirring, scraping, cutting, or beating during food preparation, consumption, or cleaning of vessels (Hally 1983; Skibo 1992:40–41; Skibo et al. 1997). Another common focus of attrition studies is pitting, which can result from thermal shock, chemical corrosion, or physical abrasion (Arthur 2002; Hally 1983; Jones 1989).

I view as major inspiration for this analysis David Hally's (1983, 1986) inferences about the function of Barnett phase Lamar pottery forms. In brief, Hally (1983, 1986) summarized the mechanical performance characteristics of vessels and compared these data to evidence of use in the form of sooting, oxidation discoloration, and surface pitting. By comparing with ethnohistorical accounts of vessel use, Hally (1986) was able to convincingly show how each of 13 Barnett phase vessel forms was used for various purposes. I have taken a similar approach to the analysis of Woodland period pottery, albeit with less reliance on ethnohistorical data. Attributes pertaining to vessel form were employed to infer trends in vessel function and evidence of use was defined by the occurrence of soot adhering to vessel surfaces and presence of drilled holes for mending and/or suspension.

## Considering Style

The data recorded in this study are useful not only in delineating the technological and functional parameters of Swift Creek earthenware vessels but also in making inferences about the history and culture of pot production and use. The consideration of style, in a broad sense, is germane to this endeavor. There have been myriad and competing expositions on the definitions and functions of style in material culture, especially pottery (reviews by Hegmon 1992; Rice 1996). Proponents of the "ceramic sociology" of the 1960s and 1970s, which inspired a surge of interest in style, held that similarity in material culture was directly related to levels of social interaction and shared learning contexts (e.g., Hill 1970; Longacre 1970). This passive view of style was attacked through more active theories of style, most notably by proponents of the information-exchange theory of Martin Wobst (1977). Wobst argued that style functions within cultures as a form of communication. Although a perspective of style as part of social strategies of identity and communication is now commonplace, several of Wobst's (1977) original tenets that rested on functionalist and systems-theory approaches have been repeatedly criticized (Hegmon 1992:520). Among Wobst's ideas that have been disputed are his claims that stylistic messages will operate within the limits of optimal efficiency, that unambiguous, simple, and recurrent messages are most commonly communicated with style, and that stylistic messages will be found primarily in the most visible contexts. The most parsimonious perspectives on style acknowledge that learning and interaction ("ceramic sociology") and information exchange are not mutually exclusive theoretical perspectives. Indeed, information exchange only emphasizes one dimension of style, namely, the mobilization of particular symbolic aspects of objects in some social contexts (Hegmon 1992).

The learning/interaction and information-exchange debate in many ways coalesced in the disputes between James Sackett (1985) and Polly Wiessner (1983). Sackett (1985) argues that style is the result of choices made from functionally equivalent alternatives; this he calls "isochrestic variation," which he suggests is learned or otherwise socially transmitted because options (e.g., "styles") are dictated by the craft traditions within social groups. Sackett (1985) contrasts isochrestic style with iconological style, with Wiessner's (1983) description of style as an example. Drawing largely on Wobst's (1977) ideas, Wiessner (1983) classifies style into two categories that relate to the conveyance of different kinds of information: emblemic style communicates information about group identity and social boundaries while assertive style relates to individual expression and identity. In essence, the arguments proffered by Sackett and Wiessner are debates about the passive versus active nature of style in material culture.

In an overview of the subject, Rice (1996) laments that many debates on style are merely reworking half-century-old debates about typology, whether types are heuristic abstractions created by the researcher or inherent to the artifacts (e.g., Ford 1954; Spaulding 1954). Yet the more recent debates about style, as clarified by Wiessner (1985, 1989) and Sackett (1986, 1990), are not over whether all style is best defined as emblemic, assertive, or isochrestic variation, but rather over which of these coexisting kinds of style pertain to specific contexts. It is the specificities of local context and particular histories that should ultimately guide studies of style (Carr and Nietzel 1995:4; Shanks and Tilley 1987:148–149).

A theoretical concept that posits the importance of social context in both technological and stylistic choices is technological style (Lechtman 1977; Lemmonier 1986, 1993; Stark 1998). According to proponents of technological style, technology itself has a style because "the activities which produce the artifacts" are stylistic (Lechtman and Merrill 1977:5). Thus, it is differences in social practice that reproduce differences in material culture that can be recognized as style. A useful way to examine culturally embedded systems of production is through analysis of the operational sequence or *chaine operatoire* (Lemmonier 1993; Leroi-Gourhan 1943, 1945). Technological style is essentially alternative ways of doing (cf. Sackett's [1985] isochrestic variation), and each step of the operational sequence of production can be examined in an attempt to determine or infer reasons for particular choices. Although the chaine operatoire is now often used in archaeology as simply a method to detail past technological strategies, sequences, and practices, a more holistic perspective comes from the heritage of Marcel Mauss's (1935) *enchainement organique,* which links the simultaneous becoming of artifacts and technical agents (Dobres 2000:155–156). In his "Les Techniques du Corps," Mauss (1935) describes how technological practice is socially embedded to the extent that making and using material culture is a process that constitutes agents as meaningful members of society, especially through everyday acts of bodily comportment that are conditioned through social tradition. Thus, the structural features of technological systems are reflections of, and indeed reproduce, the structure of social relations.

Through the legacy of Mauss (1935), the concept of technological style and the chaine operatoire method approach the idea of *habitus,* especially in terms of bodily praxis and the reproduction of social structure (e.g., Bourdieu 1977). Style is a sort of technological performance of social (re)production that need not carry observable or communicable meaning, although it certainly can serve this purpose (Lechtman 1977; Lemonnier 1993). In the concept of technological style, analysis is focused on how production "fits" into broader social and symbolic systems and cognitive structure is often privileged: different technological styles may represent different "mental processes that underlay and direct actions on the material world [and] are embedded in a broader, symbolic system" (Lemonnier 1993:3).

The cognitive focus of some applications of the technological style concept in itself fails to explain all aspects of material variation, but I find it to be a useful heuristic in examining differences within and among pottery assemblages. The fundamental contribution of technological style is in the recognition that all aspects of technologies are at least in part cultural constructions and thus social and historical context and contingency are critical parameters in defining style. Importantly, each step of the manufacturing sequence, or chaine operatoire, is potentially situated differently within social structure so that similar geographical or temporal patterns in two attributes of a class of material culture may reflect very different phenomena.

For example, some steps in the production sequence of pottery are perhaps more likely than others to be the reflection of distinct learning environments and fields of interaction. Those parts of the manufacturing sequence that depend on ingrained motor habits are more likely to preserve the routines of a potter's initial training during her or his formative years. In particular, the shaping stage of vessel manufacture has proven to be particularly conservative and resistant to change in a way that corresponds to social identities in many ethnographic studies (Arnold 1998:358; Reina and Hill 1978:230; Rice 1984; van der Leeuw et al. 1992). Alternatively, other steps in the manufacturing sequence, such as clay processing, firing, and applying surface treatments (i.e., "decoration"), can be more deliberately acquired by potters for various social reasons and are therefore more sensitive to change (Gosselain 2000:191–193). In sum, through changes in residence in the course of marriage alliance or migration, the vessel-shaping process is most likely to preserve the signatures of a potter's initial learning environment while other attributes of pottery might be easily changed to accommodate new social contexts.

Thus, there may be both habitual and purposeful (i.e., conscious) aspects of ceramic technological style that can leave archaeological residues. Some manufacturing steps reflect learning environments (as proposed by ceramic sociologists) while other attributes might be used in active messaging or become identity markers in certain contexts. The parameters that influence and inhibit a potter's technical choices are important considerations in studying interactive contexts in which alternative views of the "correct" socially accepted way to make and use pottery might collide. For example, among Swift Creek village assemblages, the mobility of potters through marriage alliances might be reflected in particular attributes of pottery that correspond with processes relying heavily on ingrained motor skills such as vessel-forming techniques. Indeed, the work of "outsiders" might be identified by looking for subtle anomalies in how clay coils were formed and bonded or how vessels were scraped and trimmed to achieve their final shape.

## Methods

Inferences about vessel form were a central part of the pottery analysis. Consequently, the vessel, as opposed to the sherd, was the unit of analysis chosen for this study. A vessel unit of analysis has the advantage of not only better approximating the number of vessels in an assemblage (e.g., minimum number of vessels, or MNV) but also inferring the relative frequencies of vessel forms. Determining a minimum number of vessels (MNV) is analogous to zooarchaeological techniques for determining minimum number of individuals (MNI) for faunal specimens (Rice 1987:292). In the present study, an attempt to identify a MNV for each assemblage began by isolating all rim sherds. These were combined or separated into numbered "vessel lots" representing individual vessels according to similarities or differences in lip form, rim form, surface treatment, and paste composition. Using surface treatment and paste composition only, each body and basal sherd was inferred to be either part of an existing numbered vessel lot or a new vessel lot. Every attempt was made to mend individual sherds that appeared similar based on the above criteria. In this way, vessel numbers were eventually assigned to individual sherds or groups of sherds that were inferred to be representative of individual vessels.

The technique described above usually underestimates the number of vessels in an assemblage (Rice 1987:292), probably among some types of sherds more than others. Body sherds, having fewer recorded attributes than rim sherds (lip form, lip fold depth, orifice diameter, rim form, etc.), are more susceptible to being incorrectly grouped into too few vessel lots. However, the uniqueness of each complicated stamped design on Swift Creek sherds allowed for better than normal precision in differentiating body sherds from separate vessels. Sand-tempered plain body sherds, with only paste composition and sometimes surface smoothing to differentiate them, were the most difficult to assign to individual vessel lots and were therefore underrepresented according to MNV to a greater degree than other types of sherds. In all, 1,222 "vessels" from 30 sites were identified and analyzed.

Recorded vessel-form data included orifice diameter, rim thickness, vessel height, lip form, rim form, lip fold depth, and basal form. In addition, rim profiles were drawn for all rims greater than 3 centimeters in length. For the majority of the vessel lots with rims, orifice diameter was calculated using a rim diameter template. Vessels exhibiting less than 5 percent of the total orifice were generally considered to give unreliable estimates of total diameter. For comparability, rim thickness was recorded at the same point on each specimen, exactly 3 centimeters below the lip of the vessel. Accurate vessel-capacity measurements were impractical due to the fragmentary nature of most vessels. Among the reconstructed vessels, volume was estimated using a version of the "summed cylinders" method, in which one-centimeter-high cylinders were "stacked" inside a vessel profile and then the volume ($V = \pi r^2 h$) of each was added together (Rice 1987:222).

Surface treatments (impressed, incised, painted, punctated, scraped, slipped, smoothed, stamped) were recorded for both exterior and interior portions of each vessel. Recorded use-alteration data included both the relative amount and location of soot adhering to vessel surfaces and the number of perforations through vessel walls, both suspension and mend holes. Using fresh breaks at sherd edges and a binocular (70X) microscope, the paste of each vessel was characterized according to the relative frequencies, size (Wentworth Scale), and shape of aplastic inclusions.

## Vessel Forms

Gordon Willey (1949:496–506) provides an overview of vessel forms from the Florida Gulf Coast, many from Weeden Island and Swift Creek contexts. With some variations discussed below, the vessel forms outlined by Willey (1949) are largely similar to the contemporaneous forms found on the Atlantic coast. I have used these Gulf Coast descriptions as a comparative guide in differentiating vessel forms.

Determining the range of vessel forms is difficult without large portions of vessels and large sample sizes. Fortunately, mortuary mound contexts that contain whole and reconstructable vessels can provide the framework through which to infer vessel dimensions from collections of smaller sherds. Based on the 102 substantially whole or reconstructed vessels from mortuary mounds on the Lower St. Johns River, at least 15 vessel forms can be differentiated. In addition, 7 vessels from village middens can be definitively assigned to one of these forms. Although the remaining vessels from both mortuary mounds and middens cannot be distinguished as specific forms, rim profiles reveal that standard cooking forms predominate, including open pots and bowls and restricted pots and bowls. Outlined in this section and summarized in Table 6.1, Table 6.2, and Table 6.3 are the morphological and functional attributes of each of the vessel forms identified from the analyzed mortuary assemblages and the few definitive specimens from middens.

### Open Bowls

The open bowl form is not defined by Willey (1949), but only differs from his "simple bowl" form in generally having greater vessel height. The widest diameter of the vessel, always at the mouth in this form, is greater than the vessel's height. The tallest of these specimens are morphologically similar to the open pot form. Bases are rounded or, in the shallowest versions, flattened. There are nine complete examples of this vessel form from mounds on the Lower St. Johns River. The form is somewhat difficult to identify among

Table 6.1. Vessel form summary statistics

| | Orifice diameter (cm) | Height (cm) | Rim thickness (mm) | Volume (l) |
|---|---|---|---|---|
| **Open bowls (n = 14)** | | | | |
| Range | 17.0–40.5 | 13.0–27.5 | 5.1–7.4 | 1.5–15.0 |
| Mean (standard deviation) | 25.70 (8.11) | 18.75 (4.99) | 6.39 (0.80) | |
| **Restricted bowls (n = 5)** | | | | |
| Range | 12.0–30.0 | 11.0–28.0 | 5.3–9.1 | 1.5–18.0 |
| Mean (standard deviation) | 19.7 (8.15) | 21.25 (7.27) | 6.68 (1.54) | |
| **Restricted pots (n = 16)** | | | | |
| Range | 12.3–28.0 | 19.0–41.0 | 4.8–9.8 | 2.5–13.5 |
| Mean (standard deviation) | 20.67 (5.00) | 25.42 (6.31) | 6.48 (1.38) | |
| **Open pots (n = 12)** | | | | |
| Range | 12.0–26.0 | 13.8–27.0 | 4.5–7.0 | 1.0–7.0 |
| Mean (standard deviation) | 16.86 (4.31) | 19.80 (4.01) | 5.88 (0.75) | |
| **Flattened-globular bowls (n = 9)** | | | | |
| Range | 7.0–17.5 | 10.0–19.0 | 4.7–8.5 | 0.5–4.0 |
| Mean (standard deviation) | 11.72 (3.07) | 13.19 (3.25) | 6.83 (1.25) | |
| **Collared jars (n = 7)** | | | | |
| Range | 9.0–18.0 | 16.0–27.0 | 4.6–9.7 | 0.8–2.5 |
| Mean (standard deviation) | 11.21 (3.12) | 21.60 (4.35) | 6.59 (1.83) | |
| **Small cups and bowls (n = 15)** | | | | |
| Range | 5.2–16.5 | 3.2–13.0 | 4.0–9.0 | 0.1–0.8 |
| Mean (standard deviation) | 10.13 (2.93) | 8.12 (3.05) | 5.54 (1.27) | |

| | | | | |
|---|---|---|---|---|
| Small jars (n = 11) | | | | |
| Range | 1.8–13.0 | 3.0–19.0 | 4.0–8.1 | 0.02–1.0 |
| Mean (standard deviation) | 5.92 (3.70) | 9.47 (4.67) | 6.08 (1.64) | |
| Boat-shaped bowls (n = 5) | long/short axis | | | |
| Range | 6.85–18.0/4.0–11.0 | 2.2–9.0 | 4.5–6.0 | 0.02–1.0 |
| Mean (standard deviation) | 11.91 (4.30)/7.13 (3.08) | 6.08 (2.96) | 5.12 (0.58) | |
| Double bowls (n = 3) | | | | |
| Range | 4.4–5.7 | 3.0–8.0 | 3.0–7.0 | 0.15–0.2 |
| Mean (standard deviation) | 5.03 (0.66) | 5.83 (2.57) | 4.50 (2.18) | |
| Multi-compartment trays (n = 5) | | | | |
| Range | 4.5–12.0 | 6.0–10.4 | 2.0–11.5 | 0.2–1.5 |
| Mean (standard deviation) | 7.63 (2.96) | 8.09 (1.78) | 5.74 (3.68) | |
| Beakers (n = 3) | | | | |
| Range | 6.8–9.2 | 15.0–18.0 | 4.6–5.2 | 0.4–0.9 |
| Mean (standard deviation) | 8.05 (1.23) | 17.00 (1.73) | 4.88 (0.28) | |
| Bottle (n = 1) | 4.5 | 4.9 | 19.2 | 1.1 |
| Shallow bowl (n = 1) | 17.0 | 4.5 | 4.0 | 0.7 |
| Double-globed jar (n = 1) | 8.0 | 6.0 | 30.0 | 4.3 |

Table 6.2. Soot and mend hole frequencies in each vessel form

| Vessel type | Soot | Mend holes |
|---|---|---|
| Open bowls (n = 14) | | |
| Frequency | 6 | 4 |
| Percent | 43 | 29 |
| Restricted bowls (n = 5) | | |
| Frequency | 2 | 2 |
| Percent | 40 | 40 |
| Restricted pots (n = 16) | | |
| Frequency | 11 | 2 |
| Percent | 69 | 13 |
| Open pots (n = 12) | | |
| Frequency | 11 | 1 |
| Percent | 92 | 8 |
| Flattened-globular bowls (n = 9) | | |
| Frequency | 3 | 1 |
| Percent | 33 | 11 |
| Collared jars (n = 7) | | |
| Frequency | 2 | 5 |
| Percent | 29 | 71 |
| Small cups and bowls (n = 15) | | |
| Frequency | 1 | 1 |
| Percent | 7 | 7 |
| Small jars (n = 11) | | |
| Frequency | 1 | 0 |
| Percent | 9 | 0 |
| Boat-shaped bowls (n = 5) | | |
| Frequency | 1 | 0 |
| Percent | 20 | 0 |
| Double bowls (n = 3) | | |
| Frequency | 0 | 0 |
| Percent | 0 | 0 |
| Multi-compartment trays (n = 5) | | |
| Frequency | 0 | 0 |
| Percent | 0 | 0 |
| Beakers (n = 3) | | |
| Frequency | 0 | 0 |
| Percent | 0 | 0 |
| Bottle (n = 1) | 0 | 0 |
| Shallow bowl (n = 1) | no data | 0 |
| Double-globed jar (n = 1) | 1 | 0 |

Table 6.3. Frequency of vessel form by surface treatment and pottery type

| Vessel form | Plain CP | Plain STP | Plain STJ | Plain GRG | Stamped ESC | Stamped LSC | Stamped SC | Stamped Other S | Incised/punctated WII | Incised/punctated CRI | Incised/punctated Other IP | Painted WIR | Painted DCR | Total |
|---|---|---|---|---|---|---|---|---|---|---|---|---|---|---|
| Open bowls | 3 | 7 | 1 | | 1 | 1 | | | | | | | 1 | 14 |
| Restricted bowls | 1 | 3 | | | | | | | | | | 1 | | 5 |
| Restricted pots | 4 | 7 | 1 | | | 2 | 2 | | | | | | | 16 |
| Open pots | 2 | 1 | | | 4 | | 1 | 3 | | | | 1 | | 12 |
| Flattened-globular bowls | 1 | 3 | | | | | | | 2 | 1 | | 2 | | 9 |
| Collared jars★ | | | | | | 6 | | | | 2 | | | | 8 |
| Small cups and bowls | 3 | 4 | 1 | | 1 | 2 | | | 1 | | 1 | | 2 | 15 |
| Small jars | | 2 | | 1 | | 2 | | | | 2 | 4 | | | 11 |
| Boat-shaped bowls | 2 | | | | | | | | | | | | 3 | 5 |
| Double bowls | | 2 | | | | | | | | | | 1 | | 3 |
| Multi-compartment trays | 1 | 3 | | | | | | | | | | 1 | | 5 |
| Beakers | | 2 | | | 1 | | | | | | | | | 3 |
| Bottle | | | 1 | | | | | | | | | | | 1 |
| Shallow bowl | | 1 | | | | | | | | 1 | | | | 1 |
| Double-globed jar | | | | | | | | | | | | | | 1 |
| TOTAL | 17 | 35 | 4 | 1 | 7 | 13 | 3 | 3 | 3 | 6 | 5 | 6 | 6 | 109 |

*Note:* Column headings are as follows: CP, charcoal-tempered plain; STP, sand-tempered plain; STJ, St. Johns Plain; GRG, grog-tempered plain; ESC, Early Swift Creek (charcoal-tempered); LSC, Late Swift Creek; SC, Swift Creek Complicated Stamped (cannot be defined as Early or Late); OtherS, other stamped (simple stamped, dentate stamped); WII, Weeden Island Incised; CRI, Crystal River Incised; OtherIP, non–diagnostic incised and/or punctuated; WIR, Weeden Island Red; DCR, Dunns Creek Red.

★Includes one collared bowl.

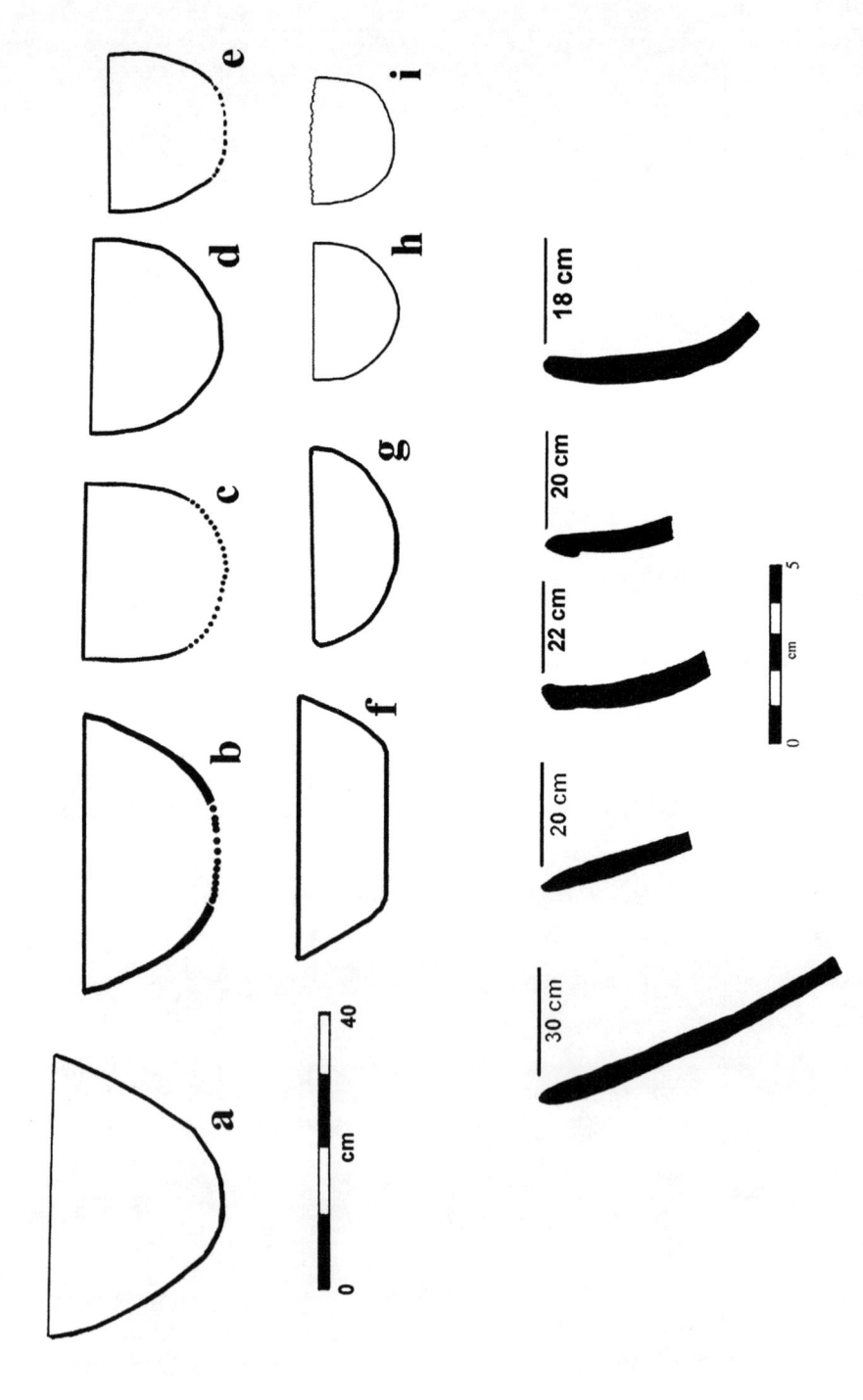

Figure 6.1. Open bowl profiles. *Top*: vessels (wall thickness not to scale) from Dent (*a, d, e, f, h, i*), Mayport (*b, c*), and Beauclerc (*g*); *bottom*: rims with estimated orifice diameters.

collections of small sherds because a steep-sided open bowl is indistinguishable from an open pot without more than half of the vessel wall present. However, the dramatic outward slope of vessel walls among the shallowest examples can be identified using smaller rim sherds. Among collections from middens, five vessels were identified as having this form. Due to the difficulties of identification, the actual frequency of open bowls among the vessels deposited in middens is assumed to be much higher.

Open bowls were made in a range of sizes, from medium to very large (Figure 6.1). The orifice diameter of open bowls ranges from 17.0 centimeters to 40.5 centimeters with a mean of 26.0 centimeters. Among the 9 substantially complete vessels, height ranges from 13.0 centimeters to 27.5 centimeters with a mean of 18.8 centimeters. This vessel form is not correlated with a particular temporal range or type. The total 14 vessels of this form include charcoal-tempered plain (n = 3), Early Swift Creek Complicated Stamped (charcoal-tempered) (n = 1), Dunns Creek Red (n = 1), sand-tempered plain (n = 7), St. Johns Plain (n = 1), and Late Swift Creek Complicated Stamped (n = 1).

Nearly half (n = 6) of open bowls have soot adhering to exterior surfaces, thus demonstrating that this vessel form was commonly used for cooking over fire. Four of the vessels have mend holes while another vessel has suspension holes drilled into the rim. Open bowls provided an alternative cooking container that was generally stable without extra supports (particularly the flatter and shallower examples) and in which contents were easily accessed and manipulated but consequently also easily spilled (cf. Hally 1986:283). Given these features, these vessels may have been used to cook food that needed frequent turning or stirring and that could be shared straight out of the vessel after preparation.

### Restricted Bowls

The restricted bowl form is largely similar to the open bowl form but differs in exhibiting its greatest width below the lip. This vessel form is not defined by Willey (1949) but is a variation of his "simple bowl." As with all bowls, the widest diameter of the vessel is greater than the vessel's height. The tallest of these specimens approaches the form of restricted pots. There are only four complete specimens from mounds on the Lower St. Johns River. Restricted bowls could be definitively identified only once within the midden assemblages owing to the lack of large portions of vessels. Indeed, the upper portions of restricted bowls near the rim are identical to restricted pots, and thus small sherds prevent their differentiation into specific vessel forms.

The limited sample of restricted bowls shows a large array of sizes with

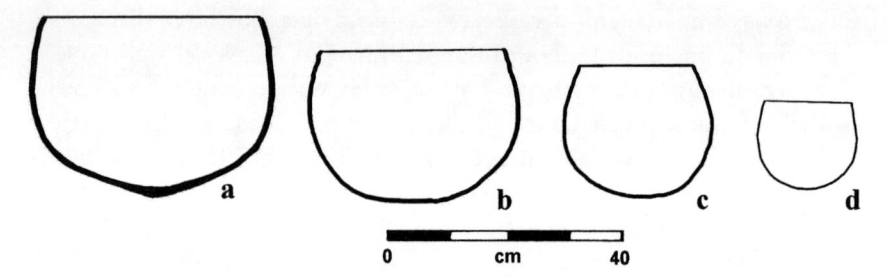

Figure 6.2. Restricted bowl profiles. Vessels (wall thickness not to scale) from Mayport (*a, b*) and Dent (*c, d*).

orifice diameters ranging from 12 centimeters to 30 centimeters with a mean of 20 centimeters (Figure 6.2). Four of the vessels are simply smoothed on exterior surfaces, three are sand tempered, and one is charcoal tempered. The fifth specimen is a painted Weeden Island Red vessel. The two largest vessels of this form were used for cooking over fire and have soot adhering to their rim exteriors. The three smaller versions of this vessel form have no evidence of soot. Thus, there are at least two sizes of restricted bowl that may each correspond with different functions: the larger was for cooking while the smaller served some non-cooking function. The orifices of these vessels are not conducive to sealing, making a storage function unlikely. While the slightly restricted orifice of these bowls served to reduce heat loss and spillage of contents (cf. Hally 1986:288–289), whether these vessels were employed differently than open bowls is unclear.

## Restricted Pots

Willey makes a distinction between "simple jars" and "pots" (1949:498–502). This distinction pertains to the degree of restriction at the orifice and the location of the maximum width of the vessel. However, Willey (1949) defines no measurable attributes to differentiate the two forms. Given the rather dubious definitional parameters, the uncertain functional differences between jars and pots in this context, and the small number of ostensible "jar" forms in the study collections, all restricted vessels that are taller than they are wide are included as restricted pots here.

There are a total of 16 restricted pots from mound assemblages on the Lower St. Johns River (Figure 6.3). This vessel form also appears to be common in the sherd assemblages from middens but cannot be confidently differentiated from restricted bowls without the majority of a vessel wall present.

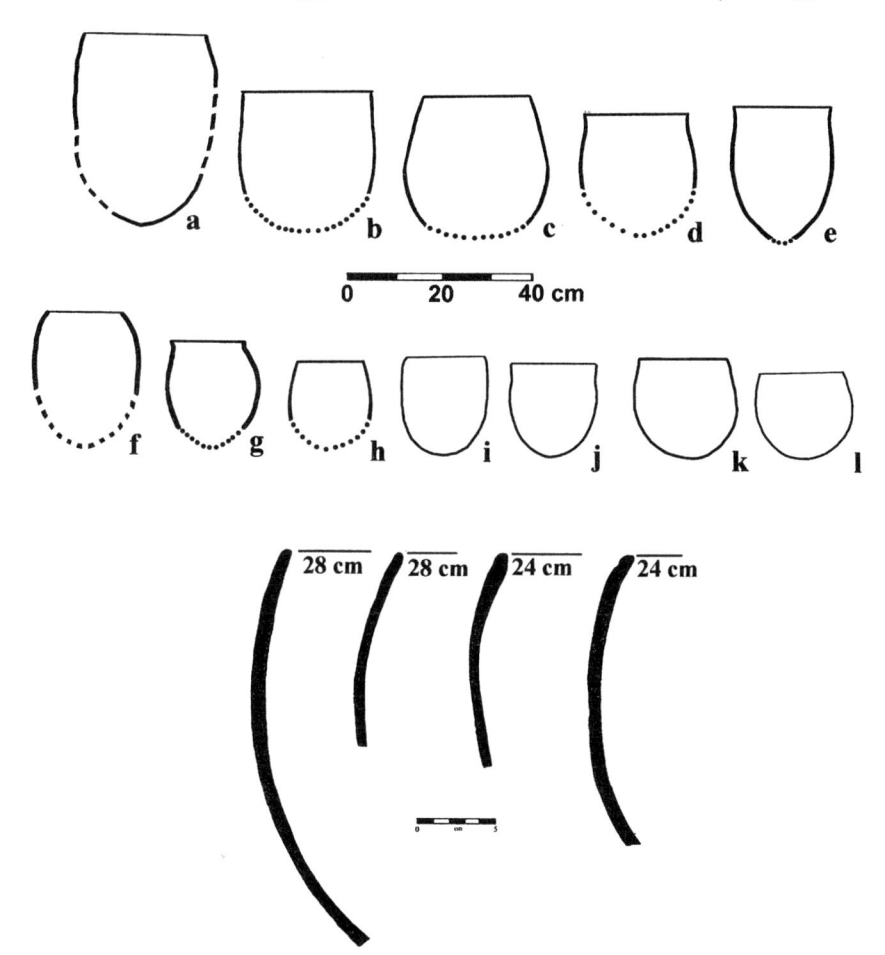

The Form, Technology, and Function of Swift Creek Pottery / 153

Figure 6.3. Restricted pot profiles. *Top:* vessels (wall thickness not to scale) from Mayport (*a–h*) and Dent (*i–l*); *bottom:* rims with estimated orifice diameters.

The restricted pots from mounds range from 12.3 centimeters to 28.0 centimeters in orifice diameter with a mean of 20.7 centimeters. They include charcoal-tempered plain (n = 4), sand-tempered plain (n = 7), St. Johns Plain (n = 1), and Swift Creek Complicated Stamped (n = 4), two of which are definitively Late Swift Creek. Restricted pots were primarily used as cooking vessels, with 11 (69 percent) from the mound sample having soot adhering to exterior rims or vessel walls. Only two (13 percent) have mend holes, demonstrating that these vessels were not commonly repaired.

These slightly restricted vessels and largely similar open pots (discussed below) were apparently very common cooking pot forms during the Woodland period in general and among many Swift Creek groups in particular (Sears 1962; Willey 1949:379). The smooth transition between base, wall, and rim provides an excellent conductive surface for cooking food and lends a high thermal shock resistance for cooking over fire. The restricted orifice varies only slightly from the morphology of open pots, and, in fact, the least restricted versions grade into open pot forms. A slightly restricted orifice may have reduced spillage and heat loss but only to a negligible degree. Restricted pots may merely be a morphological variation of open pots that served the same cooking functions.

## Open Pots

The open pot form is similar to the restricted pot but with an open, unrestricted orifice (Figure 6.4). There are 12 vessels represented in the mound assemblages, although open pots are assumed to be very numerous in both mound and midden assemblages. As with restricted pots and bowls, open pots cannot be differentiated from open bowls without major portions of the vessel wall. The mound sample of open pots is similar to restricted pots in orifice diameter size, ranging from 12 centimeters to 26 centimeters with a mean of 17 centimeters. These vessels include many pottery types, including Early Swift Creek Complicated Stamped (charcoal tempered; n = 4), charcoal-tempered plain (n = 2), sand-tempered plain (n = 1), Deptford Simple Stamped (n = 1), Mayport Dentate Stamped (n = 2), Swift Creek Complicated Stamped (n = 1), and Weeden Island Red (n = 1).

The open pot is quite possibly the quintessential cooking form among Swift Creek populations. All but one (92 percent) of these is sooted in the mound sample. The only unsooted vessel is of the type Weeden Island Red, which is nearly exclusive to mortuary contexts in northeastern Florida and appears to have been rarely used in cooking. Only one (8 percent) open pot in the sample contains mend holes, showing that these mostly utilitarian pots were not commonly repaired.

## Flattened-Globular Bowls

Willey defines this vessel form as a "medium-deep to deep bowl with maximum diameter at about midpoint of [the] vessel and with inturned sides and constricted orifice" (1949:496–498). Flattened-globular bowls are somewhat variable in their appearance owing to a variety of heights that range from half to nearly equal the maximum diameter of the vessel (Willey 1949:498). However, the defining characteristic of this vessel form is the sharply incur-

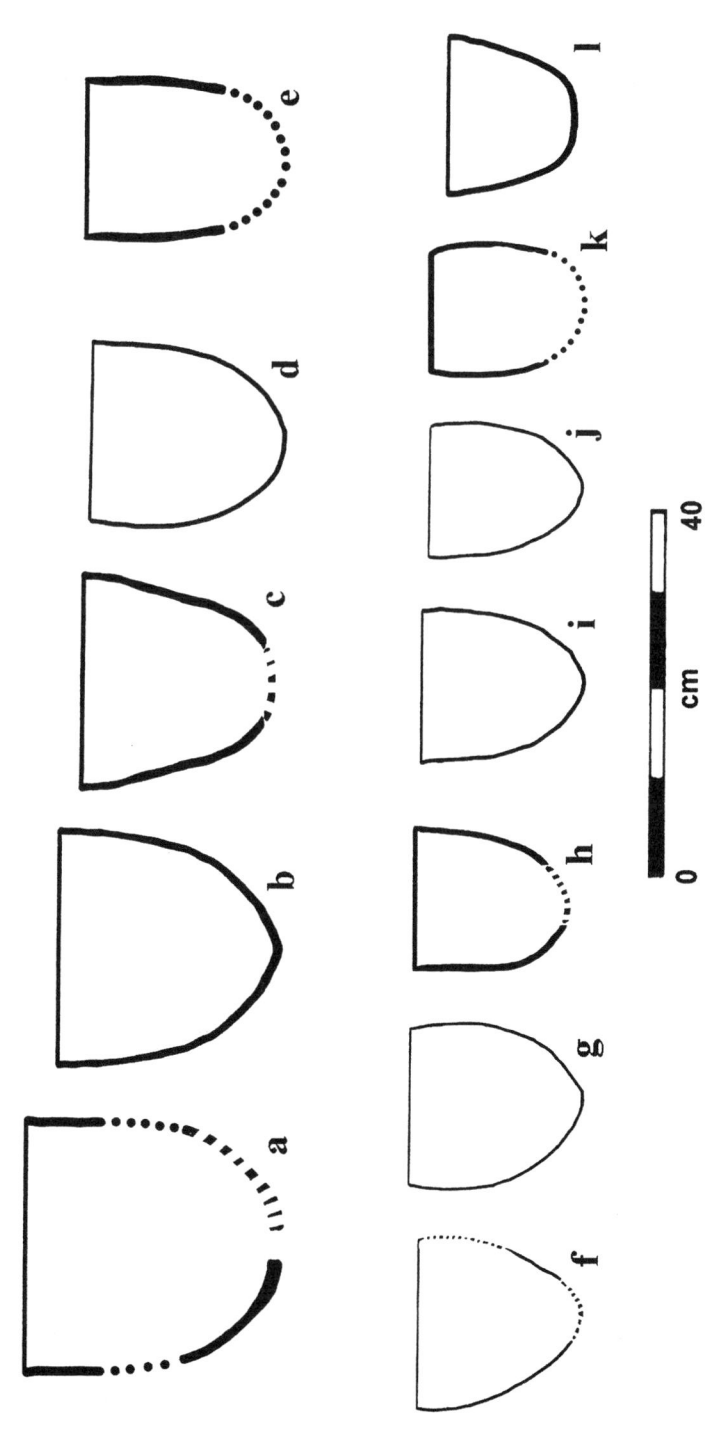

Figure 6.4. Open pot vessel profiles (wall thickness not to scale) from Mayport (*a–c, e, h*), Dent (*d, f, g, i, j*), Grant (*k*), and Grant E (*l*).

vate vessel wall near the rim. The tallest of these specimens grade into Willey's (1949:498) simple jar form.

On the Lower St. Johns River, flattened-globular bowls were made in a variety of sizes with orifice diameters ranging from 7.0 centimeters to 17.5 centimeters (mean of 11.7 centimeters). However, the mean vessel size in this case closely mirrors the mode: more than half (n = 5) of the nine specimens have orifice diameters between 11 centimeters and 12 centimeters. This vessel form, particularly this modal size, appears to have been used for cooking over fire at least some of the time as evidenced by soot adhering to the exterior surfaces of three of the nine (33 percent) vessels. Interestingly, the three sooted vessels are all of the moderate modal size (see vessels b, d, and e in Figure 6.5). The smaller vessels that are not sooted were presumably not used for cooking. Flattened-globular bowls of all sizes appear not to have been extensively repaired; only one of the nine (11 percent) vessels contains mend holes.

Flattened-globular bowls are strongly correlated with Weeden Island series pottery. Nearly half of the sampled vessels are Weeden Island Red (n = 2) or Weeden Island Incised (n = 2), and another is Crystal River Incised. The remaining vessels are sand-tempered plain (n = 3) and charcoal-tempered plain (n = 1). Thus, the idea of flattened-globular bowls and possibly the vessels themselves are likely to have come from the west along with other items of early Weeden Island and Crystal River material culture. Indeed, the flattened-globular bowl is a form quite common to Weeden Island contexts but rare in contemporaneous cultures throughout the Eastern Woodlands (Willey 1945:249). These vessel forms are notably absent from non-mortuary contexts in northeastern Florida regardless of their comparatively facile identification with small sherds. Only one of the nine vessels comes from a non-mortuary context and it, too, is Weeden Island Incised. Moreover, there may have been a functional difference between the diagnostic Weeden Island types and vessels that were not painted or incised. All three of the sooted vessels of this form are plain in surface treatment.

Thus, flattened-globular bowls were ceremonial wares that seem to have been reserved for use and deposition in mortuary contexts. This is one of several vessel forms found in northeastern Florida that substantiates a sort of "sacred" and "secular" dichotomy akin to William Sears's (1973) description of Weeden Island contexts in western Florida. Although neither Sears (1973) nor Jerald Milanich and colleagues (1997:127) found "globular bowls" to be restricted to mortuary contexts within and among Weeden Island sites, populations in northeastern Florida limited their deposition, and presumably their use, mostly to mortuary mounds.

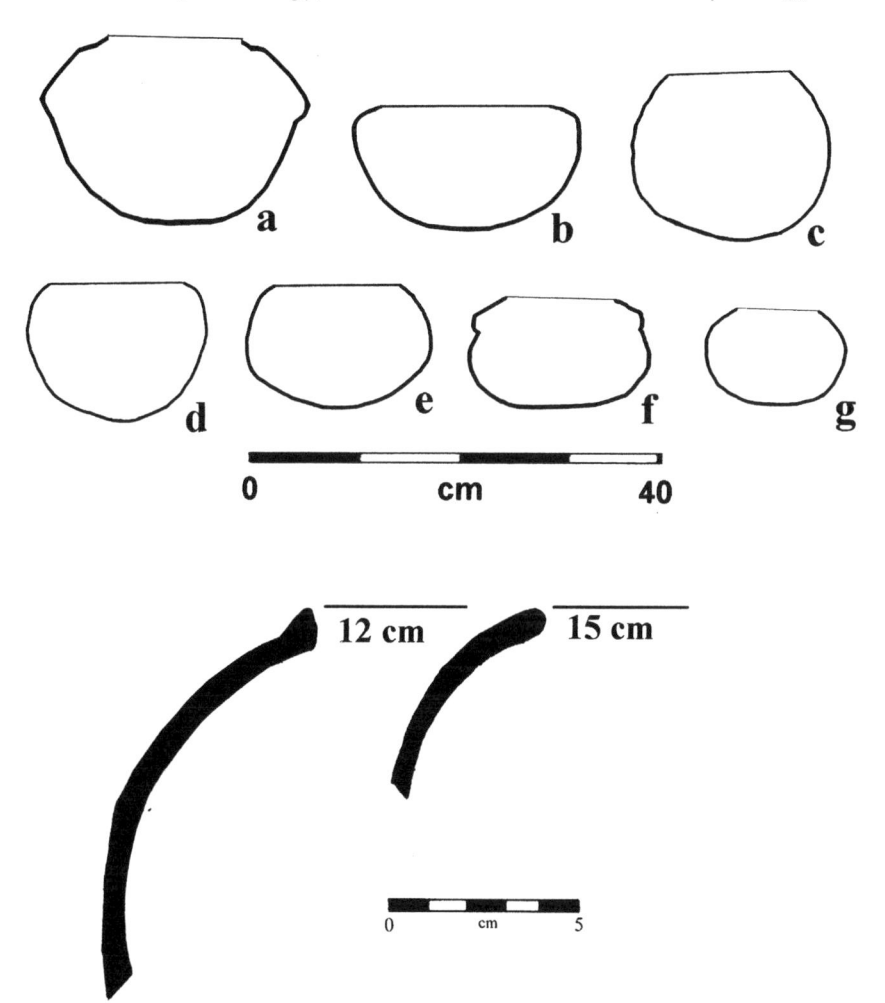

The Form, Technology, and Function of Swift Creek Pottery / 157

Figure 6.5. Flattened-globular bowl profiles. *Top:* vessels (wall thickness not to scale) from Denton (*a*), Low Grant (*b*), Dent (*c–e*), Alicia (*f*), and Arlington (*g*); *bottom:* rim profiles with estimated orifice diameters.

Collared Jars

Willey (1949:498–502) divides collared jars into two categories: "long" collared jars, in which the length of the vessel neck is between one-third and two-thirds of the total vessel height, and "short" collared jars, in which the vessel neck comprises between one-fourth and one-fifth of the vessel height. The Lower St. Johns River specimens (n = 7) do not conform to these parameters, with some necks much longer than two-thirds of the total height and others definitively between the length ranges specified by Willey (1949). Therefore, all vessels with collars are included in the same category here (Figure 6.6). Further, a single "double-globed jar"—Willey's terminology (1949:503)—with a distinct collar is also included in this category due to its overall morphological similarity.

The morphology and overall size of collared jars is variable on the Lower St. Johns River, but orifice diameters are consistently similar across vessels, with six of the seven vessels ranging between 9.0 centimeters and 11.5 centimeters. A single short-collared vessel with an orifice diameter of 18.0 centimeters is an outlier in this limited sample. While the collared jars grouped together here show a wide range of morphological variability, they are also unified by common surface treatments. Five of the vessels are Late Swift Creek Complicated Stamped, and the remaining two are Crystal River Incised. All are from mortuary mound contexts.

Collared jars appear to have been mortuary-specific wares that were an important part of the Swift Creek ceremonial complex that manifested in northeastern Florida. These vessels appear uniformly to have been expertly constructed and carefully used and repaired. Five (71 percent) of the vessels contain mend holes. Some collared jars were used over fire as evidenced by soot adhering to the shoulders of two (29 percent) of the vessels. The long-collared jars with restricted midsections and flaring orifices would have been well-suited for quickly heating liquids and transporting and pouring these contents without spilling. Given the mortuary-specific recovery context for all of these vessels, their function is likely to have been in preparing and distributing ceremonial beverages. Several vessels have a thick angular rim fold suitable for tying covers across vessel openings for secure transport (Figure 6.7).

There is a single example of a collared bowl form that may be differentiated from the collared jars by having an overall width that is greater than maximum height. The vessel approximates the shape of a shorter collared jar. This vessel is also from a mortuary context and is likely to have served functions similar to those of collared jars.

## Small Cups and Bowls

Small cups and bowls take the forms of larger pots and bowls, respectively, but differ in their diminutive size. Willey defines no such category but does mention "miniature vessels," which he describes as "very small vessels, most of which are rather carelessly made" (1949:506). Willey (1949:506) also estimates that these miniature vessels mostly conform to the morphological

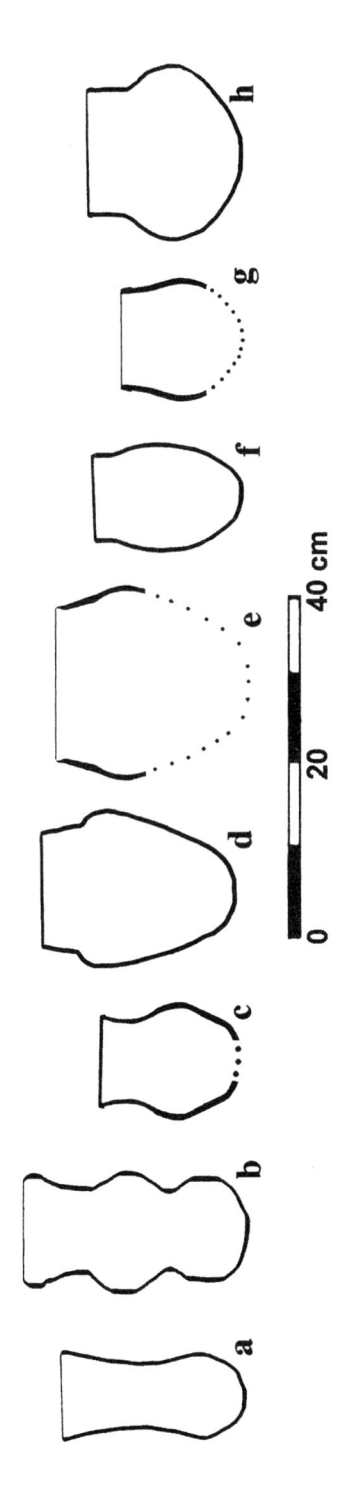

Figure 6.6. Collared jar and collared bowl (*h* only) vessel profiles (wall thickness not to scale) from Alicia (*a*), Dent (*b*, *d*, *g*, *h*), Mayport (*c*), Reddie Point (*e*), and Grant E (*f*).

Figure 6.7. Sooted collared jar with folded rim from Mayport Mound. Artifact held in the collection of the Timucuan Ecological and Historic Preserve, National Park Service, Jacksonville, Florida (image by the author).

categories of larger vessels. While there are "miniature vessels" in the Lower St. Johns mound assemblages that might fit Willey's definition (see below), the cups and bowls described here do not conform to this description, being neither "very small" nor "carelessly made." Rather than being miniature versions of large functional vessels, small cups and bowls are likely to have served a particular function, namely, to consume individual portions of food and drink and as containers for mortuary offerings.

The Form, Technology, and Function of Swift Creek Pottery / 161

There are 15 whole or nearly whole small cups and bowls among the mound assemblages from the Lower St. Johns River (Figure 6.8). As with other vessel forms, a considerable portion of the vessel wall must be present in order to differentiate between vessel forms, with small rim sherds potentially conflating identifications of small cups, bowls, and jars with beakers, bottles, and multi-compartment trays. Consequently, small cups and bowls are not specifically defined for any midden assemblages, but the extremely low relative frequency of small orifice diameters among midden assemblages indicates their rarity. The orifice diameters of small cups and bowls range mostly from 5.2 centimeters to 13.0 centimeters (mean of 10.1 centimeters) with one outlier shallow bowl with an orifice diameter of 16.5 centimeters. Several of these vessels have slightly irregular (i.e., non-circular) openings but do not approach the truly elongated shape of the "boat-shaped bowl" described below. The small cup and bowl assemblage includes a wide range of pottery types: Early Swift Creek Complicated Stamped (charcoal tempered; n = 1), charcoal-tempered plain (n = 3), Dunns Creek Red (n = 2), non-diagnostic punctated and incised (n = 1), sand-tempered plain (n = 4), St. Johns Plain (n = 1), Swift Creek Complicated Stamped (n = 2), and Weeden Island Incised (n = 1). Therefore, these vessels include both "ceremonial" pottery types (e.g., Dunns Creek Red, Weeden Island series, Crystal River series) that seem to be mostly restricted to mortuary sites as well as common types found in village middens.

Notably, only one (7 percent) vessel exhibits a small amount of soot adhering to the exterior of the rim, demonstrating that small cups and bowls usually did not serve a cooking function. These vessels were also only infrequently repaired, with mend holes present on only one (7 percent) vessel.

### Small Jars

Small jars are diminutive vessels with restricted orifices and greater height than width (Figure 6.9). The larger of these vessels are similar in volume to the small cups and bowls and may have served similar functions. In contrast, the smallest jars often appear to be diminutive versions of larger vessels in other morphological categories, what Willey refers to as "miniature vessels" (1949:506). For instance, an incised vessel from the Low Grant Mound E, only 4 centimeters tall and less than 2 centimeters wide, takes the shape of the larger collared jar form described previously and seems to mimic either the zoned decoration of Swift Creek Complicated Stamped or the incising of Crystal River or Santa Rosa–Swift Creek series vessels (Figure 6.10). Likewise, a Crystal River Incised jar, just over 10 centimeters tall, is a miniature version of Willey's "jar with lobes" (1949:498) from an early Weeden Island mound in Bay County (8BY14) (Moore 1902:145; Willey 1949:239–240).

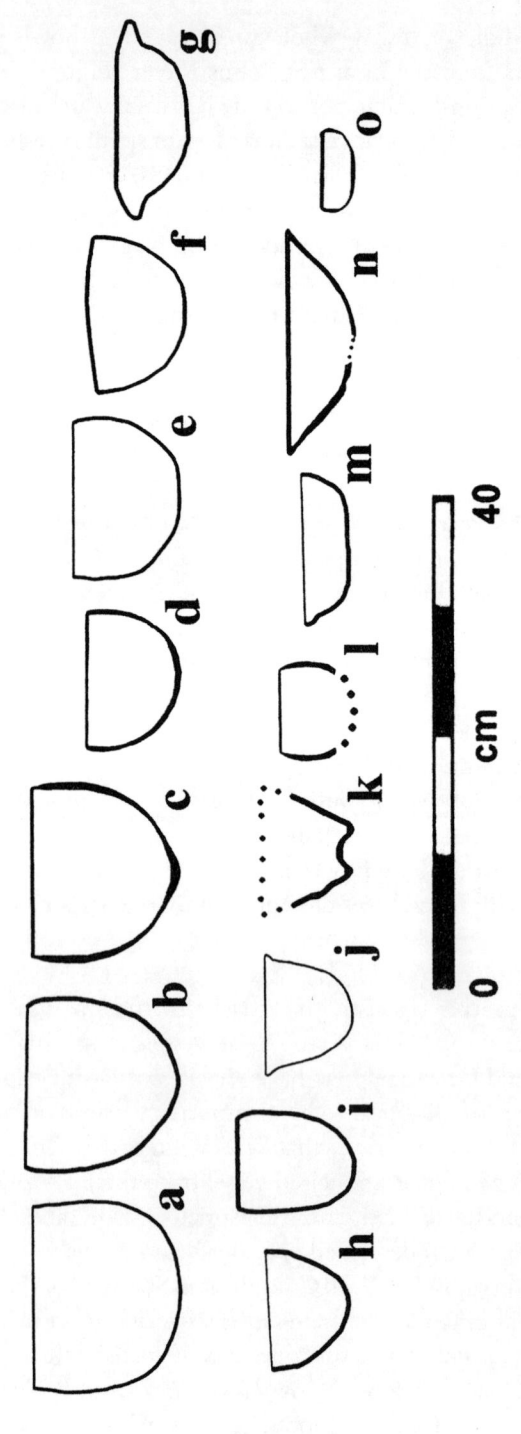

Figure 6.8. Small cup and bowl vessel profiles (wall thickness not to scale) from Dent (*a, b, e, f, j*), Mayport (*c, d, k, l, n*), Monroe (*g*), Beauclerc (*h*), Grant E (*i, o*), and Alicia (*m*).

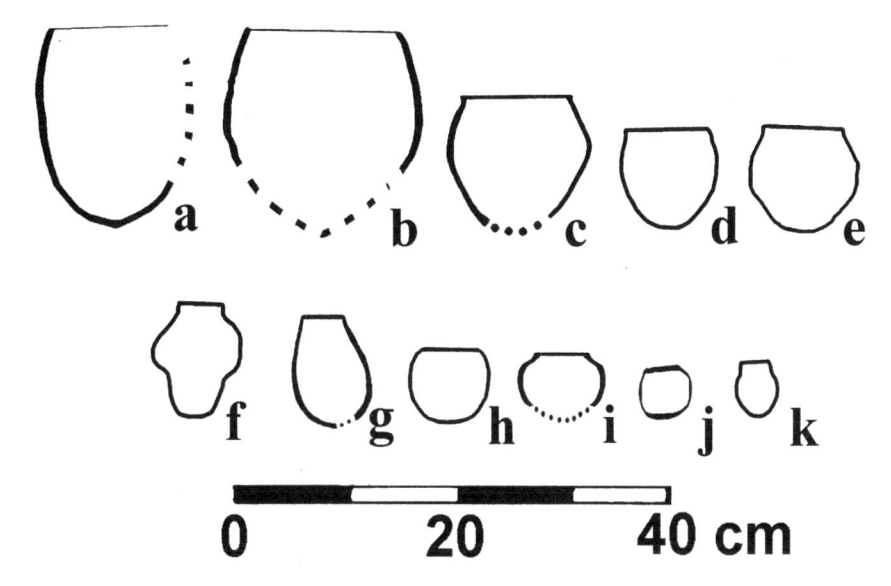

The Form, Technology, and Function of Swift Creek Pottery / 163

Figure 6.9. Small jar vessel profiles (wall thickness not to scale) from Mayport (*a, b, c, g, i*), Grant (*d, e*), Grant A (*f*), Grant E (*k*), Beauclerc (*h*), and Point La Vista (*j*).

There are 11 small jars from Lower St. Johns River mound assemblages, the largest 3 of which resemble cups and the remaining 8 which can be considered "miniature vessels." The orifice diameter of small jars ranges between 1.8 centimeters and 13.0 centimeters with a mean of 5.9 centimeters. The vessels are overwhelmingly decorated, with only three (27 percent) having entirely smoothed exterior surfaces. According to typology, the small jar assemblage includes Basin Bayou Incised (n = 1), Carrabelle Punctated (n = 1), charcoal-tempered incised (n = 1), grog-tempered plain (n = 1), Crystal River Incised (n = 2), sand-tempered plain (n = 2), Late Swift Creek Complicated Stamped (n = 2), and sand-tempered incised (non-diagnostic; n = 1).

Small jars were very rarely used for cooking; only one (9 percent) vessel contains traces of soot. While the three larger jars are well-suited for individual servings and offerings, like similar small cups and bowls, the remaining "miniature" vessels may have had an altogether different function. There are no mend holes in any of the small jars, but suspension holes near the rim are present in four (36 percent) of the miniature jars. Thus, these miniature jars were commonly suspended, perhaps with cordage, for easy carrying and display. Many of these vessels were small enough to have been attached to the body as ornamentation. As such, they may have contained materials impor-

164 / Chapter 6

Figure 6.10. Small jars with incising from Grant Mound E (*left*) and Grant Mound A (*right*). Artifacts held in the collection of the National Museum of the American Indian, Suitland, Maryland (image by the author).

tant for ceremonial events. These vessels can be easily identified in midden assemblages by their very small orifice diameters but are very rare or absent in these contexts. None are definitively identified in the midden samples of this study.

## Boat-Shaped Bowls

Willey defines boat-shaped bowls as "medium-deep or shallow" with "oval or ovate-rectangular" form (1949:498). There are five of these in the Lower St. Johns River mound assemblages (Figure 6.11). These were made in at least two distinct sizes. The larger of the two sizes (n = 3) has orifice diameters between 13.2 centimeters and 18.0 centimeters on the long axis and be-

The Form, Technology, and Function of Swift Creek Pottery / 165

Figure 6.11. Boat-shaped bowls from Low Grant (*a*), Floral Bluff (*b*), Grant (*c*), Mayport (*d*, top view), and Dent (*e*, top view). Artifacts held in the collections of the National Museum of the American Indian, Jacksonville Museum of Science and History, and Florida Museum of Natural History (images by the author).

tween 6.5 centimeters and 11.0 centimeters on the short axis. The smaller of the two vessel sizes (n = 2) is comprised of diminutive versions of the larger, with orifice diameters ranging from 7.0 centimeters to 8.0 centimeters on the long axis and 4.0 centimeters to 4.5 centimeters on the short axis. Three of the vessels, including the two miniature vessels, are Dunns Creek Red while the remaining two are charcoal-tempered plain. Only the largest vessel exhibits soot on the exterior rim. None of the specimens contain mend holes but the smallest vessel has two suspension holes.

Boat-shaped bowls served mostly non-cooking functions and may have been used in ways similar to small cups and bowls. Likewise, the smallest of these vessels could have been used as ornaments worn on the body or otherwise displayed. The use of this vessel form appears to have been limited to mortuary contexts, with none identified from non-mortuary sites and a strong association with the Dunns Creek Red type that is limited mostly to mortuary mounds.

Willey (1949:558) describes boat-shaped bowls as a distinctive feature of the St. Johns River region, where this vessel form enjoyed the greatest popularity. However, Willey (1949:558) also suggests that the idea for this vessel form may have come from the Gulf Coast, where a few such vessels have been recovered from Deptford and Early Swift Creek sites. Regardless of whether eastern Florida was mostly on the receiving end in the exchange of ideas and material culture (Willey 1949:562), all five of the vessels in the present study are presumed to have been produced either on the Lower St. Johns (charcoal-tempered) or the Middle St. Johns (Dunns Creek Red) based on their typological designations.

## Double Bowls

The double bowl vessel form, as depicted by Willey (1949:499), is made up of two conjoined bowls separated by thick compartment walls (Figure 6.12). There are three of these vessels from mound assemblages, and they are uniformly small, having orifice diameters between 4.4 centimeters and 5.7 centimeters for each "bowl." The assemblage of double bowls includes one Weeden Island Red and two sand-tempered plain vessels. None are sooted or have mend holes.

The three double bowls in the sample include a variety of unique attributes. One rather amorphous and poorly smoothed vessel has small flattened lobes, described as "handles" by C. B. Moore (1894), that protrude from the base of the vessel on either side. Another vessel has four pointed protrusions symmetrically placed on the exterior rim. The breakage pattern of this vessel is indicative of the manufacturing technique, with the bowls simply coming apart in the area where they were conjoined. The two bowls appear to have been made separately and later joined together while still wet and plastic.

Willey (1949:410–411) describes the double bowl as a Weeden Island series vessel form, comprised of Weeden Island Plain wares on the Gulf Coast. However, this temporal and cultural designation is apparently based on Moore's work on 56 "pure" Weeden Island sites in which only 2 of 248 vessels (less than 1 percent) were double bowls. In the present sample, one Weeden Island Red vessel supports a Weeden Island series affiliation.

Double bowls have not been found at midden sites on the Atlantic coast and are presumably specialized mortuary wares serving a function similar to multi-compartment trays. However, these vessels are notably different in execution, being less uniform in shape and exhibiting less smoothing and polishing than multi-compartment vessels.

## Multi-Compartment Trays

The multi-compartment tray comes in a variety of shapes and sizes (Figure 6.13). Some vessels are similar in form to double bowls but with three, rather than two, bowls conjoined. Another form with three compartments is much

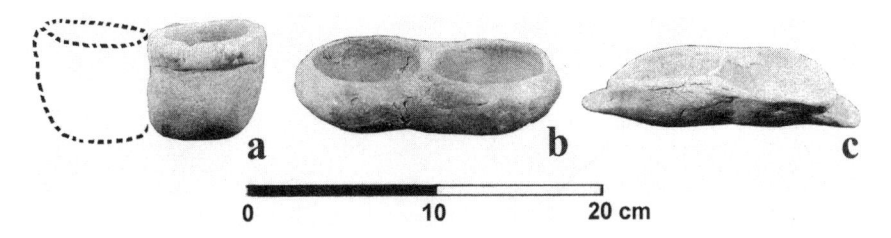

Figure 6.12. Double bowls from Beauclerc (*a*), Low Grant (*b*), and Point La Vista (*c*). Artifacts held in the collection of the National Museum of the American Indian, Suitland, Maryland (images by the author).

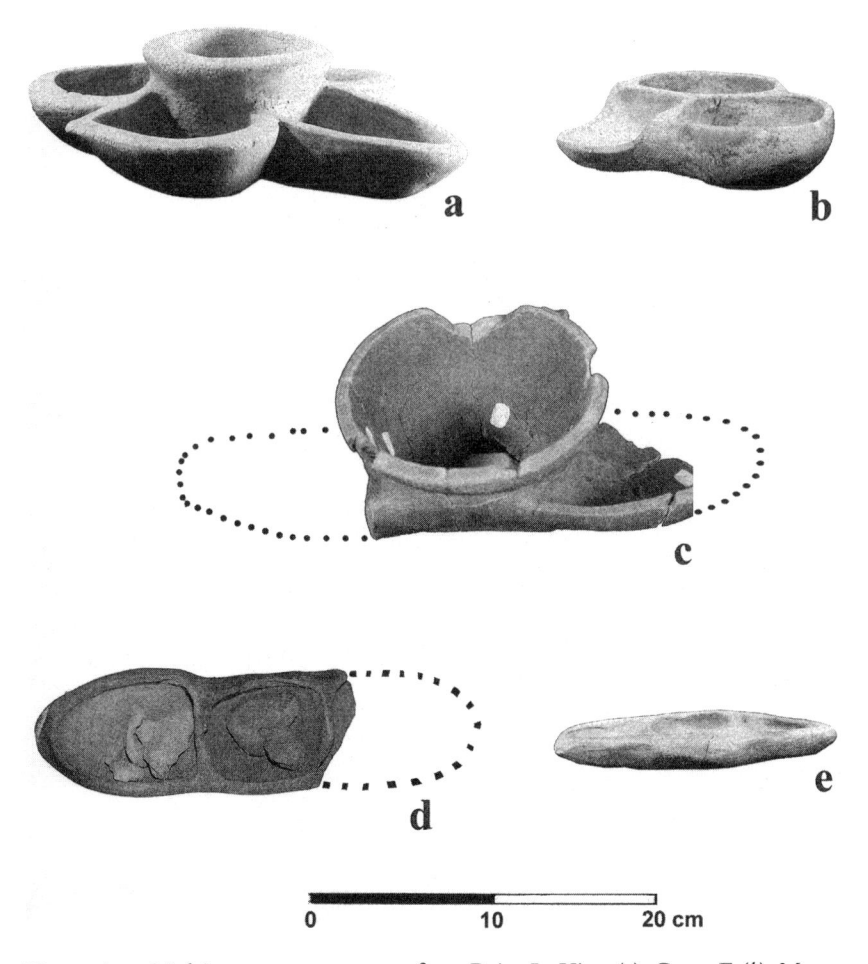

Figure 6.13. Multi-compartment trays from Point La Vista (*a*), Grant E (*b*), Mayport (*c*), Dent (*d*), and Monroe (*e*). Artifacts held in the collections of the National Museum of the American Indian, Jacksonville Museum of Science and History, and Timucuan Ecological and Historic Preserve, National Park Service (images by the author).

more reduced in height and is best described as a "tray." A third variety, which Willey describes as "common" (1949:502), consists of two or more low compartments and a single larger bowl in a raised position above the rest. The five multi-compartment vessels in the sample exhibit a variety of sizes, with individual compartments ranging from 4.5 centimeters to 12.0 centimeters (mean of 7.6 centimeters) in diameter. No soot or mend holes are observed in the sample.

As with double bowls, Willey (1949:410–411) presumes that the multi-compartment tray is a Weeden Island vessel form. Based on the same work by Moore at 56 "pure" Weeden Island sites, Willey (1945) lists 11 specimens (4.4 percent) taking this form. One Weeden Island Red vessel in the Lower St. Johns study collection corroborates this suspected Weeden Island affiliation. The remainder of the assemblage is comprised of one charcoal-tempered plain and three sand-tempered plain vessels.

Multi-compartment vessels were specialized ceremonial containers apparently designed to hold and separate important substances. At the Dent Mound, a partial multi-compartment tray was discovered with different materials in each of the two extant compartments. Found in situ, smeared on the interior of the compartments and in whole pieces within, was red ochre (hematite) in one compartment and yellow ochre (limonite) in another. Presumably, a third substance would have been contained within the missing compartment. These substances may have been important ritual items, perhaps for painting the bodies of the living and the dead in mortuary ceremony.

Beakers

The defining characteristics of beakers are straight walls and flat bases with a definite angle between the walls and base (Willey 1949:500). The three examples from Lower St. Johns River mounds conform specifically to Willey's "cylindrical beaker" form (1949:500) (Figure 6.14). Two of the beakers are nearly identical in size, 18.0 centimeters tall and between 8.2 centimeters and 9.0 centimeters in orifice diameter. The third vessel is smaller, 15.0 centimeters tall with an orifice diameter of 6.8 centimeters. Two vessels are sand-tempered plain, and one is Early Swift Creek Complicated Stamped (charcoal tempered). None were identified in the midden assemblages.

There is neither soot nor mend holes in any of the specimens. Beakers were probably not used for cooking nor were they suitable for it, with sharp profile angles that would have been particularly susceptible to thermal shock and breakage. Because they were not practical cooking containers and only fluid contents could be easily removed, beakers are likely to have served as drinking vessels.

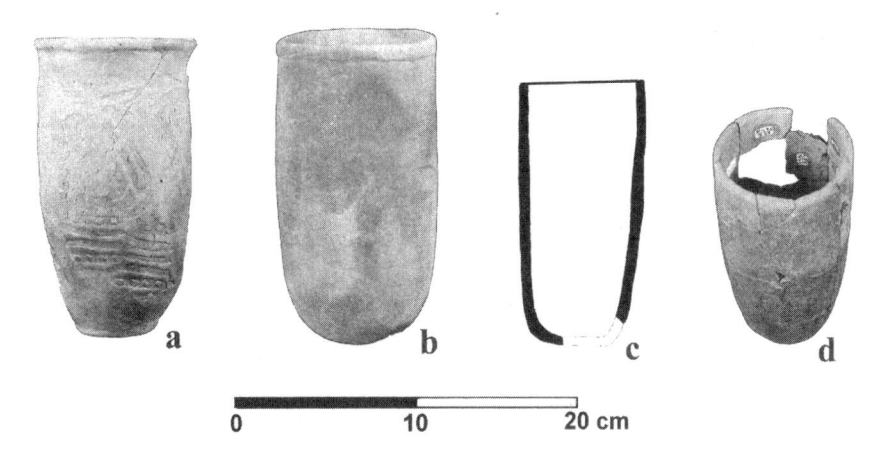

The Form, Technology, and Function of Swift Creek Pottery / 169

Figure 6.14. Beakers from Low Grant (*a* and *b*) and Mayport (*c*, profile, and *d*, oblique view). Artifacts held in the collections of the National Museum of the American Indian and the Timucuan Ecological and Historic Preserve, National Park Service, Jacksonville, Florida (images by the author).

Bottle

There is one example of a bottle vessel form. This St. Johns Plain vessel has an elongated neck with an orifice diameter (4.5 centimeters) that is markedly smaller than the maximum diameter of the vessel (18.0 centimeters). There is no soot or mend holes, but two suspension holes were drilled into the rim. With a small orifice that is easily closed, this vessel would have been well-suited for carrying liquids.

Shallow Bowl

There is one shallow bowl from the mound assemblages, with a diameter of 17 centimeters and a height of 4 centimeters. The specimen is sand-tempered plain. No other information can be garnered because a thick lacquer applied to all surfaces has unfortunately obliterated the evidence. This vessel form was popular among Weeden Island cultures to the west. For example, shallow bowls and plates are fairly common within the village and mounds at the McKeithen site (Milanich et al. 1997). This vessel form would have been suited for holding only solid foods or other non-liquid items.

Double-Globed Jar

There is one example of a double-globed jar, which Willey (1949:413) defines as a ceremonial form found at Weeden Island burial mounds along the

Figure 6.15. Double-globed jar from Grant Mound E. Artifact held in the collection of the National Museum of the American Indian, Suitland, Maryland (image by the author).

Gulf Coast. However, in the case of the Lower St. Johns River specimen, the surface treatments more closely resemble Crystal River Incised (Figure 6.15). The vessel is 30 centimeters in height, 18 centimeters in maximum width, and has a highly restricted orifice of 8 centimeters. The exceptional workmanship reflected in this vessel caused Moore to describe it as "by far the finest specimen of earthenware recovered by us from any Florida mound" (1895:491). Whatever its specific ceremonial function, this vessel was used directly over fire as demonstrated by soot adhering to exterior portions of the rim and vessel wall.

## Vessel Morphology Summary

The 15 vessel forms outlined in this chapter can be grouped into three categories: cooking vessels found in both burial mound and domestic contexts, vessels used occasionally for cooking and present only at mounds, and noncooking vessel forms restricted almost entirely to mounds.

Cooking vessel forms common to both ceremonial and domestic contexts include open pots and bowls and restricted pots and bowls. Combined, 64 percent of these vessels (30 of 47) show definitive evidence of coming into contact with fire. These vessels are moderate to large in size and were most likely used for boiling meat and vegetable foods and in some contexts, perhaps, beverages such as black drink. The morphological variations among these cooking vessel forms may correspond to practical considerations of content accessibility during cooking, serving, or eating and stability on the ground without external supports. Indeed, the use of pots versus bowls may have varied: soot is more frequent among pots (ca. 80 percent) than bowls (ca. 40 percent) while, conversely, bowls (ca. 30 percent) have a higher frequency of mend holes than pots (ca. 10 percent). Whether these attributes pertain to the nature of the food or drink being prepared or to the conventions of use in particular cultural contexts is a question addressed below with closer comparison of mound and village assemblages.

The remaining vessel forms appear to be mainly restricted to mound assemblages. Of these, the flattened-globular bowl, collared jar, and double-globed jar assemblages show at least occasional cooking functions. Combined, just over one-third (6 of 17) of these vessels have soot adhering to exterior rims or walls. The morphology of all of these vessels would have limited the type of cuisine that could have been prepared. In particular, a highly restricted orifice would have prevented access to contents during cooking tasks such as stirring that might prevent burning meats and vegetables during boiling. Alternatively, teas can be boiled without risk of charring and a restricted orifice makes heating faster and more efficient. Consequently, some of these vessels were probably used for preparation of ceremonial beverages such as black drink. In fact, a vessel form resembling the flattened-globular jar was still used to prepare black drink during early colonial times in St. Augustine according to Father Francisco Ximénez's 1615 description (Sturtevant 1979:150–151). During the Woodland period, collared jars may have been used for black drink as well; and because of their reduced ability to withstand thermal shock due to somewhat angular profiles, they were especially susceptible to cracks. The high frequency of mend holes among this vessel form (70 percent) indicates not only their fragility but also the cultural importance of keeping them in use. Also notable is the correlation between the flattened-globular bowl, collared jar, and double-globed jar forms and the Crystal River Incised type (n = 4). Willey (1949:389) lists these vessel forms, along with cylindrical beakers and composite-silhouette jars, as the most common vessel forms for Crystal River Incised along the Gulf Coast. Either garnered from the Gulf Coast or made locally as copies, these vessels likely carried considerable ceremonial importance on the Lower St. Johns River.

Several vessel forms restricted to mound assemblages had almost entirely non-cooking functions. These include small cups and bowls, small jars, boat-shaped bowls, double bowls, multi-compartment trays, beakers, bottles, and, possibly, shallow bowls. Combined, only 7 percent (n = 3) contain evidence of soot. In addition, only one vessel shows evidence of repair with mend holes, corresponding with the possibility that many of these vessels were not heavily used. Indeed, many of these vessels, particularly the multi-compartment trays, double bowls, and various miniature vessels, are clearly ceremonial forms intended for only specific ritual tasks. The comparably high frequency of incised and painted pottery types among these vessel forms, rarely found in midden contexts on the Atlantic coast, corroborates their special function.

In sum, contained within mortuary mounds were numerous vessel forms ostensibly designed for various specific functions and particular cultural contexts. Based on many rim profiles from Swift Creek middens along the Atlantic coast, the vast majority of domestic cooking vessels were identical in shape and size to the sooted pots and bowls placed in mortuary mounds. In contrast, many vessels with special cooking functions and non-cooking functions in mound assemblages are apparently absent in village and midden contexts. As noted, the limitations of small sherds, as are typical at middens, impede the conclusive identification of many vessel forms. However, the disparity between vessel forms among mound and midden assemblages can be understood through comparisons of vessel orifice diameter.

## Orifice Diameter, Soot, and Mend Holes

Among assemblages from mortuary mounds, whole or nearly whole vessels were not uncommon, and overall morphology and vessel capacity could be accurately estimated. However, the majority of vessels in this study were each represented by only small sherds, and vessel dimensions were much more difficult to infer. In the absence of whole vessels, orifice diameter estimates from rim sherds were used as a general proxy for vessel size. Orifice diameter corresponds most directly with overall vessel size when all vessels being compared have similar morphology. As noted, the midden assemblage consists overwhelmingly of open and slightly restricted pots and bowls, simple vessel

Table 6.4. Mound assemblage orifice diameter and rim thickness summary statistics

|  |  | Orifice diameter (cm) | Rim thickness (mm) |
|---|---|---|---|
| Dent (8DU68) | n | 60 | 53 |
|  | Mean | 18.28 | 5.93 |
|  | Standard deviation | 7.29 | 1.08 |
|  | Minimum | 8.00 | 3.80 |
|  | Maximum | 40.50 | 8.70 |
| Mayport (8DU96) | n | 34 | 35 |
|  | Mean | 16.40 | 6.26 |
|  | Standard deviation | 9.32 | 2.62 |
|  | Minimum | 3.50 | 4.10 |
|  | Maximum | 39.00 | 10.35 |
| Other Lower St. Johns Mounds | n | 47 | 50 |
|  | Mean | 11.76 | 6.87 |
|  | Standard deviation | 7.46 | 1.65 |
|  | Minimum | 1.80 | 3.00 |
|  | Maximum | 30.00 | 10.30 |
| TOTAL | n | 141 | 138 |
|  | Mean | 15.68 | 6.22 |
|  | Standard deviation | 8.18 | 1.37 |
|  | Minimum | 1.80 | 3.00 |
|  | Maximum | 40.50 | 10.35 |

forms whose orifice diameters correspond more or less directly with overall size. Other vessel forms identified in the mound assemblages have variable vessel morphologies that make for poor predictions of vessel size based on orifice diameters. For example, bottles, collared jars and bowls, and beakers have greater capacities than their orifice diameters might suggest because of highly restricted orifices or great height, while the opposite is true of shallow bowls. Thus, differences in orifice diameters between assemblages can at once reflect both distinctions in the overall volume of vessels and differences in the frequency of particular vessel forms.

Out of 1,222 total vessels, 517 orifice diameters were recorded, including 141 from mortuary mounds and 376 from midden contexts. Taken as a whole, the combined mound assemblages have a much smaller mean orifice diameter (15.7 centimeters) and a much larger standard deviation (8.2) than the combined midden assemblages (Table 6.4; Table 6.5). These differences reflect the

Table 6.5. Midden assemblage orifice diameter and rim thickness summary statistics

|  |  | Orifice diameter (cm) | Rim thickness (mm) |
|---|---|---|---|
| Tillie Fowler (8DU17245) | n | 78 | 60 |
|  | Mean | 19.86 | 6.23 |
|  | Standard deviation | 5.40 | 1.21 |
|  | Minimum | 8.00 | 3.90 |
|  | Maximum | 31.00 | 9.20 |
| Greenfield #7 (8DU5543) | n | 79 | 45 |
|  | Mean | 20.05 | 5.85 |
|  | Standard deviation | 4.67 | 0.98 |
|  | Minimum | 10.00 | 4.15 |
|  | Maximum | 29.00 | 8.30 |
| Greenfield #8/9 (8DU5544/5) | n | 64 | 78 |
|  | Mean | 23.50 | 6.86 |
|  | Standard deviation | 5.59 | 1.00 |
|  | Minimum | 10.00 | 5.10 |
|  | Maximum | 34.00 | 9.80 |
| McArthur (8DU32) | n | 14 | 12 |
|  | Mean | 19.93 | 6.80 |
|  | Standard deviation | 5.50 | 1.63 |
|  | Minimum | 10.00 | 3.60 |
|  | Maximum | 30.00 | 9.80 |
| Cathead Creek (9MC360) | n | 30 | 22 |
|  | Mean | 20.40 | 7.60 |
|  | Standard deviation | 5.25 | 1.39 |
|  | Minimum | 9.00 | 5.15 |
|  | Maximum | 30.00 | 10.00 |
| Evelyn (9GN6) | n | 24 | 17 |
|  | Mean | 19.80 | 7.95 |
|  | Standard deviation | 4.93 | 1.22 |
|  | Minimum | 10.00 | 5.50 |
|  | Maximum | 28.00 | 9.51 |
| Hallows Field (9CM25) | n | 7 | 8 |
|  | Mean | 22.86 | 7.39 |

|  |  | Orifice diameter (cm) | Rim thickness (mm) |
|---|---|---|---|
|  | Standard deviation | 6.89 | 1.53 |
|  | Minimum | 13.00 | 5.45 |
|  | Maximum | 32.00 | 9.25 |
| Kings Lake | $n$ | 5 | 6 |
|  | Mean | 21.00 | 6.42 |
|  | Standard deviation | 5.83 | 1.13 |
|  | Minimum | 14.00 | 5.35 |
|  | Maximum | 28.00 | 7.30 |
| Lewis Creek (9MC16) | $n$ | 10 | 11 |
|  | Mean | 19.89 | 8.50 |
|  | Standard deviation | 7.98 | 1.56 |
|  | Minimum | 10.00 | 5.80 |
|  | Maximum | 36.00 | 10.90 |
| Sidon (9MC372) | $n$ | 51 | 34 |
|  | Mean | 20.51 | 8.09 |
|  | Standard deviation | 5.29 | 1.23 |
|  | Minimum | 8.00 | 5.18 |
|  | Maximum | 34.00 | 11.10 |
| Florida residual | $n$ | 8 | 6 |
|  | Mean | 19.25 | 5.90 |
|  | Standard deviation | 5.42 | 1.07 |
|  | Minimum | 14.00 | 4.55 |
|  | Maximum | 28.00 | 7.50 |
| Georgia residual | $n$ | 6 | 6 |
|  | Mean | 22.83 | 7.71 |
|  | Standard deviation | 5.31 | 0.62 |
|  | Minimum | 18.00 | 6.70 |
|  | Maximum | 32.00 | 8.40 |
| TOTAL | $n$ | 376 | 305 |
|  | Mean | 20.68 | 6.91 |
|  | Standard deviation | 5.43 | 1.39 |
|  | Minimum | 8.00 | 3.90 |
|  | Maximum | 36.00 | 11.10 |

higher frequency at mounds of small vessels such as small cups, bowls, and jars, as well as vessel forms with small restricted orifices such as flattened-globular bowls and collared jars. In comparison, the orifice diameters recorded from midden assemblages are distributed almost entirely within the range of variation among the reconstructed cooking vessels from mounds. At middens, no orifice diameter smaller than 8 centimeters was recorded, revealing that miniature vessels, double bowls, and multi-compartment trays rarely, if ever, were broken or deposited in domestic contexts. Furthermore, only 4 percent of vessels (n = 15) from middens have orifices smaller than 12 centimeters compared to 37 percent (n = 52) in the combined mound assemblages. Because cooking vessel forms in the mound assemblages were determined to be universally larger than 12 centimeters in diameter, rims with estimated orifice diameters less than 12 centimeters are very likely to be from vessels other than the basic cooking forms. The rim profiles among the few small vessels within the midden assemblages indicate that they take the form of small cups, bowls, and jars, although beakers and collared jars cannot be completely ruled out for some of these small-rim sherds (Figure 6.16). Regardless of whether rim sherds with small estimated orifice diameters represent small vessels like cups or bowls or larger vessels with highly restricted orifices, the relative frequency of both is demonstrably limited in domestic contexts, where simple cooking vessel forms predominate.

A comparison of the frequency of sooted vessels within both midden and mound assemblages corroborates the hypothesized functions of various vessel forms (Table 6.6). In both midden and mound assemblages the relative frequency of soot by approximate orifice diameter conforms to a bell-shaped curve in which frequency is greatest among vessels with orifice diameters between 20 and 24 centimeters and frequencies diminish toward either end of the size distribution. Thus, the relative frequency of soot among very small and very large vessels is low among both midden and mound assemblages. The consistent discrepancy of soot frequency between midden and mound assemblages of all sizes is very likely due to sampling biases. Specifically, the smaller portions of vessels represented from village assemblages leads to lower frequencies of soot identification than within mound assemblages in which the entire rim of a vessel is often available. This sampling bias results in a sort of logarithmic effect in the midden assemblage data, decreasing the order of magnitude by which size classes differ in the frequencies of recorded soot (Figure 6.17). Many small sherds that lack soot are likely to have come from vessels that contained soot on other portions of the rim or wall. The frequency by which sooted vessels were misclassified using sherds that lacked soot appears to have increased as the actual occurrence of soot in-

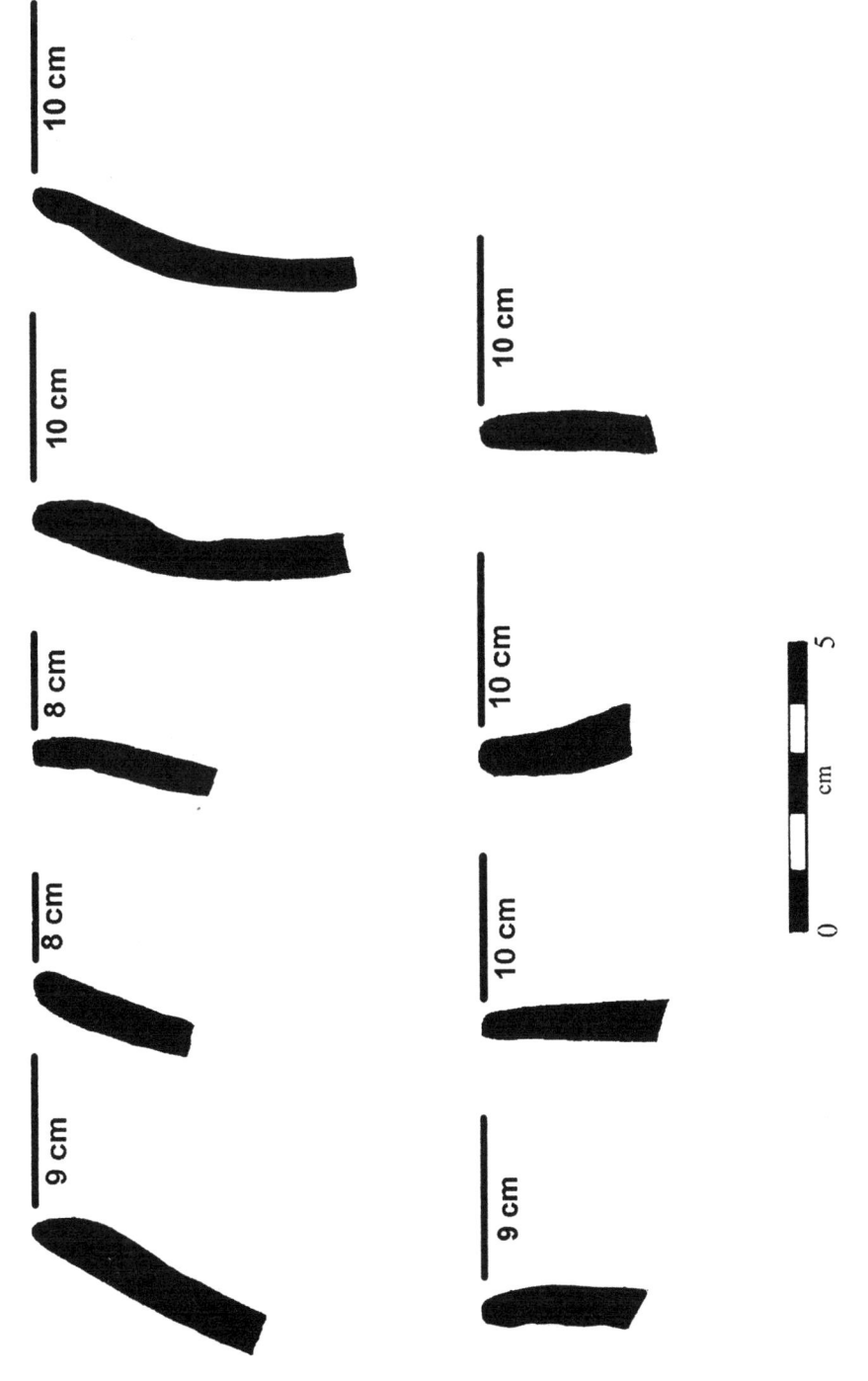

Figure 6.16. Rim profiles of small cups, bowls, and jars from midden contexts.

Table 6.6. Soot frequency grouped by orifice diameter (cm)

|  | <12.0 | 12.0–16.0 | 16.1–20.0 | 20.1–24.0 | 24.1–28.0 | 28.1–32.0 | >32.0 | TOTAL |
|---|---|---|---|---|---|---|---|---|
| **Midden** | | | | | | | | |
| # sooted | 1 | 7 | 15 | 14 | 9 | 1 | 0 | 47 |
| total vessels | 15 | 66 | 117 | 84 | 64 | 25 | 5 | 376 |
| % | 7.0 | 10.6 | 12.8 | 16.7 | 14.1 | 4.0 | 0 | 12.5 |
| **Mound** | | | | | | | | |
| # sooted | 5 | 9 | 10 | 11 | 13 | 2 | 0 | 50 |
| total vessels | 52 | 29 | 19 | 13 | 20 | 5 | 3 | 141 |
| % | 9.6 | 31.0 | 52.6 | 84.6 | 65.0 | 40.0 | 0 | 35.5 |

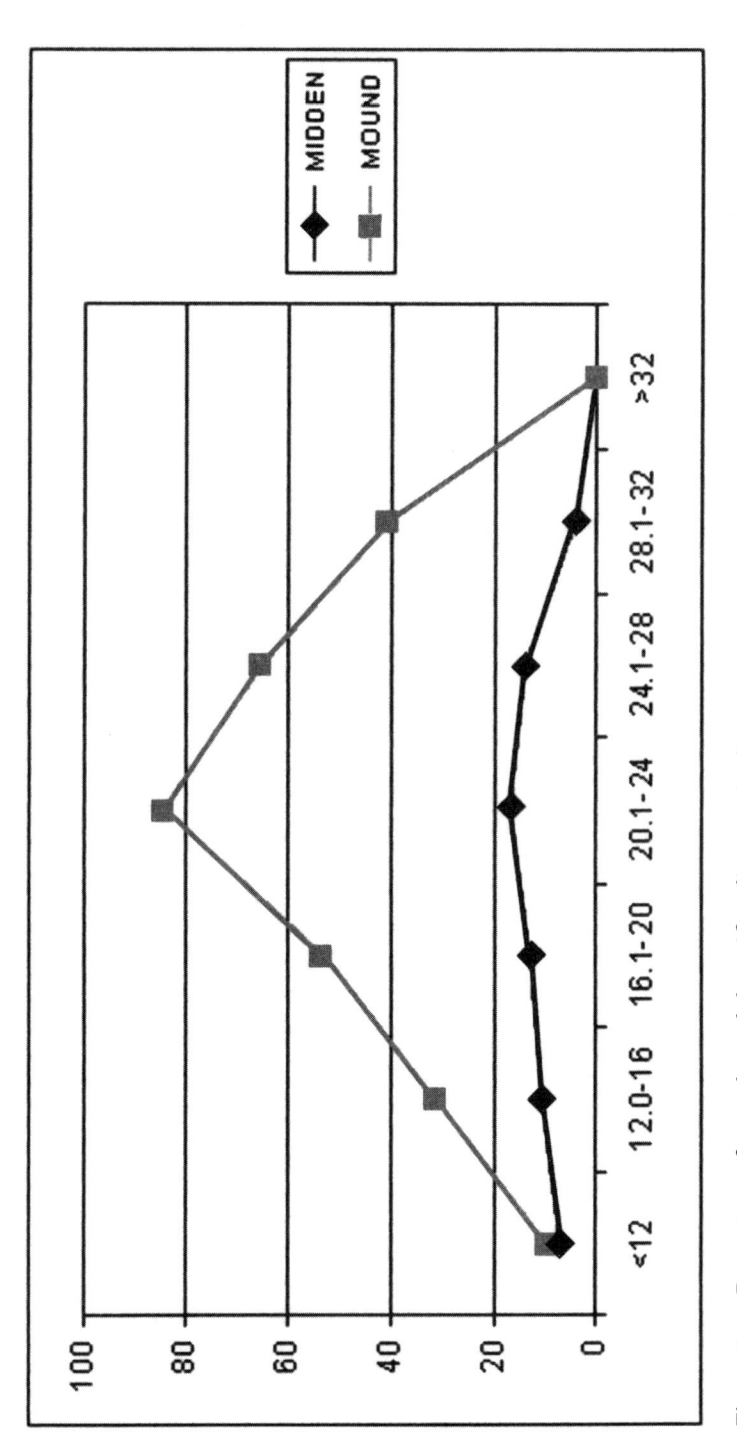

Figure 6.17. Percentage of sooted vessels by orifice diameter (cm).

creased in the whole vessel sample. Yet this bias was not great enough to conceal the relative trend of soot frequency among small sherds that mirrors the whole vessel assemblage.

In sum, vessels with small orifice diameters from midden assemblages appear to correspond with the small cups, bowls, and jars from mound assemblages that were very rarely used in cooking. On the other end of the size distribution, very large vessels in both mound and midden assemblages have a lower frequency of soot that may also indicate a non-cooking function. Notably, among whole or reconstructed vessels, only open bowls have recorded orifice diameters greater than 28 centimeters; therefore, sherds with the largest orifice diameters from middens are likely to have come from open bowls as well. Given the comparatively low frequency of soot on these vessels, many open bowls clearly served non-cooking functions.

Mend holes were recorded for their potential in discriminating the breakage rates and relative cultural importance of different kinds of vessels (DeBoer and Lathrap 1979; Senior 1994). Most important, the number of mend holes in a vessel is likely to reflect its longevity, an important aspect of an object's biography that could reveal some of its symbolic density. Mend hole data have proven useful for distinguishing some vessel forms, such as the collared jars that appear to have been repaired with some frequency; however, the combined number of vessels with mend holes from all assemblages (n = 39) provides too small a sample to reveal significant differences in frequencies between size classes or pottery types. There is a general correlation between mend holes and larger vessel sizes, but the sample size makes this trend statistically insignificant. In addition, the same sampling biases that pertain to soot data are far more detrimental with such a small sample and inhibit useful comparisons between the frequencies of mend holes in mound (n = 17, 11 percent) and village (n = 22, 2 percent) assemblages. While I have previously argued, based on just two assemblages, that mound assemblages have a higher frequency of mend holes than village assemblages (Wallis 2007), this statistic disregards the formidable sampling bias inherent in comparing small sherds to whole vessels. Whatever the degree of mathematical misrepresentation in comparisons of entire assemblages, there are two vessels from mound assemblages that deserve special mention. One St. Johns Plain vessel, from the Mayport Mound, contained over two dozen mend holes along its bottom half that seem to have been an attempt to repair coil breaks (Wallis 2007:226). A Dunns Creek Red vessel from the Dent Mound contained 12 mend holes that were oriented to repair a large portion of the vessel rim. Both of these vessels are large open pots, nearly 40 centimeters in orifice diameter. The large number of mend holes in these specimens indicates both the fragility of spiculate paste wares and the cultural concern for extending the lives of these particular vessels. For the Mayport Mound vessel especially, this concern may have surpassed consideration of the object's functional capabilities in order to keep the heirloom alive.

To summarize, assemblages from mortuary mounds and middens are clearly comprised of different vessel forms, with mounds containing many small vessel forms that are very uncommon or absent at villages. Frequencies of soot on vessel surfaces corroborate the non-cooking function of smaller-sized vessels at all sites and further bolster the much higher proportion of non-cooking vessel forms at mounds. Small sample size limits the comparability of mend holes among assemblages, although particular vessel forms such as collared jars appear to have been repaired more often than other vessels, and two large open bowls from mounds are notable for exceptional numbers of holes. Combined, these data delineate a suite of special-use vessels nearly exclusively deposited in ceremonial contexts as well as cooking pots and bowls that are common to both mound and midden contexts.

Importantly, this pattern is evident by the Early Swift Creek phase, as clearly indicated by the range of mound-specific vessel forms that contain temporally diagnostic charcoal-tempered paste. Charcoal tempering is found in flattened-globular bowls; small cups, bowls, and jars; boat-shaped bowls; multi-compartment trays; and beakers, all forms restricted mostly or exclusively to mounds. In contrast, there are no examples of collared jars with charcoal tempering, although Crystal River Incised examples are presumed to be contemporaneous with Early Swift Creek. In comparison to vessels in mound assemblages, midden vessels with charcoal temper are restricted almost exclusively to standard domestic cooking forms. Thus, a sort of dichotomy between mortuary and domestic forms was well established by the Early Swift Creek phase, and many of the unique mound vessels were made in the local paste tradition.

## Rim Thickness

Rim thickness was measured 3 centimeters below the lip on a total of 443 vessels, including 138 vessels from mounds and 305 from middens (see Table 6.4; Table 6.5). There is a wide range of variation in rim thickness across the combined assemblages, ranging from 3.0 millimeters to 11.1 millimeters. While there are small differences in the rim thicknesses of mound and midden assemblages on the Lower St. Johns River, the most notable differences appear between midden assemblages themselves and correspond with both geography and temporality. There is a significant difference between Lower

St. Johns River midden rims, which are generally thin (mean = 6.39 millimeters), and Lower Altamaha River rims, which are comparatively much thicker (mean = 7.83 millimeters). This geographic difference is especially clear between village sites in each area that are likely to have been contemporaneous, based on radiocarbon assays. Each dating to the seventh century, Greenfield #8/9 (8DU5544/5) on the Lower St. Johns River and Sidon (9MC372) on the Lower Altamaha River have mean rim thicknesses of 6.9 millimeters and 8.1 millimeters, respectively. Sample sizes are regrettably small for assemblages from sites in the areas between Greenfield #8/9 and Sidon, but rim thicknesses appear to vary between the thin and thick extremes of the southern and northern sites. However, analysis of larger assemblages from Camden and Nassau counties may demonstrate a graduated continuum in the distribution of rim thickness. Rebecca Saunders (1986), for example, recorded mean thicknesses of 7.2 millimeters (n = 20) and 7.6 millimeters (n = 18) for the two most common vessel forms at the Late Swift Creek site of Kings Bay (9CM171). Because thickness was not measured according to the same parameters in Saunders's (1986) work ("just below the lip") as the current one (3 centimeters below the lip), these data are not directly comparable. However, the profiles of the vast majority of vessels from Swift Creek sites on the Atlantic coast indicate that thickness increases with distance from the lip. Therefore, the Kings Bay data are likely to underestimate the rim thickness at 3 centimeters below the lip.

Variation in rim thickness is also highly correlated with temporal change. Assemblages from predominantly Early Swift Creek sites, such as Greenfield #7 (8DU5543) and Tillie Fowler (8DU17245), are comprised of mostly thin vessels, with rim thickness means of 5.9 millimeters (n = 45) and 6.2 millimeters (n = 60), respectively. In comparison, Late Swift Creek assemblages from sites nearby have significantly thicker rims, such as at Greenfield #8/9 (mean = 6.9 millimeters). The correlation between temporality and rim thickness becomes more pronounced when comparison between assemblages is limited to vessels that are irrefutably Early Swift Creek and Late Swift Creek. Charcoal-tempered vessels, which clearly date to the Early Swift Creek phase on the Lower St. Johns River, have a mean thickness of 5.8 millimeters (n = 118). In comparison, Late Swift Creek Complicated Stamped vessels with hallmark folded rims from Lower St. Johns River sites have a mean rim thickness of 6.9 millimeters (n = 34).

Thus, on the Lower St. Johns River rims were thin during Early Swift Creek times and became thicker with the emergence of Late Swift Creek pottery. Not coincidentally, this increase in rim thickness corresponds with

Late Swift Creek paddle matches that link sites on the Lower St. Johns River to sites as far north as the Altamaha River, Georgia, where rims are very thick. A logical conclusion is that increasingly thicker rims in Lower St. Johns River assemblages are a consequence of social interactions with populations to the north where thick rims were more common, combined with the actual import of thick-rimmed vessels made in Georgia. Indeed, all of the measurable vessels on Lower St. Johns sites that were identified by INAA and petrographic analysis as originating from near the Altamaha River have rim thicknesses greater than average, ranging from 7.0 millimeters to 9.8 millimeters (average of 8.15 millimeters, n = 6). At the same time, however, thicker rims are partly a consequence of slightly increasing vessel size over time. There is some positive correlation between rim thickness and orifice diameter. In a general sense, as rim thickness increases so does orifice diameter, but this correlation does not explain a large portion of variation in rim thickness ($\rho = .303$). In fact, among midden assemblages rim thickness is more strongly correlated with the latitude where a vessel was recovered ($\rho = .551$) than it is with orifice diameter. Comparisons of all midden assemblages from the Atlantic coast reveal that most have a mean orifice diameter near 20 centimeters, while rim thickness averages vary widely. Unless there were differences in height that could not be measured in this sample, coastal Swift Creek populations from north to south were producing roughly the same size sub-conoidal cooking pot regardless of rim thickness. The comparability of cooking vessel size along the coast might be expected if family and village sizes were similar.

Although thicker walls on vessels would have been less efficient in conducting heat, soot frequencies indicate that cooking pots in a variety of thicknesses were all used in direct-heat cooking over fire. The differences in thickness are not likely to have been related to differences in diet or cuisine, at least based on available zooarchaeological data that indicate a consistent diet dominated by the same species of fish and shellfish all along the Georgia Bight (deFrance 1993; Fradkin 1998; Reitz 1988; Reitz and Quitmyer 1988). The majority of variation in rim thickness must be explained by other, presumably cultural, factors. More specifically, the thickness of vessels is likely to correspond with the habitual vessel-forming routines that are acquired in a potter's original learning environment (Arnold 1998:358; Gosselain 2000; Reina and Hill 1978:230; Rice 1984; van der Leeuw et al. 1992). Vessel thickness may be the residue of ingrained bodily practice, with generations of Swift Creek populations along the Georgia coast having learned to make thick vessels while their counterparts in coastal Florida inherited the technique of making thin vessels. Thus, rim thickness may provide critical data for differentiating social groups within the Swift Creek archaeological culture and investigating interaction between them.

## Paste Characteristics

Using a binocular microscope (70X), the paste of vessels was analyzed in order to identify the frequency and size of a variety of aplastics. As reviewed in chapter 5, aplastics in the paste of vessels may represent intentionally added temper, natural inclusions in the clay, or both (Rice 1987:409–411). In general, charcoal, grog, and bone are almost certainly intentional additions to the paste because these constituents do not occur with any frequency in natural clays (Rice 1987:410). Depending on their frequency in the paste, sponge spicules may be either natural constituents of the clays used for pottery (Cordell and Koski 2003; Espenshade 1983; and see chapter 5) or added temper (Rolland and Bond 2003). I concur with Vicki Rolland and Paulette Bond (2003) that the density of spicules within the paste of most St. Johns vessels denotes an intentionally added temper in Northeast Florida. In contrast, mica, calcite, and fine quartz particles are naturally abundant in some natural clay deposits and might have been incorporated into the paste of vessels with selection of particular clays. The present discussion concerns the results of analysis that characterized vessel paste constituents by relative abundance and size. Abundance was recorded on an ordinal scale (absent, rare, moderate, common, abundant), and size was grouped by the Wentworth Scale for sand (very fine, fine, medium, coarse, very coarse).

Variation in the aplastic paste constituents in the sample can be usefully separated into five temper categories: spiculate, charcoal, fine sand, medium sand, and coarse sand-tempered pastes (Table 6.7). Bone, limestone, and, especially, grog were also observed in a few samples but were never the dominant temper and therefore were not separated by category. Spiculate pastes are characterized by common to abundant sponge spicules and, on occasion, angular or sub-angular very fine or fine sand. Charcoal-tempered pastes contain occasional to common charcoal fragments ranging in size from very fine to very coarse, often within the same sample. Bone fragments occur on occasion, as well as grog to a more limited extent. Very fine and fine sand that is angular or sub-angular is quite common. Fine sand pastes mostly contain abundant very fine and fine sand that is angular to sub-angular in shape. Mica is normally absent but in rare instances is common, usually corresponding with uncommon pottery types like Weeden Island Red. Medium sand and coarse sand pastes contain a majority of medium- or coarse-sized sand, re-

Table 6.7. Aplastic constituents of gross paste categories

| Paste category | Vessel count | Percent | Description |
|---|---|---|---|
| Spiculate | 38 | 3.3 | Common to abundant sponge spicules |
| | | | None to common sub-angular very fine to fine sand |
| | | | Rare ferruginous lumps |
| | | | No mica |
| | | | One sample with grog |
| Charcoal | 238 | 20.7 | Occasional to common charcoal fragments: very fine to very coarse |
| | | | Rare to occasional bone fragments |
| | | | Rare grog |
| | | | Common to abundant angular to sub-angular very fine sand |
| | | | Occasional to common angular to sub-angular fine sand |
| | | | Rare instances of medium and coarse sand |
| | | | None to occasional mica |
| | | | Rare to occasional ferruginous lumps |
| Fine sand | 543 | 47.1 | Common to abundant angular to sub-angular very fine sand |
| | | | Occasional to abundant sub-angular fine sand; rare rounded fine sand |
| | | | None to occasional mica; in rare instances common |
| | | | None to occasional ferruginous lumps; in rare instances common |
| Medium sand | 127 | 11.1 | None to common angular to sub-angular very fine sand |
| | | | Occasional to common sub-angular to sub-rounded fine sand |
| | | | Occasional to common sub-angular to rounded medium sand |

*Continued on the next page*

Table 6.7. *Continued*

| Paste category | Vessel count | Percent | Description |
|---|---|---|---|
| | | | Rare coarse and very coarse sand |
| | | | No mica |
| | | | None to rare ferruginous lumps |
| | | | One sample with grog |
| Coarse sand | 204 | 17.8 | None to common angular to sub-angular very fine and fine sand |
| | | | None to common sub-angular to rounded medium sand |
| | | | Occasional to common sub-angular to rounded coarse sand |
| | | | None to occasional sub-angular to rounded very coarse sand |
| | | | None to rare mica |
| | | | None to rare ferruginous lumps; in rare instances common |
| Total★ | 1,150 | 100.0 | |

★When fresh breaks on vessels were not permitted, no paste category was assigned.

spectively, with these large grains tending to have a sub-rounded or rounded shape. Very fine and fine sands are common in these pastes as well and tend to be more angular than the larger grains.

Based on the ubiquity of angular and sub-angular quartz grains in all paste categories, these may have been natural inclusions in the clays rather than added temper. Spiculate, charcoal, medium sand, and coarse sand pastes commonly contain abundant very fine and fine sand. This hypothesis is also supported by the angular shape of most small sand particles. Rounded and water-worn grains are not common in clay bodies, particularly in Florida (Ann Cordell, personal communication, 2006; Shepard 1968). On the other hand, the medium and coarse pastes with more rounded grains may have been added to clay bodies that already contained smaller and more angular quartz grains. The results of petrographic analysis of a limited number of samples were used to corroborate the temper categories assigned to the entire assemblage. The petrography confirmed the gross temper categories in all but three cases: one instance of charcoal temper identified under low magnification but

# The Form, Technology, and Function of Swift Creek Pottery / 187

not observed in petrographic thin section and two instances in which coarse sand was identified under low magnification but only fine sand was identified in petrographic thin section.

An important pattern that emerged from this analysis was in the distribution of the major paste constituents of vessels among sites. As expected, charcoal-tempered paste occurs only in northeastern Florida and comprises the majority of assemblages from Early Swift Creek sites like 8DU5543 and 8DU17245 (Table 6.8). Spiculate pastes are a consistent minority at sites in northeastern Florida and seem to have been more frequent at mounds than middens. Finally, sand temper or inclusions are ubiquitous within most assemblages, but the size of the grains shows consistent geographic distributions. Fine sand temper predominates on sites in northeastern Florida while medium and coarse sand temper is most common on sites in southeastern Georgia. Interestingly, sites near the Florida–Georgia border in Nassau and Camden counties may yield a more equal distribution of grain size. The McArthur site (8NA32) contained roughly equal proportions of fine and coarse quartz temper. An increasing frequency of coarse grain temper is apparent just to the north: the Kings Bay site (9CM171) assemblage is reported to have been "predominantly grit-tempered [1.0–3.0 millimeters], with sand and shell being minority tempers" (Espenshade 1985:304). Thus, moving north along the coast from the St. Johns River there is a general trend toward increasing grit temper within Swift Creek assemblages.

This geographic trend may be the result of both geological and cultural factors. Overall, sand grain sizes are likely to be smaller on the St. Johns River compared to the Altamaha River due to differences in gradient and consequent sediment load. At the same time, however, individual sand bars and different parts of a river channel might have widely varying grain sizes (Orrin Pilkey, personal communication, 2008). In fact, Christopher Espenshade notes sand and "grit" in a wide range of sizes found together on sand bars of the Crooked River near the Kings Bay site (1985:302). Thus, sand grain size in earthenware pastes may be related, in part, to the regional availability of sand sizes but is also likely to correspond with cultural prescriptions for appropriate tempering agents.

There is a notable correlation between medium and coarse sand pastes and thick rims (Table 6.9). While this pattern mostly corresponds simply with the parallel geographical distribution of grain size and rim thickness, vessels from northeastern Florida sites demonstrate this relationship as well. This correlation within northeastern Florida samples denotes nonlocal vessels made in coastal Georgia or the work of potters from coastal Georgia accustomed to coarse tempers and thick vessel walls. Based on the provenance stud-

Table 6.8. Frequency of gross paste groups by site

|  | Charcoal | | Fine sand | | Medium sand | | Coarse sand | | Spiculate | | Other* | | Total | |
| --- | --- | --- | --- | --- | --- | --- | --- | --- | --- | --- | --- | --- | --- | --- |
|  | # | % | # | % | # | % | # | % | # | % | # | % | # | % |
| 8DU5543 | 85 | 52.8 | 62 | 38.5 | 6 | 3.7 | 6 | 3.7 | 2 | 1.2 |  |  | 161 | 100.0 |
| 8DU17245 | 93 | 66.0 | 37 | 26.2 | 5 | 3.5 | 1 | 0.7 | 5 | 3.5 |  |  | 141 | 100.0 |
| 8DU5544/5 | 26 | 6.1 | 316 | 74.2 | 38 | 8.9 | 20 | 4.7 | 23 | 5.4 | 3 | 0.7 | 426 | 100.0 |
| 8NA32 | 3 | 7.9 | 14 | 36.8 | 2 | 5.3 | 18 | 47.4 |  |  | 1 | 2.6 | 38 | 100.0 |
| 8DU14683/14686 | 4 | 20.0 | 15 | 75.0 |  |  |  |  | 1 | 5.0 |  |  | 20 | 100.0 |
| 8DU68 | 14 | 38.9 | 12 | 33.3 | 4 | 11.1 | 6 | 16.7 |  |  |  |  | 36 | 100.0 |
| 8DU96 | 6 | 14.6 | 21 | 51.2 | 3 | 7.3 | 5 | 12.2 | 4 | 9.8 | 2 | 4.9 | 41 | 100.0 |
| Other LSJ mounds | 6 | 11.8 | 26 | 51.0 | 7 | 13.7 | 9 | 17.6 | 3 | 5.9 |  |  | 51 | 100.0 |
| Other Florida middens | 1 | 16.7 | 4 | 66.7 | 1 | 16.7 |  |  |  |  |  |  | 6 | 100.0 |
| *Northeastern Florida* | *238* | *25.9* | *507* | *55.1* | *66* | *7.2* | *65* | *7.1* | *38* | *4.1* | *6* | *0.7* | *920* | *100.0* |
| 9MC360 |  |  | 5 | 10.4 | 13 | 27.1 | 30 | 62.5 |  |  |  |  | 48 | 100.0 |
| 9GN6 |  |  | 3 | 13.0 | 3 | 13.0 | 17 | 73.9 |  |  |  |  | 23 | 100.0 |
| 9MC25 |  |  | 4 | 26.7 | 4 | 26.7 | 7 | 46.7 |  |  |  |  | 15 | 100.0 |
| 9MC16 |  |  | 3 | 13.0 | 4 | 17.4 | 16 | 69.6 |  |  |  |  | 23 | 100.0 |
| 9MC372 |  |  | 19 | 19.8 | 32 | 33.3 | 45 | 46.9 |  |  |  |  | 96 | 100.0 |
| Kings Lake |  |  | 1 | 5.3 | 2 | 10.5 | 16 | 84.2 |  |  |  |  | 19 | 100.0 |
| Other Georgia middens |  |  | 1 | 7.7 | 3 | 23.1 | 8 | 61.5 |  |  | 1 | 7.7 | 13 | 100.0 |
| *Southeastern Georgia* | *0* | *0.0* | *36* | *15.2* | *61* | *25.7* | *139* | *58.6* | *0* | *0.0* | *1* | *0.4* | *237* | *100.0* |

*Includes grog, sponge spicule and grog, sand and bone, and limestone.

Table 6.9. Rim thickness summary statistics by gross paste groups

|  | Fine sand | Medium sand | Coarse sand |
|---|---|---|---|
| All pottery | n = 162 | n = 47 | n = 56 |
| Mean rim thickness | 6.65 | 7.75 | 7.66 |
| Standard deviation | 1.23 | 1.41 | 1.45 |
| Minimum | 3.00 | 5.20 | 4.70 |
| Maximum | 9.90 | 11.10 | 10.90 |
| Florida pottery | n = 148 | n = 18 | n = 23 |
| Mean rim thickness | 6.50 | 7.30 | 7.40 |
| Standard deviation | 1.20 | 1.50 | 1.40 |
| Minimum | 3.00 | 5.20 | 4.70 |
| Maximum | 9.80 | 10.40 | 9.80 |

ies outlined in chapters 4 and 5, most of the grit-tempered, thick-rimmed vessels on the Lower St. Johns probably were made in Georgia near the Altamaha River and were ultimately exchanged.

## Summary and Conclusions

The combined data from technofunctional analysis lead to two compelling discoveries. First, specialized forms of pottery were made for specific tasks and were deposited almost exclusively at mortuary mounds while ostensibly domestic cooking vessels were placed at both mounds and habitation sites. Second, resilient manufacturing traditions that correspond with populations in certain areas can be identified. To summarize, the 15 vessel forms defined from the assemblage of whole or nearly whole vessels were grouped into three functional categories based on their physical suitability to certain tasks and the presence or absence of soot and mend or suspension holes. These categories include vessels used primarily for cooking, those used occasionally for (ceremonial) cooking and non-cooking tasks, and those used for entirely non-cooking functions. Based on profiles, estimated orifice diameters, and soot frequency among rim sherds, midden assemblages are dominated by moderately sized cooking vessels. Mounds contain many of these cooking vessels too, but they comprise only half of mound assemblages. The remainder of mound assemblages are made up of vessels intended for specific ritual tasks, both cooking and non-cooking. Many of these non-cooking vessels were small cups and bowls that may have had serving functions while other forms had other functions as containers of potent ritual substances.

Based on the prevalence of rare pottery types among these special-function vessels (Crystal River, Weeden Island, Dunns Creek Red, etc.), many may have been made nonlocally. Unfortunately, chemical and mineralogical data were not generated from any of these presumably foreign vessels. Finally, geographic patterns in average rim thickness and the size of quartz temper in vessels are likely to reflect the unconscious, ingrained aspects of technological style that correspond with particular learning environments in at least two different pottery traditions, one located on the Lower St. Johns River and the other centered around the Altamaha River.

Thus, the story that is emerging from Middle and Late Woodland pottery on the Atlantic coast is reminiscent of the "sacred and secular" dichotomy that William Sears (1973) used to rather simplistically describe Weeden Island pottery assemblages. Yet exactly how these objects operated in social life may have been quite different from the classic Weeden Island contexts of the Gulf Coast area. Sears (1973) clearly viewed the ornate and fantastic earthenware vessels from Weeden Island mounds as ceremonial rather than purely mortuary forms, arguing that the vessels were used for some period of time in various non-secular contexts and periodically buried all at once in caches. In comparison, the "continuous use" type of mound was predominant on the Lower St. Johns River, and there were not east side caches of vessels or other artifacts (Sears 1967). Instead, at many of the mounds, vessels were deposited continuously over time, often over a period of several centuries. Many of these vessels were clearly not produced for immediate burial—they were used repeatedly, as indicated by soot and mend holes in many specimens. While there is presently no way to determine whether individual special-use vessels eventually buried at mounds were used exclusively (and repeatedly) at mounds or whether their roles in social life extended to events at other locations, the periodic deposition of individual vessels, compared to the caching of entire assemblages, may relate to a more obvious heterogeneity in the biography of objects. Rather than an assemblage of vessels that were used repeatedly for the same periodic events, it seems more likely that some of the special-use vessels deposited at mounds along the Lower St. Johns River were used for a variety of rituals (perhaps involving healing, divination, various initiations, etc.) at multiple locations. For some of these vessels, it may have been only their last use that took place at mounds, thus invoking and mobilizing object biographies in particularly salient social events.

Notably, the vessels identified as foreign-made from the Georgia coast are nearly all domestic cooking pot forms. They bear the chemical, mineralogical, and morphological trademarks of cooking vessels made by potters local to the Altamaha River for use in domestic cooking. It appears, then, that Swift Creek vessels represent an unusual kind of gift, one that was drawn out of domestic and mundane contexts to make manifest its latent symbolic potential. These were a special kind of gift that achieved symbolic transformation through dramatic contextual shifts—the significance and meaning of which are discussed in the final chapter.

# 7

# The Swift Creek Gift

The exchange of Swift Creek Complicated Stamped vessels was an important social practice that, on the Lower St. Johns River at least, became inextricable from mortuary ceremony. The specific contexts of production and deposition and the apparent functions of these vessels reveal the signatures of gifts that were transformed into significant citations from the seemingly mundane material of everyday practice. This conclusion emerges out of a genealogy of the material practices of pottery production, use, and deposition that has been developed in preceding chapters. This final chapter synthesizes the sourcing and technofunctional data from pottery assemblages in order to construct an outline of material practice and interpret evident patterns of exchange.

## A Genealogy of Swift Creek Materiality on the Atlantic Coast

At first glance, Swift Creek Complicated Stamped pottery seems to have been initially adopted on the Atlantic coast as simply a different stamping technique that was added to existing pottery technology. Indeed, where complicated stamping first occurred on the Lower St. Johns River, simple, check, and a variety of other stamping forms had undergone periods of florescence amidst a persistent sand-tempered plain pottery tradition that spanned several centuries (Ashley and Wallis 2006). Judging by limited data from earlier contexts, cooking vessels in the form of sub-conical pots and open bowls were widespread by at least the Deptford phase and persisted through the adoption of complicated stamping (DePratter 1979; Kirkland and Johnson 2000). Cooking vessel forms did not change, yet the adoption of complicated stamping was coincident with a number of new material practices. First was the development of a locally distinctive temper that consisted of pounded charcoal fragments. Charcoal-tempered pottery is found only within a circumscribed area around the Lower St. Johns River and seems to have corresponded with production by social groups that shared close cultural ties to one another. As the incorporation of hearth contents from households or villages into vessels that were moved across the Lower St. Johns landscape, charcoal tempering may signify a growing concern with descent groups and their distribution. Second, the adoption of complicated stamping was coincident with the initiation of a series of mortuary mounds along the Lower St. Johns River, some of which continued to serve as mortuary repositories for centuries. Third and finally, with complicated stamping, charcoal tempering, and mortuary mounds came many new vessel forms that were deposited only in mound contexts. Along with human interments, shells, exotic objects of copper, mica, and stone, and many plain and complicated stamped cooking pots that were identical to local village forms were flattened globular bowls, boat-shaped bowls, multi-compartment trays, beakers, collared jars, and small cups, bowls, and jars. Many of these new vessel forms were made with charcoal-tempered paste and were therefore produced locally. However, a few vessels had Crystal River series surface treatments and may have derived from the Gulf Coast, although these could not be sampled by INAA or petrography.

Therefore, upon closer examination, the adoption of Swift Creek pottery brought a revolution of material practice, particularly in "hearth-tempered" pottery, the construction of a mortuary landscape, and in the range of vessel forms that were buried exclusively at mortuary mounds. The initiation of each of these material practices arguably entrenched peoples' concerns with descent groups and their standing vis-à-vis one another, a point to which I will return later. The distinction between mound and village pottery forms was likely a significant departure from earlier Deptford-phase ceramic traditions on the Atlantic coast (e.g., DePratter 1979) but followed in the tradition of the various "sacred-secular" divisions of the Gulf Coast Yent and Green Point complexes that culminated in later Weeden Island contexts (Sears 1962, 1973). Even as the mortuary tradition and ceremonial life that included specific vessel forms seemed obviously to derive much inspiration from populations to the west, most Early Swift Creek vessels in both mounds and middens were locally produced along the Lower St. Johns River. Instrumental Neutron Activation Analysis and petrography confirm local production origins for nearly all vessels that are demonstrably Early Swift Creek. However, this sample consists primarily of charcoal-tempered specimens and includes no Crystal River series examples that may have been made near the Florida Gulf Coast.

Swift Creek Complicated Stamped pottery on the Georgia coast also developed out of the Deptford tradition that lingered there until relatively late, with apparent influences from the interior of central and southern Georgia. Presently unclear is whether there was a wide-scale migration of Swift Creek pottery-making populations into the Georgia coastal zone from further inland (Wayne 1987). Regardless of population movement, Swift Creek groups were permanent residents of the Georgia coast and developed in their carved designs distinctive elements that are distinguished from the corpus of interior Georgia paddle designs (Ashley et al. 2007; Kelly and Smith 1975). Nevertheless, social ties between populations on the coast and the interior are evident in several paddle matches between the two areas as well as moundbuilding practices at Evelyn that resemble interior traditions. There is no evidence to suggest that the ceremonial attributes found at mounds like Evelyn were autochthonous developments. Rather, these practices seem clearly to represent a departure from Deptford mortuary traditions (cf. Thomas and Larsen 1979).

Thus, complicated stamping was adopted along the Atlantic coast in two separate historical processes. Swift Creek Complicated Stamped pottery came early (ca. AD 200) to the Lower St. Johns River from the Florida Gulf Coast, along with a whole host of new material practices. By all accounts, Swift Creek pottery on the Lower Altamaha River also came with other cultural changes, but these new ideas came from central and southern Georgia several centuries later (ca. AD 500). These distinct historical trajectories are important because between AD 200 and 500 there appear to be no material connections between Lower St. Johns River and Lower Altamaha River populations. Instead, Early Swift Creek Lower St. Johns River populations are characterized by the stalwart maintenance of material practices that were distinct but in some aspects borrowed from populations living along the Gulf Coast of Florida.

These separate historical trajectories along the Atlantic coast are evident in the village pottery assemblages of the subsequent Late Swift Creek phase. Two attributes distinguish between Lower St. Johns River and Altamaha River midden assemblages. First, there are differences in temper, with grit temper more prevalent along the Georgia coast and fine sand temper predominant in the Lower St. Johns River area. Second, Lower Altamaha River vessels are on average significantly thicker than Lower St. Johns River vessels, even in the context of identical vessel capacities and similar diet and cuisine. Temper and vessel thickness both seem to correspond with long-standing divergent cultural traditions that were inculcated for several centuries. While type of temper may have been consciously chosen, the thickness of vessel walls may very well have corresponded with habitual ways of making pots that were ingrained in somatic memory.

The advent of Late Swift Creek rim forms and designs was the result of a global phenomenon in the sense that style changes affected the entire Swift Creek pottery-making world. Indeed, thick, folded rims are diagnostic of Late Swift Creek pottery across the lower Southeast. Concomitant with folded rims on the Atlantic coast are paddle designs that seem to be more systematically carved and more carefully applied on vessel surfaces compared to "sloppy" Early Swift Creek examples (Ashley and Wallis 2006:8). This difference between Early and Late Swift Creek designs may be due, in the former, to lack of concern for clearly registering designs on vessels as well as the effect of charcoal tempering that left design-obliterating holes in vessel surfaces. The more systematic carving and careful execution of Late Swift Creek designs make the identification of paddle matches much easier for archaeologists, and it seems that this is what they were intended to do in the past as well. The distinctive and recognizable qualities of designs were ultimately mobilized by people to act as powerful material citations on the Atlantic coast.

In the context of this widespread stylistic shift, Swift Creek pottery was introduced to the Altamaha River and southward down the Georgia coast, charcoal tempering was abandoned on the Lower St. Johns River, and vessels made at Altamaha River sites were brought to the Lower St. Johns River. In this way social connections and a semblance of cultural continuity spread across southeastern Georgia and northeastern Florida for the first time in at least several centuries. There is no clear dividing line between the pottery traditions that characterize the Altamaha and St. Johns River regions during the Late Swift Creek phase. Instead, assemblages from sites between the two rivers appear to contain a mixture of the two styles. However, the Altamaha-based tradition, with thick rims and grit temper, had a notably stronger influence toward the south than did Lower St. Johns styles toward the north. For instance, many Swift Creek sites on Amelia Island, just 15 kilometers north of the mouth of the St. Johns River, are characterized by assemblages made up of more than 50 percent vessels with grit temper, some with very thick rims. There are also paddle matches between Georgia interior sites and sites in extreme southeastern Georgia that indicate continued social interactions. The southernmost distribution of Late Swift Creek pottery, which is characteristic of the Georgia coast and has paddle matches with the Georgia interior, does not overlap with the extent of Early Swift Creek manifestations on the Lower St. Johns River. This correspondence is not coincidental. Rather, the distribution is likely to reflect the continued social cohesion of groups living along the Lower St. Johns River for centuries. Even with the broad changes in Swift Creek pottery styles, there was significant continuity in the material practices of Late Swift Creek populations on the Lower St. Johns River, continuing to use the same mortuary mounds initiated during the Early Swift Creek phase and continuing to produce similar ceremonial vessel forms.

But there were new social interactions that took place along the Atlantic coast with the spread of Late Swift Creek materiality. Instrumental Neutron Activation Analysis and petrography together indicate that at least nine vessels from two Lower St. Johns River mounds, comprising 19 percent of the mound sample, were likely made somewhere near the Altamaha River. Three of these foreign vessels correspond with paddle matches that link them to specific village sites on the Altamaha River. In comparison, two vessels from midden contexts on the Lower St. Johns were made at Altamaha River sites, comprising 2 percent of the sample. The data from Altamaha River midden contexts are basically identical: three vessels, comprising 3 percent of the sample, may have been made near the Lower St. Johns River. Unfortunately, no mortuary mound assemblages were sampled from the Altamaha River for this study, which might have manifested a pattern similar to St. Johns mound assemblages.

Due to the multi-phase nature of mound assemblages on the Lower St. Johns River, the frequency calculations are sure to underestimate the proportion of foreign pottery at mounds. The mound assemblages used in the analysis, from Dent and Mayport, span several centuries of both the Early and Late Swift Creek phases, from circa AD 300 to 800. Therefore, roughly half of these assemblages may date to the Early Swift Creek phase, which predates interaction with populations in southeast Georgia. If we remove from the calculations the charcoal-tempered samples, which come from Early Swift Creek contexts, nearly 27 percent of vessels at Lower St. Johns River mounds were made near the Altamaha River. However, this is still too conservative an estimate, because at least half of Early Swift Creek assemblages were tempered with fine sand rather than charcoal. This means that the relative frequency of Georgia-made vessels in Lower St. Johns mounds may be much higher, up to half of the Late Swift Creek Complicated Stamped and sand-tempered plain assemblages. After AD 500, foreign vessels derived from other regions also seem to have become more common in mounds. These include Weeden Island series vessels, possibly from the Gulf Coast or north-central Florida, and St. Johns series vessels, probably from the Middle St. Johns River area, although none of these received adequate testing in the INAA or petrographic studies. While some of these vessels may be local renditions of foreign wares, macroscopic differences in the paste constituents of many may indicate distant production origins. Moreover, vessels of some of these nonlocal types, such as Weeden Island Red, are demonstrated by petrographic analysis of north-central Florida and Gulf Coast assemblages to have been carried considerable distances (Cordell 2006; Rice 1980).

Thus, in the purview of ceremonial material practices, Late Swift Creek phase populations on the Lower St. Johns River increasingly emphasized "the unique and the foreign" in ways that mirrored Weeden Island cultures to the west (Sears 1973). Yet unlike some Weeden Island populations, for these Swift Creek pottery-making peoples "the foreign" was manifested not just in ceremonial forms but also in domestic cooking vessels that were superficially similar to local village pots. From the available data, each of the vessels demonstrated to have been carried from the Altamaha River area and deposited at mounds on the Lower St. Johns River were domestic cooking forms. Based on the occurrence of coarse sand temper, some other special-use vessel forms may have been brought to mounds as well, including small cups and bowls, beakers, and collared jars. However, the foreign cooking vessels are especially important as recontextualized materials that became a new kind of citation in ceremonial contexts.

## The Forms and Meanings of the Swift Creek Gift

On the Lower St. Johns River, domestic cooking vessels were deposited in mounds for centuries. During the Early Swift Creek phase these were nearly all locally produced within the immediate region. However, these locally made cooking vessels deposited at mounds are not likely to have all simply come from the nearest village site. As dramatically demonstrated by an Early Swift Creek paddle design shared among vessels deposited at the Dent, Alicia B, and Beauclerc mounds, transporting vessels some distance to mounds may not have been unusual. In the heightened context of ceremony, in which other vessels were important for ritually specific tasks, the salience of cooking vessels seems to have derived mostly from where they were made, who made them, and other recognizable aspects of biography. There may have been important biographical qualities of plain cooking vessels that were eventually buried at mounds, but complicated stamping enabled biographic specificity to become indelibly attached through the differentiation of design. Indeed, among Late Swift Creek phase assemblages, the overwhelming majority (82 percent) of foreign-made vessels identified in the sourcing analyses were complicated stamped. Thus, the citational capabilities of complicated stamped vessels were employed during the Early Swift Creek phase, but the distance and frequency of these citations appears to have increased dramatically during the Late Swift Creek phase. This increase in the spatial extent of references corresponded with the culmination of distinctively clear and unadulterated paddle impressions. In short, the deliberate use of complicated stamped vessels as citations was related to the increased visual impact of designs.

Complicated stamping was, and continues to be, an exceptionally effective technology of citation that conferred upon simple cooking pots new capabilities of enchainment (Chapman 2000; Jones 2001). As a wet clay vessel was stamped with a carved wooden paddle, it became connected to the paddle by becoming a copy of its image and preserving evidence of contact (e.g., Frazer 1922; Mauss 1972). Through the impression of many vessels during manufacture, a carved wooden paddle was an effective tool for the creation of a recognizable chain of associations in objects that could be distributed across the landscape. In this way, the biography of a stamped vessel could become linked not only to a carved wooden paddle but also to every other vessel that was stamped with the same paddle. The fingerprinting capabilities of complicated stamping, making vessels that preserved an exact copy of an image and evidence of direct contact with it, arguably transferred the unmodified essence of whatever was depicted on the wooden paddle. Indeed, part of the power of mimesis is in the inability to distinguish the copy from the original (Taussig 1993:53). Given the distribution of nonlocal vessels, found almost exclusively at mortuary mounds on the Lower St. Johns River, these were capabilities recognized by people who made and used Swift Creek vessels. Through complicated stamping, cooking vessels became material citations or indexes of persons who made and used the design. These qualities made complicated stamped vessels parts of a quintessential distributed object, an image with many spatially separated manifestations across the landscape, each with a unique micro-history (Gell 1998:221). As distributed objects, complicated stamped vessels were not merely representations that symbolically "stood for" the wooden paddle that bore the same design. Rather, each image was manifested in a corpus of vessels that were moved across the landscape and distributed independently of one another. The power of these distributed objects culminated in their functions as indexes of bodily presence of an image and a person (e.g., Gell 1998:231; Munn 1990).

Distributed objects are often fundamental to the constitution of distributed persons. So it is, for example, that an arm-shell or necklace exchanged through Kula networks does not just represent a renowned person who owns it, but rather the object itself *is* the person of renown in the sense that it is conceived as embodying the age, influence, and "wisdom" of that person

(Gell 1998:231). Thus, distributed objects incorporate the substance of a human subject in a way that allows them not only to represent a person but also to embody personhood in a corporeal way. The interpretation of exchanged Swift Creek Complicated Stamped vessels as distributed objects, and hence vehicles of distributed personhood, provides a cogent explanation for the data presented in previous chapters: designs depicting faces and animals and their rendering by split representation, the high frequency of nonlocal vessels at mortuary mounds, and the apparent symbolic importance of nonlocal domestic cooking vessels amidst many special-use vessel forms in mortuary mound assemblages.

Carved paddle designs that were impressed into vessels often clearly depicted faces and animals, and as I argued in chapter 2, these images were rendered by split representation. This representational technique is significant because it tends to indicate an inextricability of an image and what it represents (e.g., signifier and signified, in semiotic terms). Split representation renders images that *are* faces or animals as subjects, rather than as objects symbolically standing for the real-life versions of them. Split representation is common among "tattooing cultures" in which images are viewed not only as indelible on the skin but also as constitutive of the skin of social persons (Gell 1998:195). Because images literally *are* what they represent, to be represented in two dimensions, a three-dimensional body must be conceived as cut into sections and spread apart. The result is an image that embodies and is part of the thing it represents. Faces, animals, and other designs rendered by split representation impressed into an earthenware vessel could have conferred a degree of personhood to a vessel, making cooking pots into persons and objects into subjects. This explanation for the symbolic efficacy of complicated stamped designs resonates with the qualities often ascribed to long-distance exchanged objects such as Kula necklaces and arm-shells. With a carved design embodying a social person, Swift Creek Complicated Stamped vessels were vehicles of distributed personhood, disseminating the image, and therefore the person, across the landscape and through time.

The fact that nonlocal complicated stamped vessels, as vehicles of distributed personhood, would be most often deposited at mortuary mounds is not surprising because this is where distanciations of personhood are most common. Indeed, as Alfred Gell conveys, "The idea of personhood being spread around in time and space is a component of innumerable cultural institutions and practices. Ancestral shrines, tombs, memorials, ossuaries, sacred sites, etc. all have to do with the extension of personhood beyond the confines of biological life via indexes distributed in the milieu" (1998:223). If Swift Creek Complicated Stamped vessels were conceived as persons, what sorts of persons were being distributed via the pots and what does their deposition at mortuary mounds signify? The answer, I believe, lies in marriage alliances and the social obligations established between descent groups, the wife-givers and wife-takers.

Claude Levi-Strauss argues that split representation corresponds cross-culturally with societies that are obsessed with competition over genealogical credentials that link men to gods because of "the strict conformity of the actor to his role and of social rank to myths, ritual, and pedigree" (1969:264). The persons distributed via complicated stamped pots are likely to have had genealogical significance as important ancestors whose possession by a lineage or clan legitimated the descent group's identity and rank. Swift Creek societies along the Atlantic coast were almost certainly not hierarchical to the degree that Levi-Strauss (1969:264) associates with split representation. However, given the age distributions of burial populations, with very few sub-adults interred in mounds, not everyone had access to mound burial and at least some degree of ranking is apparent. While there were probably limited degrees of achieved status for individuals (Thunen and Ashley 1995), the premier concern in mortuary ritual was likely membership in and ranking of descent groups, with burial in a mortuary mound restricted to members of higher-ranking lineages or clans. The ranking of descent groups was reproduced by claiming important ancestors and coordinating advantageous marriages and exchange networks with other ranked descent groups. Thus, not only the split representation of the designs themselves, but also the placement of Swift Creek Complicated Stamped vessels within and on top of mortuary mounds reveals their symbolic density as genealogical representations that may have been exchanged in the context of marriage alliances or in the event of a death that recalled the obligations of affinal kin.

Without data from mortuary mound contexts along the Altamaha River and in the absence of other (especially perishable) forms of material culture besides pottery, determining whether these were asymmetric affinal alliances and which descent groups were wife-givers and which were wife-takers is quite difficult. If descent groups located on the Lower St. Johns River were wife-givers to Altamaha River descent groups, then vessels may have been "exchanged" in a reciprocal way as distributed persons exchanged for biological persons (wives). When a descent group on the Altamaha River accepted a wife, the gifting of a complicated stamped cooking vessel to a descent group on the Lower St. Johns River was probably one constituent of creating affinal bonds. Thus, as a woman moved north through patrilocal residence, a person was extended south through the exchange of a vessel that embodied the apical ancestor or some other important person of the wife-taking descent group. The vessels may have been exchanged in the event of a marriage and kept as the physical presence (through a totem) of the descent group whom had taken a woman as a wife. If this were the case, the gifted vessel was carefully guarded and not often used in village contexts, as very few nonlocal vessels were identified in village assemblages in the analysis. Alternatively, vessels may have been given in the event of a death, in which the death of affinal kin recalled debts accrued through histories of exchange and provisioning that are typical of marriage alliances (e.g., Battaglia 1983, 1990; Kan 1989; Weiner 1992). In either case, the end result was the same: the extension of the social person embodied in the vessel was ritually killed and placed in (or on top of) a mortuary mound. The ritual death of the vessel did not signify the dissolution of the relationships that had been developed between descent groups. More likely, placing a piece of the affinal descent group into a cemetery was a way to ensure the retention of past alliances and extension of future ones (e.g., Husserl 1962, 1964; Munn 1990). By placing a piece of an allied descent group within a mortuary mound, ancestors were commingled and a permanent point of reference to these social connections was inscribed onto the landscape (e.g., Joyce 2000b).

As the embodiment of important social persons claimed by descent groups, the designs and the carved paddles used to distribute them on vessels were inalienable (e.g., Weiner 1992). They could not be given away. On the Atlantic coast there is no evidence to suggest that carved paddles were exchanged or used outside of local villages. Instead, the paddles seem to have been jealously guarded even as stamped vessels were broadly distributed. In fact, by overstamping and smoothing stamped impressions on vessels, a prohibition against unauthorized reproduction of the image was enforced. For the most part, enough of the design was registered on an earthenware vessel for a clan or lineage ancestor to be recognized, but not enough of the design was present on a vessel to make an exact replica from sherds and thereby steal the capability of reproducing it. The apparent rarity of negative impressions made by sherds in vessel production reveals the power of these prohibitions. Swift Creek vessels with designs were likely understood as embodying social persons, but the full extent of the design remained partially concealed through overstamping, thus protecting the distributed person from co-option by other descent groups.

With its bewildering effect on those trying to precisely interpret designs, overstamping may also have imparted an apotropaic function to vessels, acting as a protective device (i.e., Gell 1998:83–90). As Gell summarizes, apotropaic patterns are "demon-traps" that act by compelling evil spirits to be fascinated by intricacy or sheer multiplicity (1998:84). Spirits become so engaged in attempting to comprehend a design, such as a maze, that they are distracted from their malicious plans. The complexity of overstamped Swift Creek designs on vessels exemplifies these mystifying qualities, as anyone attempting to reconstruct designs knows well. What is more, the multiplicity of each design on Swift Creek vessels is metaphorically linked to the protection of the vessel in functional terms: paddles were used to bond clay coils during manufacture, creating a solid earthenware body, and thus protecting the vessel from death (i.e., breakage). It seems highly likely that these designs adorned people's bodies for the same reason, as a way to ward off dangerous forces. By exchanging Swift Creek vessels, the protective devices that were rendered potent on the skin could be loaned to allied descent groups without giving up control of them. Given the prominence of exchanged vessels at mortuary mounds, these designs may have been especially important in death, as persons negotiated transitions into the ancestral and spirit world.

In light of this interpretation of exchanged vessels as distributed persons, it is worth mentioning some other person-like qualities of vessels. Copying is often synonymous with reproduction (Taussig 1993:112), and in this sense both wooden paddles and earthenware vessels might be viewed as having procreative power. Along these lines, a particularly compelling way to interpret the (re)production of complicated stamped vessels is as multiply-authored by two genders. Domestic pottery production is likely to have been the domain of women (Vincentelli 2000, 2004). However, carving wooden paddles may have been the responsibility of men. In fact, wood carving seems to have been widely associated with men in North America according to ethnohistoric accounts (Driver and Massey 1957:371). If these gendered divisions of labor pertained to Swift Creek phase populations, there may have been metaphorical and metonymical conceptions of these gendered technologies that paralleled ethnographic Southeastern Indian understandings, such as among the Creek Indians. For Creeks, women are associated with uncontrolled, generative force (water and corn) while men are identified with structuring forces (fire, wood, and bone) (Bell 1990). In the production of Swift Creek Complicated Stamped pottery, the generative capacity of women in molding wet clay into a vessel and the structuring capacity of men in finishing the vessel with stamped designs may have been an act of reproduction that paralleled human biological conception. The logical conclusion of this idea is that once the vessel was "conceived" through paddle stamping (by men or by women using an object made by men), it went through a gestation period in the drying and firing process, whereby it emerged as a functional vessel. This vessel was essentially a completed person that represented the agency and the substance of at least two persons. This interpretation of pottery production paralleling the constitution of persons appears more plausible in the context of paddle stamps that took the form of faces and in the likely commonality of both people and pots becoming cultural subjects through the rendering of designs on their surfaces.

Conceived in a way that parallels biological reproduction, and often given faces, complicated stamped vessels might also have been seen to act with person-like qualities. First, through the production process that included stamping many vessels with a distinctive image, vessels could be seen to have procreative powers whereby they reproduced themselves. Indeed, many vessels in a village appear to have shared the same paddle stamp impression (Wallis 2007). The fecundity of vessels was also demonstrated by their function in cooking, repeatedly producing nourishing cooked food out of an orifice. Second, vessels had mobility and traveled across the landscape with people through residential moves and, most importantly, to important places for ceremony. Because of the unique and recognizable impressions of each design, the movements of complicated stamped vessels could be more easily traced than among other types of vessels. Finally, vessels died, either during use at villages or as they were deliberately dispatched at mound ceremonies. The spirit of the object may have been released through the death of its image in salient acts of destruction (Taussig 1993:135).

In light of their importance in mortuary ceremony, where webs of social relations between both living and deceased persons were (re)constructed and differences between persons in terms of kinship and status were given currency (e.g., Joyce 2001), exchanged complicated stamped vessels represent a recontextualization and inversion of the significance of ordinary cooking pots. At mounds, among a corpus of special-use vessels that were not used in daily life, were the very same cooking pots that were strewn across the garbage heaps at distant village middens. Exchanged vessels were taken out of the corpus of stamped vessels bearing the same (clan?) design within a village, and in this way a part was extricated from the social body of the descent group. The everyday ubiquity of a design on cooking vessels within the villages of a particular descent group was likely part of its biographic power in manifesting a distributed person, making reference not just to an ethereal ancestor but to an organic, living, working descent group. As parts of distributed persons, exchanged vessels could quite literally give bodily presence to social persons who were not otherwise present within mortuary mounds.

The use of complicated stamped vessels as enlivened descent emblems seems to have begun with the initial adoption of Swift Creek pottery on the Lower St. Johns River, but the spatial scale and intensity of their exchange, along with the clarity of designs, increased during the Late Swift Creek phase.

In the context of incipient social complexity, this escalation is presumably linked to increasing competition among descent groups that struggled over claims to ancestry and desirable alliances in marriage. Thus, marriage patterns and economic alliances are likely to have contributed to patterns of paddle matches between distant sites (e.g., Stoltman and Snow 1998), but I contend that vessels carried across the landscape do not represent the de facto refuse of these practices. Rather, I find that utilitarian cooking wares seem to have been caught up in political processes as citations of social relationships during momentous mortuary events. This transformation of value for cooking pots was contextual and historical: at a time and place where material references to places, people, and genealogies became most important, complicated stamping on domestic cooking pots offered material that was especially suitable for these purposes. This co-option and transformation of ostensibly mundane material culture reinforces the arbitrariness of cultural attributions of value that anthropologists have long recognized. Just as the choice of seashells, banana leaf bundles, and cloth as important items of exchange in Melanesia are embedded in cultural practice (Myers and Kirshenblatt-Gimblett 2001), so too are the reasons why cooking vessels became important items of exchange on the Lower St. Johns River.

## Future Directions

I hope that this research has built a foundation for future studies of Swift Creek cultures as well as archaeological considerations of exchange more generally. To begin with the foregoing case study, several practical limitations could be successfully addressed with future work. In the nascent stages of the project, I set out to analyze pottery assemblages from mortuary mound and village midden sites along the Atlantic coast from the St. Johns River to the Altamaha River. However, these goals were compromised when I was unable to locate mortuary mound assemblages from Antonio Waring and Preston Holder's (1968) excavations at the Evelyn site (9GN6) or any assemblages from Swift Creek mortuary sites along the Georgia coast. This deficiency in the sample prevents comparison between mortuary assemblages and potential identification of exchanges of complicated stamped vessels in reciprocation of vessels brought to the Lower St. Johns River. While many mounds have been destroyed and their collections lost, a few mortuary sites remain for future excavations, including unexcavated portions of Mound B and Mound C at Evelyn and one or more potential Swift Creek mounds at Lewis Creek (Cook 1966).

Another sampling limitation was introduced by the institutional restrictions placed on many collections. Because whole or especially ornate vessels were mostly off limits to destructive sampling by INAA and petrographic thin sections, specialized mortuary mound vessels were not represented in the chemical or mineralogical data. As a consequence, the samples from mounds were limited mostly to sand-tempered plain and Swift Creek Complicated Stamped cooking vessels and excluded the incised and painted wares as well as diminutive vessels that had been recovered whole or had been completely reconstructed. The provenance portion of this research therefore only discovered significant exchange relationships between the Lower St. Johns River and Altamaha River. However, many of the unsampled specialized vessels may have been made along the Gulf Coast (Crystal River and Weeden Island types) or Middle St. Johns River (St. Johns types) where these pottery types are more common. Discovering provenance for these ostensibly nonlocal vessels will require some destructive analysis as well as a large comparative sample of vessels and clays from suspected source areas.

Even in the areas along the coast where patterns in chemical and mineralogical data were fairly conclusive, more clay samples would be beneficial for outlining the range of compositional variability within the region. Clays from along the coast in the areas between the St. Johns and Altamaha rivers appear to be particularly variable in chemical composition, necessitating a much larger sample to begin to outline spatial distributions of elements. Future work might also benefit from a greater focus on ceramic ecology, sampling not only potential clay sources but also potential temper sources, particularly sand. Although quartz sands are likely to make only minimal contributions to the elemental composition of pottery (except in hafnium and zirconium), determining the geographic availability of various grain sizes in itself might contribute to our understanding of tempering traditions along the coast.

There is tremendous potential for future research of Swift Creek interaction and exchange in other areas of the lower Southeast and beyond. Future development of a searchable digital database of paddle matches is necessary for realizing this potential on a larger scale. There have been some attempts to create a digital database of designs, but today Frankie Snow's (2007) unpublished manuscript that compiles reconstructed designs and paddle matches is the primary resource for design studies. The application of technology, such as fingerprinting software for design recognition, will be critical for making paddle-match identification more efficient and for standardizing design reconstructions. Ultimately, design data should be combined in a database with other vessel attributes such as vessel morphology and chemical and mineralogical composition.

Finally, more excavations at Swift Creek village sites would be beneficial to explore intrasite patterns in the use of designs and, ultimately, to test inferences about the social structure and reproduction of descent groups that seem to have been the driving forces of vessel exchange, at least on the Atlantic coast. Aside from work at Kings Bay (Saunders 1986, 1998), opportunities to identify and excavate multiple discrete households have been limited. Restricted budgets often restrict the scope of work on threatened sites and ethical considerations limit excavations at protected sites; nonetheless, thorough excavation of a multi-household Swift Creek village holds great potential to build on our understandings of social structure.

For future studies of the Swift Creek archaeological culture, I advocate analyses of large assemblages across many sites in order to reconstruct the contextual details of material practice. I have suggested that the data presented in this study indicate the exchange of "used" village cooking vessels as indexes of persons and descent groups that operated as material for constituting social relationships on momentous occasions at mortuary mounds. This conclusion does not negate the possibility that the contents of exchanged vessels may have also been important, but empirical evidence to support this idea is currently lacking. Regardless of the significance of vessel contents in exchange, the data presented here indicate that vessels were not mere containers but held symbolic importance themselves. However, the material practices outlined for the Atlantic coast were not necessarily shared among other Swift Creek populations across the lower Southeast. I have emphasized that complicated stamping was embraced on the Lower St. Johns in specific ways that made cooking vessels appropriate as meaningful citations for reworking social relationships. Given the lack of data from mortuary mounds along the Altamaha River, the region where exchanged Swift Creek vessels on the Lower St. Johns derived, I have been reticent to make conjectures about the ways material culture at Altamaha River mounds may have been mobilized in reciprocal ways. It may be even less likely in other areas of the Eastern Woodlands that Swift Creek pottery was distributed by similar social practices with analogous logics of value. Swift Creek Complicated Stamped pottery was a global-scale phenomenon that was incorporated differently across space and through time. To assert that Swift Creek pottery was moved by the same practices or had similar meanings across thousands of kilometers ignores the possibilities of recontextualization, whereby even mass-produced objects in a globalized market take on local connotations of identity (e.g., Miller 1995a). In the particular case of populations on the Lower St. Johns River, I have argued that the indexical capabilities of cooking vessels as vehicles of distributed personhood were appropriated for constructing webs of social connections between descent groups. With continued empirical research, I believe we will find that Swift Creek Complicated Stamped vessels were frequently exchanged by other populations as well, but that the specific ways that the items were mobilized and the manifestation of their citational potential were quite variable with context.

# References

Adams, William Hampton, ed.
　1985　Aboriginal Subsistence and Settlement Archaeology of the Kings Bay Locality, vol. 1. University of Florida, Department of Anthropology Reports of Investigations No. 1, Gainesville.

Allen, Catherine J.
　1998　When Utensils Revolt: Mind, Matter, and Models of Being in the Pre-Colombian Andes. RES: Anthropology and Aesthetics 33:19–27.

Anderson, David G.
　1985　Middle Woodland Societies on the Lower South Atlantic Slope: A View from Georgia and South Carolina. Early Georgia 13:29–66.
　1995　Paleoindian Interaction Networks in the Eastern Woodlands. In Native American Interactions, edited by Michael Nassaney and Kenneth Sassaman, pp. 3–26. University of Tennessee Press, Knoxville.
　1998　Swift Creek in a Regional Perspective. In A World Engraved: Archaeology of the Swift Creek Culture, edited by Mark Williams and Daniel T. Elliott, pp. 274–300. University of Alabama Press, Tuscaloosa.

Anderson, David G., and Glen T. Hanson
　1988　Early Archaic Settlement in the Southeastern United States: A Case Study from the Savannah River Valley. American Antiquity 53:262–286.

Anderson, David G., and Robert C. Mainfort Jr.
　2002　An Introduction to Woodland Archaeology in the Southeast. In The Woodland Southeast, edited by David G. Anderson and Robert C. Mainfort Jr., pp. 1–19. University of Alabama Press, Tuscaloosa.

Anderson, Warren, and D. A. Goolsby
　1973　Flow and Chemical Characteristics of the St. Johns River at Jackson-

ville, Florida. State of Florida, Department of Natural Resources, Information Circular No. 82, Tallahassee.

Appadurai, Arjun
  1986  Introduction: Commodities and the Politics of Value. *In* The Social Life of Things: Commodities in a Cultural Perspective, edited by Arjun Appadurai, pp. 3–63. Cambridge University Press, Cambridge.

Arnold, Dean E.
  1998  Ancient Andean Ceramic Technology: An Ethnoarchaeological Perspective. *In* Andean Ceramics: Technology, Organization, and Approaches, edited by Izumi Shimada, pp. 353–367. MASCA Research Papers in Science and Archeology, Supplement to vol. 15, 1998. Museum Applied Science Center for Archaeology, University of Pennsylvania of Archaeology and Anthropology, Philadelphia, PA.

Arthur, John W.
  2002  Pottery Use-Alteration as an Indicator of Socioeconomic Status: An Ethnoarchaeological Study of the Gamo of Ethiopia. Journal of Archaeological Method and Theory 9(4):331–355.

Ashley, Keith H.
  1992  Swift Creek Manifestations along the Lower St. Johns River. The Florida Anthropologist 45:127–138.
  1995  The Dent Mound: A Coastal Woodland Period Burial Mound near the Mouth of the St. Johns River. The Florida Anthropologist 48:13–35.
  1998  Swift Creek Traits in Northeastern Florida: Ceramics, Mounds, and Middens. *In* A World Engraved: Archaeology of the Swift Creek Culture, edited by M. Williams and D. T. Elliott, pp. 197–221. University of Alabama Press, Tuscaloosa.
  2003  Interaction, Population Movement, and Political Economy: The Changing Social Landscape of Northeastern Florida. Ph.D. dissertation, Department of Anthropology, University of Florida, Gainesville.

Ashley, Keith H., and Greg S. Hendryx
  2008  Archaeological Site Testing and Data Recovery and Mitigation at the Dolphin Reef Site (8DU276), Duval County, Florida. Report on file, Division of Historical Resources, Tallahassee.

Ashley, Keith, Keith Stephenson, and Frankie Snow
  2007  Teardrops, Ladders, and Bull's Eyes: Swift Creek on the Georgia Coast. Early Georgia 35(1):3–28.

Ashley, Keith H., and Neill J. Wallis
  2006  Northeastern Florida Swift Creek: Overview and Future Research Directions. The Florida Anthropologist 59:5–18.

Battaglia, Debbora
- 1983 Projecting Personhood in Melanesia. Man 18:289–304.
- 1990 On the Bones of the Serpent: Person, Memory, and Mortality in Sabarl Island Society. University of Chicago Press, Chicago.

Baxter, Michael J.
- 1992 Archaeological Uses of the Biplot—A Neglected Technique? *In* Computer Applications and Quantitative Methods in Archaeology, 1991, edited by G. Lock and J. Moffett, pp. 141–148. BAR International Series (S577). Tempvs Reparatvm, Archaeological and Historical Associates, Oxford.
- 1994 Exploratory Multivariate Analysis in Archaeology. Edinburgh University Press, Edinburgh.

Baxter, Michael J., and Caitlin E. Buck
- 2000 Data Handling and Statistical Analysis. *In* Modern Analytical Methods in Art and Archaeology, edited by E. Ciliberto and G. Spoto, pp. 681–746. John Wiley and Sons, New York.

Bell, Amelia R.
- 1990 Separate People: Speaking of Creek Men and Women. American Anthropologist 92:332–45.

Bense, Judith A.
- 1998 Santa Rosa–Swift Creek in Northwest Florida. *In* A World Engraved: Archaeology of the Swift Creek Culture, edited by Mark Williams and Daniel T. Elliott, pp. 247–273. University of Alabama Press, Tuscaloosa.

Bense, Judith A., and Thomas C. Watson
- 1979 A Swift Creek and Weeden Island "Ring Midden" in the St. Andrews Bay Drainage System on the Northwest Florida Gulf Coast. Journal of Alabama Archaeology 25:85–137.

Bieber, Alan M., Jr., Dorothea W. Brooks, Garman Harbottle, and Edward V. Sayre
- 1976 Application of Multivariate Techniques to Analytical Data on Aegean Ceramics. Archaeometry 18:59–74.

Binford, Lewis R.
- 1962 Archaeology as Anthropology. American Antiquity 28:217–25.
- 1965 Archaeological Systematics and the Study of Culture Process. American Antiquity 31:203–10.

Binford, Lewis R., and Jeremy A. Sabloff
- 1982 Paradigms, Systematics, and Archaeology. Journal of Anthropological Research 38:137–153.

Bishop, Ronald L., and Hector Neff
   1989   Compositional Data Analysis in Archaeology. *In* Archaeological Chemistry IV, edited by R. O. Allen, pp. 576–586. Advances in Chemistry Series 220, American Chemical Society, Washington, DC.
Bishop, Ronald L., Robert L. Rands, and George R. Holley
   1982   Ceramic Compositional Analysis in Archaeological Perspective. *In* Advances in Archaeological Method and Theory, vol. 5, pp. 275–330. Academic Press, New York.
Blanton, Richard E., Gary M. Feinman, Stephen A Kowaleswki, and Peter Peregrine
   1996   A Dual-Processual Theory for the Evolution of Mesoamerican Civilization. Current Anthropology 37:1–14.
Boas, Franz
   1955   Primitive Art. Dover Publications, New York.
Bourdieu, Pierre
   1977   Outline of a Theory of Practice. Cambridge University Press, Cambridge.
Bradley, Richard
   2000   An Archaeology of Natural Places. Routledge, London.
Braun, David P.
   1983   Pots as Tools. *In* Archaeological Hammers and Theories, edited by J. A. Moore and A. S. Keene, pp. 108–134. Academic Press, New York.
   1986   Midwestern Hopewellian Exchange and Supralocal Interaction. *In* Peer Polity Interaction and Socio-Political Change, edited by Colin Renfrew and John F. Cherry, pp. 117–126. Cambridge University Press, Cambridge.
Braun, David P., and Stephen Plog
   1982   Evolution of "Tribal" Social Networks: Theory and Prehistoric North American Evidence. American Antiquity 47:504–525.
Brooks, Mark J., and Veletta Canouts
   1984   Modeling Subsistence Change in the Late Prehistoric Period in the Interior Lower Coastal Plain of South Carolina. Anthropological Studies 6, Occasional Papers of the South Carolina Institute of Archaeology and Anthropology, University of South Carolina, Columbia.
Brose, David
   1979a   An Interpretation of the Hopewellian Traits in Florida. *In* Hopewell Archaeology: The Chillicothe Conference, edited by David S. Brose and Naomi Greber, pp. 141–149. Kent State University Press, Kent, OH.
   1979b   A Speculative Model of the Role of Exchange in the Prehistory of

the Eastern Woodlands. *In* Hopewell Archaeology: The Chillicothe Conference, edited by David S. Brose and Naomi Greber, pp. 3–8. Kent State University Press, Kent, OH.

   1994   Trade and Exchange in the Midwestern U.S. *In* Prehistoric Exchange Systems in North America, vol. 2, ed. Timothy G. Baugh and Jonathan E. Ericson, pp. 215–240. Plenum Press, New York.

Brose, David S., and Naomi Greber (editors)
   1979   Hopewell Archaeology: The Chillicothe Conference. The Kent State University Press, Kent, OH.

Brown, James A.
   1985   Long-Term Trends to Sedentism and the Emergence of Complexity in the American Midwest. *In* Prehistoric Hunter-Gatherers: The Emergence of Cultural Complexity, edited by T. Douglas Price and James A. Brown, pp. 201–231. Academic Press, New York.

Brown, James A., R. A. Kerber, and Howard D. Winters
   1990   Trade and the Evolution of Exchange Relations at the Beginning of the Mississippian Period. *In* The Mississippian Emergence, edited by Bruce D. Smith, pp. 251–263. Smithsonian Institution Press, Washington, DC.

Broyles, Bettye J.
   1968   Reconstructed Designs from Swift Creek Complicated Stamped Sherds. Southeastern Archaeological Conference Bulletin 8:49–74. Morgantown, West Virginia.

Brumfiel, Elizabeth, and Timothy Earle
   1987   Specialization, Exchange, and Complex Societies: An Introduction. *In* Specialization, Exchange, and Complex Societies, edited by Elizabeth Brumfiel and Timothy Earle, pp. 1–9. Cambridge University Press, Cambridge.

Bullen, Ripley P., Adelain K. Bullen, and W. J. Bryant
   1967   Archaeological Investigations at the Ross Hammock Site, Florida. William L. Bryant Foundation, American Studies Report 7.

Bullen, Ripley P., and John W. Griffin
   1952   An Archaeological Survey of Amelia Island, Florida. The Florida Anthropologist 5:37–64.

Butler, Judith
   1993   Bodies That Matter: On the Discursive Limits of "Sex". Routledge, London.

Byrd, John E.
   1997   The Analysis of Diversity in Archaeological Faunal Assemblages: Complexity and Subsistence Strategies in the Southeast during the

Middle Woodland Period. Journal of Anthropological Archaeology 16:49–72.

Caldwell, Joseph R.
- 1952 The Archaeology of Eastern Georgia to South Carolina. *In* Archaeology of Eastern United States, edited by James B. Griffin, pp. 312–321. University of Chicago Press, Chicago.
- 1958 Trend and Tradition in the Prehistory of the Eastern United States. Memoir No. 88, American Anthropological Association, Scientific Papers. Vol. X, Illinois State Museum, Springfield.
- 1964 Interaction Spheres in Prehistory. *In* Hopewellian Studies, edited by Joseph Caldwell and Robert Hall, pp. 133–143. Scientific Papers 12, Illinois State Museum, Springfield.
- 1970 Chronology of the Georgia Coast. Southeastern Archaeological Conference Bulletin 13:88–92.

Carder, Nanny, Elizabeth J. Reitz, and J. Matthew Compton
- 2004 Animal Use in the Georgia Pine Barrens: An Example from the Hartford Site (9PU1). Southeastern Archaeology 23:25–40.

Carr, Christopher
- 2006a Historical Insight into the Directions and Limitations of Recent Research on Hopewell. *In* Gathering Hopewell: Society, Ritual, and Ritual Interaction, edited by Christopher Carr and D. Troy Case, pp. 51–70. Springer, New York.
- 2006b Rethinking Interregional Hopewellian "Interaction." *In* Gathering Hopewell: Society, Ritual, and Ritual Interaction, edited by Christopher Carr and D. Troy Case, pp. 575–623. Springer, New York.

Carr, Christopher, and Jill E. Nietzel
- 1995 Integrating Approaches to Material Style in Theory and Philosophy. *In* Style, Society, and Person, edited by Christopher Carr and Jill E. Nietzel, pp. 3–20. Springer, New York.

Chance, Marsha A.
- 1974 The W.P.A. Glynn County Project: A Ceramic Analysis. Unpublished M.A. thesis, Department of Anthropology, Florida State University.

Chapman, John
- 2000 Tension at Funerals: Social Practices and the Subversion of Community Structure in Later Hungarian Prehistory. *In* Agency in Archaeology, edited by Marcia-Anne Dobres and John Robb, pp. 169–195. Routledge, New York.

Chase, David W.
- 1998 Swift Creek: Lineage and Diffusion. *In* A World Engraved: Archaeology of the Swift Creek Culture, edited by Mark Williams and Daniel T. Elliott, pp. 48–60. University of Alabama Press, Tuscaloosa.

Clay, R. Berle
  1998  Essential Features of Adena Ritual and Their Implications. Southeastern Archaeology 17:1–21.
Cobb, Charles R.
  1991  Social Reproduction and the Longue Durée in the Prehistory of the Midcontinental United States. *In* Processual and Postprocessual Archaeologies: Multiple Ways of Knowing the Past, edited by R. W. Preucel, pp. 168–182. Occasional Paper No. 10. Center for Archaeological Investigations, Southern Illinois University, Carbondale.
Cogswell, James, Hector Neff, and Michael D. Glascock
  1998  Analysis of Shell-Tempered Pottery Replicates: Implications for Provenance Studies. American Antiquity 63:63–72.
Cook, Fred C.
  1966  The 1966 Excavation at the Lewis Creek Site. Report on file, Department of Anthropology, University of Georgia, Athens.
  1979  Kelvin: A Late Woodland Phase on the Southern Georgia Coast. Early Georgia 7(2):65–86.
  1995  An Archaeological Survey of Human Remains Found at Sidon Plantation. Manuscript on file, South Georgia College, Douglas.
Cordell, Ann S.
  2006  Finish What You Start: Revisiting the McKeithen Site Pottery Analysis. Paper presented at the 63rd Annual Meeting of the Southeastern Archaeological Conference, Little Rock, AR.
  2008  Explanation of Methods: Petrographic Analysis of 67 NAA Pottery/Clay Samples. Report on file, Florida Museum of Natural History, Gainesville, FL.
Cordell, Ann S., and Steven H. Koski
  2003  Analysis of a Spiculate Clay from Lake Monroe, Volusia County, Florida. The Florida Anthropologist 56:113–125.
Crocker, Mark D.
  1999  Geochemical Mapping in Georgia, USA: A Tool for Environmental Studies, Geologic Mapping, and Mineral Exploration. Journal of Geochemical Exploration 67:345–360.
Crown, Patricia L.
  2007  Life Histories of Pots and Potters: Situating the Individual in Archaeology. American Antiquity 72:677–690.
David, Nicholas, and Hilke Hennig
  1972  The Ethnography of Pottery: A Fulani Case Seen in Archaeological Perspective. Module 21. Addison–Wesley, Reading, MA.
Davis, Richard A., Jr.
  1997  Geology of the Florida Coast. *In* The Geology of Florida, edited

by A. F. Randazzo and D. S. Jones, pp. 155–168. University Press of Florida, Gainesville.

Davis, Richard A., and Miles O. Hayes
 1984 What Is a Wave-Dominated Coast? Marine Geology 60:313–329.

Deal, Michael, and Melissa B. Hagstrum
 1994 Ceramic Reuse Behavior among the Maya and Wanka: Implications for Archaeology. *In* Expanding Archaeology, edited by J. M. Skibo, W. H. Walker, and A. E. Neilsen, pp. 111–125. University of Utah Press, Salt Lake City.

DeBoer, Warren R., and Donald Lathrap
 1979 The Making and Breaking of Shipibo-Conibo Ceramics. *In* Ethnoarchaeology: Implications of Ethnography for Archaeology, edited by C. Kramer, pp. 102–138. Columbia University Press, New York.

deFrance, Susan D.
 1993 Faunal Material from the Greenfield Site (8DU5543), Duval County Florida. Report on file, Florida Museum of Natural History, Environmental Archaeology Laboratory.

Deleuze, Gilles, and Félix Guattari
 1987 A Thousand Plateaus: Capitalism and Schizophrenia, translated by Brian Massumi. University of Minnesota Press, Minneapolis.

DeMarrais, Elizabeth, Chris Gosden, and Colin Renfrew
 2005 Introduction. *In* Rethinking Materiality: The Engagement of Mind with the Material World, edited by Elizabeth DeMarrais, Chris Gosden, and Colin Renfrew, pp. 1–7. McDonald Institute for Archaeological Research, Cambridge.

DePratter, Chester B.
 1979 Ceramics. *In* The Anthropology of St. Catherine's Island: The Refuge-Deptford Mortuary Complex, edited by David H. Thomas and Clark S. Larsen, pp. 109–132. Anthropological Papers of the American Museum of Natural History 56(1), New York.

DePratter, Chester B., and James D. Howard
 1981 Evidence for a Sea Level Lowstand between 4500 and 2400 Years B.P. on the Southeast Coast of the United States. Journal of Sedimentary Petrology 1:1287–1295.

Derrida, Jacques
 1982 Signature, Event, Context. *In* The Margins of Philosophy, edited by J. Derrida, pp. 307–330. Harvester Press, Brighton.

Dickinson, Martin F., and Lucy B. Wayne
 1999 Island in the Marsh: An Archaeological Investigation of 8NA59 and 8NA709, the Crane Island Sites, Nassau County, Florida. Report on file, Division of Historical Resources, Tallahassee.

Dobres, Marcia-Anne
  2000   Technology and Social Agency: Outlining a Practice Framework for Archaeology. Blackwell, Oxford.

Drennan, Robert D.
  1985   Porters, Pots, and Profit: The Economics of Long-Distance Exchange in Mesoamerica. American Anthropologist 87:891–893.

Driver, Harold E., and William C. Massey
  1957   Comparative Studies of North American Indians, vol. 47, no. 2. Transactions of the American Philosophical Society, New Series, Philadelphia.

Duff, Andrew I.
  2002   Western Pueblo Identities: Regional Interaction, Migration, and Transformation. University of Arizona Press, Tucson.

Dye, David H.
  1996   Riverine Adaptation in the Midsouth. *In* Of Caves and Shell Mounds, edited by K. C. Carstens and P. J. Watson, pp. 140–158. University of Alabama Press, Tuscaloosa.

Earle, Timothy A.
  1994   Positioning Exchange in the Evolution of Human Society. *In* Prehistoric Exchange Systems in North America, edited by T. Baugh and J. Ericson, pp. 419–437. Plenum, New York.

Elliott, Daniel T.
  1998   The Northern and Eastern Expression of Swift Creek Culture: Settlement in the Tennessee and Savannah River Valleys. *In* A World Engraved: Archaeology of the Swift Creek Culture, edited by M. Williams and D. Elliott, pp. 19–35. University of Alabama Press, Tuscaloosa.

Espenshade, Christopher T.
  1983   Ceramic Ecology and Aboriginal Household Pottery Production at the Gauthier Site, Florida. Unpublished M.A. thesis, University of Florida, Gainesville.
  1985   Ceramic Technology of the Kings Bay Locality. *In* Aboriginal Subsistence and Settlement Archaeology of the Kings Bay Locality, vol. I: The Kings Bay and Devils Walkingstick Sites, edited by W. H. Adams, pp. 295–336. University of Florida, Department of Anthropology, Reports of Investigations 1, Gainesville.

Espenshade, Christopher T., Linda Kennedy, and Bobby G. Southerlin
  1994   What Is a Shell Midden? Data Recovery Excavations of Thom's Creek and Deptford Shell Middens, 38BU2, Spring Island, South Carolina. Submitted to Spring Island Plantation by Brockington and Associates, Atlanta, GA.

Fairbanks, Charles H.
  1952   Creek and Pre-Creek. *In* Archaeology of Eastern United States, ed-

ited by J. B. Griffin, pp. 285–300. University of Chicago Press, Chicago.

Farnsworth, Kenneth B., and Karen A. Atwell
N.d. The Blue Island and Naples-Russell Mounds and the Origins of Hopewell in the Illinois River Valley. Manuscript in production for the Illinois Transportation Archaeological Research Program.

Fie, Shannon M.
2000 An Integrative Study of Ceramic Exchange during the Illinois Valley Middle Woodland Period. Unpublished Ph.D. dissertation, State University of New York, Buffalo.
2006 Visiting in the Interaction Sphere: Ceramic Exchange and Interaction in the Lower Illinois Valley. *In* Recreating Hopewell, edited by D. K. Charles and J. E. Buikstra, pp. 427–445. University Press of Florida, Gainesville.

Florida Archeological Services, Inc. (FAS)
1994 Phase II Archeological Investigations at Sites 8DU5541, 8DU5542, and 8DU 5543 at the Queen's Harbour Yacht and Country Club, Duval County, Florida. Report on file, Division of Historic Resources, Tallahassee.

Ford, James A.
1954 Spaulding's Review of Ford. American Anthropologist 56:109–112.

Fowler, Chris
2004 The Archaeology of Personhood: An Anthropological Approach. Routledge, London.

Fradkin, Arlene
1998 Appendix B: Quantification of 8DU5545 Faunal Assemblage. *In* A Phase II Archeological Investigation of Florida Inland Navigation District Tract DU-7, Greenfield Peninsula, Duval County, Florida, by Robert E. Johnson, B. Alan Basinet, David N. Dickel, and Arlene Fradkin, pp. 138–156. Report on file, Division of Historical Resources, Tallahassee.

Fradkin, Arlene, and Jerald T. Milanich
1977 Salvage Excavations at the Law School Mound, Alachua County, Florida. Florida Anthropologist 30:166–178.

Frazer, James George
1922 The Golden Bough. Macmillan, New York.

Gayes, Paul T., David B. Scott, Eric S. Collins, and Douglas D. Nelson
1992 A Late Holocene Sea-Level Fluctuation in South Carolina. *In* Quaternary Coasts of the United States: Marine and Lacustrine Systems. Special Publication No. 48, edited by Charles H. Fletcher III and John F.

Wehmiller, pp. 155–160. SEPM Society for Sedimentary Geology, Tulsa, OK.

Gell, Alfred
  1998 Art and Agency: An Anthropological Theory. Clarendon Press, Oxford.

Gibson, Jon L.
  1996 Poverty Point and Greater Southeastern Prehistory: The Culture That Did Not Fit. *In* Archaeology of the Mid-Holocene Southeast, edited by Kenneth E. Sassaman and David G. Anderson, pp. 288–305. University Press of Florida, Gainesville.

Gillespie, Susan D.
  2001 Personhood, Agency, and Mortuary Ritual: A Case Study from the Ancient Maya. Journal of Anthropological Archaeology 20:73–112.

Gilman, Antonio
  1981 The Development of Social Stratification in Bronze Age Europe. Current Anthropology 22:1–23.

Glascock, Michael D.
  1992 Characterization of Archaeological Ceramics at MURR by Neutron Activation Analysis and Multivariate Statistics. *In* Chemical Characterization of Ceramic Pastes in Archaeology, edited by H. Neff, pp. 11–26. Prehistory Press, Madison, WI.

Glascock, Michael D., ed.
  2002 Geochemical Evidence for Long-Distance Exchange. Bergin and Garvey, Westport, CT.

Goggin, John W.
  1949 Cultural Traditions in Florida Prehistory. *In* The Florida Indian and His Neighbors, edited by J. W. Griffin, 13–44. Rollins College, Winter Park, FL.
  1952 Space and Time Perspective in Northern St. Johns Archaeology, Florida. Yale University Publications in Anthropology 47, New Haven.

Gosden, Chris
  2005 What Do Objects Want? Journal of Archaeological Method and Theory 12:193–211.

Gosden, Chris, and Yvonne Marshall
  1999 The Cultural Biography of Objects. World Archaeology 31:169–178.

Gosselain, Olivier P.
  2000 Materializing Identities: An African Perspective. Journal of Archaeological Method and Theory 7:187–217.

Graves, Michael W.
  1991 Pottery Production and Distribution among the Kalinga: A Study of

Household and Regional Organization and Differentiation. *In* Ceramic Ethnoarchaeology, edited by William A. Longacre, pp. 112–143. University of Arizona Press, Tucson.

Gregory, Chris
 1982   Gifts and Commodities. Academic Press, London.

Griffin, James B.
 1965   Hopewell and the Dark Black Glass. Michigan Archaeologist 11:115–155.

Gudeman, Stephen
 2001   The Anthropology of Economy. Blackwell, Malden, MA.

Hackney, C. T., W. D. Burbanck, and O. P. Hackney
 1976   Biological and Physical Dynamics of a Georgia Tidal Creek. Chesapeake Science 17:271–280.

Hally, David J.
 1983   Use Alteration of Pottery Surfaces: An Important Source of Evidence for the Identification of Vessel Function. North American Archaeologist 4:3–26.
 1986   The Identification of Vessel Function: A Case Study from Northwest Georgia. American Antiquity 51:267–295.

Handley, Brent M., Steve Ferrell, and Neill J. Wallis
 2004   Addendum To: Data Recovery at 8NA32, the McArthur Estates Tract, Nassau County, Florida. Report on file, Division of Historical Resources, Tallahassee.

Harbottle, Garman
 1976   Activation Analysis in Archaeology. Radiochemistry 3:33–72. The Chemical Society, London.

Hardin, Kenneth, John Ballo, and Michael Russo
 1988   Cultural Resource Assessment Survey of the Crossings at Fleming Island, DRI, Clay County, Florida. Report on file, Division of Historical Resources, Tallahassee.

Hardin, Kenneth, and Michael Russo
 1987   Phase II Test Excavations at the Piney Point Site, 8NA31, Amelia Island, Florida. Report on file, Division of Historical Resources, Tallahassee.

Harry, Karen G.
 2003   Economic Organization and Settlement Hierarchies: Ceramic Production and Exchange among the Hohokam. Praegger Press, Westport, CT.

Hart, Keith
 2007   Marcel Mauss: In Pursuit of the Whole. Comparative Studies of Society and History 49:1–13.

Hayden, Brian
 1995   The Emergence of Prestige Technologies and Pottery. *In* The Emer-

gence of Pottery Production: Technology and Innovation in Ancient Societies, edited by W. Barnett and J. Hoopes, pp. 257–265. Smithsonian Institution Press, Washington, DC.

1998 Practical and Prestige Technologies: The Evolution of Material Systems. Journal of Archaeological Method and Theory 5:1–55.

Hegmon, Michelle
1992 Archaeological Research on Style. Annual Review of Anthropology 21:517–536.

Helms, Mary W.
1988 Ulysses' Sail: An Ethnographic Odyssey of Power, Knowledge, and Geographical Distance. Princeton University Press, Princeton, NJ.

Hendon, Julia A.
2000 Having and Holding: Storage, Memory, Knowledge, and Social Relations. American Anthropologist 102(1):42–53.

Hendryx, Greg S.
2004 The Honey Dripper Site (8NA910): A Late Swift Creek Encampment in Northeastern Florida. The Florida Anthropologist 57:299–310.

Hendryx, Greg S., and Neill J. Wallis
2007 The Woodland Period in Northeastern Florida: A View from the Tillie Fowler Site. The Florida Anthropologist 60:179–200.

Hill, James N.
1970 Broken K Pueblo: Prehistoric Social Organization in the American Southwest. University of Arizona Anthropological Papers 18. University of Arizona Press, Tucson.

Houston, Stephen D., and David Stuart
1998 The Ancient Maya Self: Personhood and Portraiture in the Classic Period. RES: Anthropology and Aesthetics 33:73–101.

Husserl, Edmund
1962 Ideas: General Introduction to Pure Phenomenology. Collier Books, New York.
1964 The Phenomenology of Internal Time and Consciousness. Indiana University Press, Bloomington.

Jefferies, Richard W.
1994 The Swift Creek Site and Woodland Platform Mounds in the Southeastern United States. In Ocmulgee Archaeology, 1936–1986, edited by David J. Hally, pp. 71–83. University of Georgia Press, Athens.
1996 The Emergence of Long-Distance Exchange Networks in the Southeastern United States. In Archaeology of the Mid-Holocene Southeast, edited by Kenneth E. Sassaman and David G. Anderson, pp. 222–234. University Press of Florida, Gainesville.

Jennings, Jesse D., and Charles H. Fairbanks
  1939   Pottery Type Description for Swift Creek Complicated Stamped. Southeastern Archaeological Conference Newsletter 1(2).

Johnson, Robert E.
  1988   An Archeological Reconnaissance Survey of the St. Johns Bluff Area of Duval County, Florida. Report on file, Division of Historical Resources, Tallahassee.
  1994   An Archeological and Historical Survey of the Wood-Hopkins Tract on Dames Point, Duval County, Florida. Report on file, Division of Historic Resources, Tallahassee.
  1998   A Phase II Archeological Investigation of Florida Inland Navigation District Tract DU7, Greenfield Peninsula, Duval County, Florida. Report on file, Division of Historic Resources, Tallahassee.

Johnson, Robert E., Myles C. P. Bland, B. Alan Basinet, and Bob Richter
  1997   An Archeological Investigation of the Ocean Reach Site (8NA782), Nassau County, Florida. Report on file, Division of Historical Resources, Tallahassee.

Jones, Andrew
  2001   Drawn from Memory: The Aesthetics of Archaeology and the Archaeology of Aesthetics in the Earlier Bronze Age and the Present. World Archaeology 33:334–356.
  2005   Lives in Fragments? Personhood and the European Neolithic. Journal of Social Archaeology 5:193–224.

Jones, Bruce A.
  1989   Use-Wear Analysis of White Mountain Redwares at Grasshopper Pueblo, Arizona. The Kiva 54(4):353–361.

Joyce, Rosemary
  1998   Performing the Body in Prehispanic Central America. RES: Anthropology and Aesthetics 33:147–65.
  2000a  Girling the Girl and Boying the Boy: The Production of Adulthood in Ancient Mesoamerica. World Archaeology 31:473–483.
  2000b  Heirlooms and Houses: Materiality and Social Memory. *In* Beyond Kinship: Social and Material Reproduction in House Societies, edited by Rosemary Joyce and Susan Gillespie, pp. 189–212. University of Pennsylvania Press, Philadelphia.
  2001   Burying the Dead at Tlatilco: Social Memory and Social Identities. *In* Social Memory, Identity, and Death: Anthropological Perspectives on Mortuary Rituals, edited by M. S. Chesson, pp. 12–26. Archaeological Papers of the American Anthropological Association 10, Arlington, VA.

2003  Concrete Memories: Fragments of the Past in the Classic Maya Present (500–1000 AD). *In* Archaeologies of Memory, edited by Ruth M. van Dyke and Susan E. Alcock, pp. 104–125. Oxford: Blackwell.

Kan, Sergei
  1989  Symbolic Immortality: The Tlingit Potlatch of the Nineteenth Century. Smithsonian Institution Press, Washington, DC.

Kellar, James H.
  1979  The Mann Site and "Hopewell" in the Lower Wabash-Ohio Valley. *In* Hopewell Archaeology: The Chillicothe Conference, edited by David Brose and Naomi Greber, pp. 100–107. Kent State University Press, Kent, OH.

Keller, Cynthia, and Christopher Carr
  2006  Gender, Role, Prestige, and Ritual Interaction across the Ohio, Mann, and Havana Hopewellian Regions, as Evidenced by Ceramic Figurines. *In* Gathering Hopewell: Society, Ritual, and Ritual Interaction, edited by C. Carr and D. T. Case, pp. 428–460. Springer, New York.

Kelly, Arthur
  1938  A Preliminary Report on Archaeological Explorations at Macon Georgia. Smithsonian Institution, Bureau of American Ethnology Bulletin 119, Washington, DC.

Kelly, Arthur R., and Betty A. Smith
  1975  The Swift Creek Site, 9-Bi-3, Macon, Georgia. Report submitted to the Southeast Archeological Center, National Park Service, Atlanta, GA.

Kelly, Richard L.
  1995  The Foraging Spectrum: Diversity in Hunter-Gatherer Lifeways. Smithsonian Institution Press, Washington, DC.

Kirkland, S. Dwight.
  2003  Human Prehistory at the Sadlers Landing Site, Camden County, Georgia. Early Georgia 31:107–192.

Kirkland, S. Dwight, and Robert E. Johnson
  2000  Archeological Data Recovery at Greenfield Site No. 5, 8DU5541. Report on file, Division of Historical Resources, Tallahassee.

Knight, Vernon James, Jr.
  2001  Feasting and the Emergence of Platform Mound Ceremonialism in Eastern North America. *In* Feasts: Archaeological and Ethnographic Perspectives on Food, Politics, and Power, edited by Michael Dietler and Brian Hayden, pp. 311–333. Smithsonian Institution Press, Washington, DC.

Knight, Vernon J., and Timothy S. Mistovich
  1984  Walter F. George Lake: Archaeological Survey of Fee Owned Lands,

Alabama and Georgia. University of Alabama Office of Archaeological Research, Report of Investigations 42, Tuscaloosa.

LaFond, Arthur A.
1983 The Queen Mound, Jacksonville, Florida. Manuscript on file, Florida Museum of Natural History, Gainesville.

Latour, Bruno
1999 Pandora's Hope: Essays on the Reality of Science Studies. Harvard University Press, Cambridge.

Leach, Edmond
1976 Culture and Communication: The Logic by Which Symbols Are Connected. Cambridge University Press, Cambridge.

Lechtman, Heather
1977 Style in Technology: Some Early Thoughts. *In* Material Culture: Styles, Organization, and Dynamics of Technology, edited by H. Lechtman and R. S. Merrill, pp. 3–20. American Ethnological Society, St. Paul, MN.

Lechtman, Heather, and Robert S. Merrill
1977 Material Culture, Styles, Organization, and Dynamics of Technology. 1975 Proceedings of the American Ethnological Society. West, St. Paul, MN.

Leese, Morven N., and Peter L. Main
1994 The Efficient Computation of Unbiased Mahalanobis Distances and Their Interpretation in Archaeometry. Archaeometry 36:307–316.

Lemonnier, Pierre
1986 The Study of Material Culture Today: Toward an Anthropology of Technical Systems. Journal of Anthropological Archaeology 5:147–186.
1992 Elements of an Anthropology of Technology. Anthropological Papers of the Museum of Anthropology, vol. 88. University of Michigan, Ann Arbor.
1993 Introduction. *In* Technological Choices: Transformation in Material Culture since the Neolithic, edited by Pierre Lemmonier, pp. 1–35. Routledge, London.

Leroi-Gourhan, André
1943 L'Homme et la Matière. Albin Michelle, Paris.
1945 Milieu et Technique. Albin Michelle, Paris.

Levi-Strauss, Claude
1963 Structural Anthropology, translated by C. Jacobson and B. C. Schoepf. Basic Books, New York.
1969 The Elementary Structures of Kinship, revised edition, translated by James Harle Bell, John Richard von Sturmer, and Rodney Needham. Beacon Press, Boston.

Lindauer, Owen, and John H. Blitz
  1997    Higher Ground: The Archaeology of North American Platform Mounds. Journal of Archaeological Research 5:169–207.
Linton, Ralph
  1944    North American Cooking Pots. American Antiquity 9:369–380.
LiPuma, Edward
  1998    Modernity and Forms of Personhood in Melanesia. *In* Bodies and Persons: Comparative Perspectives from Africa and Melanesia, edited by M. Lambek and A. Strathern, pp. 53–79. Cambridge University Press, Cambridge.
Longacre, William A.
  1970    Archaeology as Anthropology: A Case Study. University of Arizona Anthropological Papers 17. University of Arizona Press, Tucson.
MacKenzie, Maure
  1991    Androgynous Objects: Strong Bags and Gender in Central New Guinea. Harwood Academic Press, Melbourne, Australia.
Mainfort, Robert C., Jr.
  1988    Middle Woodland Ceremonialism at Pinson Mounds, Tennessee. American Antiquity 53:158–173.
Mainfort, Robert C., Jr., James W. Cogswell, Michael J. O'Brien, Hector Neff, and Michael D. Glascock
  1997    Neutron Activation Analysis of Pottery from Pinson Mounds and Nearby Sites in Western Tennessee: Local Production vs. Long-Distance Importation. Midcontinental Journal of Archaeology 22:43–68.
Malinowski, Bronislaw
  1922    Argonauts of the Western Pacific. Routledge, London.
Mauss, Marcel
  1925    The Gift. W. W. Norton, New York.
  1935    Les Techniques du Corps. Journal de Psychologie 32:271–293.
  1972    A General Theory of Magic, translated by R. Brain. Routledge, London.
Meskell, Lynn
  2004    Object Worlds in Ancient Egypt: Material Biographies Past and Present. Berg, New York.
Meskell, Lynn, ed.
  2005    Archaeologies of Materiality. Blackwell, Oxford.
Meskell, Lynn, and Rosemary Joyce
  2003    Embodied Lives: Figuring Ancient Maya and Egyptian Experience. London: Routledge.
Milanich, Jerald T.
  1971    The Deptford Phase: An Archeological Reconstruction. Ph.D. disser-

tation, Department of Anthropology, University of Florida, Gainesville.
- 1973 The Southeastern Deptford Culture: A Preliminary Definition. Florida Bureau of Historic Sites and Properties, Bulletin 3:51–63.
- 1994 Archaeology of Precolumbian Florida. University of Florida Press, Gainesville.
- 1999 *Review of* A World Engraved: Archaeology of the Swift Creek Culture, edited by M. Williams and D. Elliott. American Antiquity 64:704–705.
- 2002 Weeden Island Cultures. *In* The Woodland Southeast, edited by D. G. Anderson and R. C. Mainfort Jr., pp. 352–372. University of Alabama Press, Tuscaloosa.
- 2004 Archaeology of the Lower Atlantic Coastal Region, ca. 600 B.C. to Contact. *In* Handbook of the North American Indians, vol. 14: Southeast, edited by Raymond D. Fogelson, pp. 219–228.

Milanich, Jerald T., Ann S. Cordell, Vernon J. Knight Jr., Timothy A. Kohler, and Brenda J. Sigler-Lavelle
- 1984 McKeithen Weeden Island: The Culture of Northern Florida, A.D. 200–900. Academic Press, Orlando.
- 1997 Archaeology of Northern Florida, A.D. 200–900: The McKeithen Weeden Island Culture. University Press of Florida, Gainesville.

Milanich, Jerald T., and Charles H. Fairbanks
- 1980 Florida Archaeology. Academic Press, New York.

Miller, Daniel
- 1987 Material Culture and Mass Consumption. Blackwell, Oxford.
- 1995a Coca-Cola: A Black Sweet Drink from Trinidad. *In* Material Cultures: Why Some Things Matter, edited by D. Miller, pp. 169–188. University of Chicago Press, Chicago.
- 1995b Why Some Things Matter. *In* Material Cultures: Why Some Things Matter, edited by Daniel Miller, pp. 3–21. University of Chicago Press, Chicago.
- 2001 Alienable Gifts and Inalienable Commodities. *In* The Empire of Things, edited by Fred R. Myers, pp. 91–118. School of American Research Press, Santa Fe, NM.
- 2005 Materiality: An Introduction. *In* Materiality, edited by Daniel Miller, pp. 1–50. Duke University Press, Durham, NC.

Mills, Barbara J.
- 1986 "North American Cooking Pots" Reconsidered: Some Behavioral Correlates of Variation in Cooking Pot Morphology. Paper presented at the Annual Meeting of the Society for American Archaeology, Denver.

2004  The Establishment and Defeat of Hierarchy: Inalienable Possessions and the History of Collective Prestige Structures in the Puebloan Southwest. American Anthropologist 106:238–251.

2007  Performing the Feast: Visual Display and Suprahousehold Commensalism in the Puebloan Southwest. American Antiquity 72:210–239.

Moore, Clarence B.
1894  Certain Sand Mounds of the St. Johns River, Florida, Parts I and II. Journal of the Academy of Natural Sciences of Philadelphia, Second Series 10:129–246.

1895  Certain Sand Mounds of Duval County, Florida. Journal of the Academy of Natural Sciences of Philadelphia, Second Series 10:449–502.

1896  Certain Florida Coast Mounds North of the St. Johns River. *In* Additional Mounds of Duval and Clay Counties, Florida, pp. 22–30. Privately printed.

1902  Certain Aboriginal Remains of the Northwest Florida Coast, Part II. Journal of the Academy of Natural Sciences of Philadelphia 12:127–358.

Mosko, Mark
1992  Motherless Sons: "Divine Kings" and "Partible Persons" in Melanesia and Polynesia. Man 27:697–717.

Munn, Nancy D.
1983  Gawan Kula: Spatiotemporal Control and the Symbolism of Influence. *In* The Kula: New Perspectives on Massim Exchange, edited by E. Leach and J. Leach, pp. 277–308. Cambridge University Press, Cambridge.

1986  The Fame of Gawa: A Symbolic Study of Value Transformation in a Massim (PNG) Society. Cambridge University Press, Cambridge.

1990  Constructing Regional Worlds in Experience, Kula Exchange, Witchcraft, and Gawan Local Events. Man 25:1–17.

Myers, Fred R., and Barbara Kirshenblatt-Gimblett
2001  Art and Material Culture: A Conversation with Annette Weiner. *In* The Empire of Things, edited by Fred R. Myers, pp. 269–314. School of American Research Press, Sante Fe, NM.

Nassaney, Michael S., and Kenneth E. Sassaman
1995  Introduction: Understanding Native American Interactions. *In* Native American Interactions: Multiscalar Analyses and Interpretations in the Eastern Woodlands, edited by Michael S. Nassaney and Kenneth E. Sassaman, pp. xix–xxxviii. University of Tennessee Press, Knoxville.

Neff, Hector
1992  Introduction. *In* Chemical Characterization of Ceramic Pastes in Archaeology, edited by Hector Neff, pp. 1–10. Prehistory Press, Madison, WI.

1994   RQ-mode Principal Components Analysis of Ceramic Compositional Data. Archaeometry 36:115–130.
2000   Neutron Activation Analysis for Provenance Determination in Archaeology. *In* Modern Analytical Methods in Art and Archaeology, edited by E. Ciliberto and G. Spoto, pp. 81–134. John Wiley and Sons, New York.
2002   Quantitative Techniques for Analyzing Ceramic Compositional Data. *In* Ceramic Source Determination in the Greater Southwest, edited by Donna M. Glowacki and Hector Neff. Monograph 44, Cotsen Institute of Archaeology, UCLA, Los Angeles.

Neff, Hector, Ronald L. Bishop, and Edward V. Sayre
1988   A Simulation Approach to the Problem of Tempering in Compositional Studies of Archaeological Ceramics. Journal of Archaeological Science 15:159–172.
1989   More Observations on the Problem of Tempering in Compositional Studies of Archaeological Ceramics. Journal of Archaeological Science 16:57–69.

Neff, Hector, Jeffrey Blomster, Michael D. Glascock, Ronald L. Bishop, M. James Blackman, Michael D. Coe, George L. Cowgill, Ann Cyphers, Richard A. Diehl, Stephen Houston, Arthur A. Joyce, Carl P. Lipo, and Marcus Winter
2006   Smokescreens in the Provenance Investigation of Early Formative Mesoamerican Ceramics. Latin American Antiquity 17:104–118.

Neff, Hector, and Frederick J. Bove
1999   Mapping Ceramic Compositional Variation and Prehistoric Interaction in Pacific Coastal Guatemala. Journal of Archaeological Science 26:1037–1051.

Parry, Jonathan
1986   The Gift, the Indian Gift and the "Indian Gift." Man 21:453–473.

Pauketat, Timothy R., and Susan M. Alt
2005   Agency in a Postmold? Physicality and the Archaeology of Culture-Making. Journal of Archaeological Method and Theory 12(3):213–236.

Peregrine, Peter
1991   Prehistoric Chiefdoms on the American Midcontinent: A World-System Based on Prestige Goods. *In* Core/Periphery Relations in Precapitalist Worlds, edited by C. Chase-Dunn and T. Hall, pp. 193–211. Westview, Boulder, CO.

Phelps, David S.
1969   Swift Creek and Santa Rosa in Northwest Florida. Notebook 1(6–9):

14–24. South Carolina Institute of Archaeology and Anthropology, University of South Carolina, Columbia.

Phillips, Philip
- 1970 Archaeological Survey in the Lower Yazoo Basin, Mississippi, 1949–1955. Papers of the Peabody Museum of Archaeology and Ethnology. Vol. 60, pt. 1. Harvard University, Cambridge.

Pilkey, Orrin H., and Mary Edna Fraser
- 2002 A Celebration of the World's Barrier Islands. Columbia University Press, Irvington, NY.

Pluckhahn, Thomas J.
- 2003 Kolomoki: Settlement, Ceremony, and Status in the Deep South, A.D. 350 to 750. University of Alabama Press, Tuscaloosa.
- 2007 Reflections of Paddle Stamped Pottery: Symmetry Analysis of Swift Creek Paddle Designs. Southeastern Archaeology 26:1–11.

Polanyi, Karl
- 1944 The Great Transformation. Rinehart, New York.

Price, George
- 2003 Rethinking the Lithic Assemblage from the Swift Creek Type Site (9BI3). The Profile 119:8–9.

Quitmyer, Irvy R.
- 1985 Aboriginal Subsistence Activities in the Kings Bay Locality. *In* Aboriginal Subsistence and Settlement Archaeology of the Kings Bay Locality, vol. 2. University of Florida, Department of Anthropology Reports of Investigations No. 2, Gainesville.

Raheja, Gloria Goodwin
- 1988 The Poison in the Gift: Ritual, Prestation, and the Dominant Caste in a North Indian Village. University of Chicago Press, Chicago.

Rein, Judith S.
- 1974 The Complicated Stamped Pottery of the Mann Site, Posey County, Indiana. Unpublished M.A. thesis, Indiana University.

Reina, Rubin E., and Robert M. Hill II.
- 1978 The Traditional Pottery of Guatemala. University of Texas Press, Austin.

Reitz, Elizabeth J.
- 1988 Evidence for Coastal Adaptations in Georgia and South Carolina. Archaeology of Eastern United States 16:137–158.

Reitz, Elizabeth J., and Irvy R. Quitmyer
- 1988 Faunal Remains from Two Coastal Georgia Swift Creek Sites. Southeastern Archaeology 7:95–108.

Rice, Prudence M.
- 1980 Trace Elemental Characterization of Weeden Island Pottery: Implications for Specialized Production. Southeastern Conference Bulletin 22:29–35.
- 1984 Some Reflections on Change in Pottery Producing Systems. *In* The Many Dimensions of Pottery: Ceramics in Archaeology and Anthropology, edited by S. E. van der Leeuw and A. C. Pritchard, pp. 231–293. CINGULA 7. Institute for Pre- and Proto-history, University of Amsterdam, Amsterdam.
- 1987 Pottery Analysis: A Sourcebook. University of Chicago Press, Chicago.
- 1996 Recent Ceramic Analysis: 1. Function, Style, and Origins. Journal of Archaeological Research 4:133–163.

Robb, John
- 2005 The Extended Artefact and the Monumental Economy: A Methodology for Material Agency. *In* Rethinking Materiality: The Engagement of Mind with the Material World, edited by E. DeMarrais, C. Gosden, and C. Renfrew, pp. 131–140. McDonald Institute for Archaeological Research, Cambridge.

Robb, John E.
- 1999 Secret Agents: Culture, Economy, and Social Reproduction. *In* Material Symbols: Culture and Economy in Prehistory, pp. 3–15. Center for Archaeological Investigations, Southern Illinois, Carbondale.

Rolland, Vicki L., and Paulette Bond
- 2003 The Search for Spiculate Clays near Aboriginal Sites in the Lower St. Johns River Region, Florida. The Florida Anthropologist 56:91–112.

Ruby, Bret J., and Christine M. Shriner
- 2006 Ceramic Vessel Compositions and Styles as Evidence of the Local and Nonlocal Social Affiliations of Ritual Participants at the Mann Site, Indiana. *In* Gathering Hopewell: Society, Ritual, and Ritual Interaction, edited by C. Carr and D. T. Case, pp. 553–574. Springer, New York.

Russo, Michael
- 1992 Chronologies and Cultures of the St. Marys Region of Northeast Florida and Southeast Georgia. The Florida Anthropologist 45:107–126.

Russo, Michael, Ann Cordell, Lee Newsom, and Robert Austin
- 1989 Phase III Archaeological Excavations at Edgewater Landing, Volusia County, Florida. Report on file, Division of Historical Resources, Tallahassee.

Russo, Michael, Ann S. Cordell, and Donna L. Ruhl
- 1993 The Timucuan Ecological and Historical Preserve Phase III Final Re-

port. National Park Service, Southeast Archeological Center, National Park Service, Tallahassee.

Sackett, James R.
- 1985 Style and Ethnicity in the Kalahari: A Reply to Wiessner. American Antiquity 50:154–159.
- 1986 Isochrestism and Style: A Clarification. Journal of Anthropological Archaeology 5:266–277.
- 1990 Style and Ethnicity in Archaeology: The Case for Isochrestism. In The Uses of Style in Archaeology, edited by M. Conkey and C. Hastorf, pp. 32–43. Cambridge University Press, Cambridge.

Sahlins, Marshall
- 1972 Stone Age Economics. Aldine, Chicago.

Saitta, Dean J.
- 1999 Prestige, Agency, and Change in Middle-Range Societies. In Material Symbols: Culture and Economy in Prehistory, edited by John Robb, pp. 135–149. Occasional Paper No. 26. Center for Archaeological Investigations, Southern Illinois University, Carbondale.
- 2000 Theorizing Political Economy of Southwestern Exchange. In The Archaeology of Regional Interaction, edited by Michelle Hegmon, pp. 151–166. University of Colorado, Boulder.

Sassaman, Kenneth E.
- 1993 Early Pottery in the Southeast: Tradition and Innovation in Cooking Technology. University of Alabama Press, Tuscaloosa.
- 2006 People of the Shoals: Stallings Culture of the Savannah River Valley. University Press of Florida, Gainesville.

Saunders, Rebecca
- 1986 Attribute Variability in Late Swift Creek Phase Ceramics from King's Bay, Georgia. Unpublished M.A. thesis, Department of Anthropology, University of Florida, Gainesville.
- 1998 Swift Creek Phase Design Assemblages from Two Sites on the Georgia Coast. In A World Engraved: Archaeology of the Swift Creek Culture, edited by Mark Williams and Daniel T. Elliott, pp. 154–180. University of Alabama Press, Tuscaloosa.

Schiffer, Michael B.
- 1975 Archaeology as a Behavioral Science. American Anthropologist 77:836–848.
- 1976 Behavioral Archaeology. Academic Press, New York.
- 1990 The Influence of Surface Treatment on Heating Effectiveness of Ceramic Vessels. Journal of Archaeological Science 17:373–381.

Schiffer, Michael B., and James M. Skibo
- 1987 Theory and Experiment in the Study of Technological Change. Current Anthropology 28:595–622.
- 1997 The Explanation of Artifact Variability. American Antiquity 62:25–50.

Schiffer, Michael Brian, James M. Skibo, Tamara C. Boelke, Mark A. Neupert, and Meredith Aronson
- 1994 New Perspectives on Experimental Archaeology: Surface Treatments and Thermal Response of the Clay Cooking Pot. American Antiquity 59:197–217.

Sears, William H.
- 1952 Ceramic Development in the South Appalachian Province. American Antiquity 18:101–110.
- 1956 Excavations at Kolomoki: Final Report. University of Georgia Series in Anthropology No. 5, Athens.
- 1957 Excavations on Lower St. Johns River, Florida. Contributions of the Florida State Museum 2, Gainesville.
- 1958 Burial Mounds on the Gulf Coastal Plain. American Antiquity 23:274–283.
- 1959 Two Weeden Island Period Burial Mounds, Florida. Contributions of the Florida State Museum 5, Gainesville.
- 1962 The Hopewellian Affiliations of Certain Sites on the Gulf Coast of Florida. American Antiquity 28:5–18.
- 1967 *Review of* Excavations at the Mayport Mound, Florida, by Rex K. Wilson. American Antiquity 32:120–121.
- 1973 The Sacred and the Secular in Prehistoric Ceramics. *In* Variations in Anthropology: Essays in Honor of John McGregor, edited by D. Lathrap and J. Douglas, pp. 31–42. Illinois Archaeological Survey, Urbana.

Seeman, Mark F.
- 1979 The Hopewell Interaction Sphere: The Evidence for Interregional Trade and Structural Complexity. Prehistory Research Series 5. Indiana State Historical Society, Indianapolis.
- 1995 When Words Are Not Enough: Hopewell Interregionalism and the Use of Material Symbols at the GE Mound. *In* Native American Interactions: Multiscalar Analyses and Interpretations in the Eastern Woodlands, edited by Michael S. Nassaney and Kenneth E. Sassaman, pp. 122–143. University of Tennessee Press, Knoxville.

Seip, Lisa P.
- 1999 Transformations of Meaning: The Life History of a Nuxalk Mask. World Archaeology 31:272–287.

Senior, Louise M.
- 1994 The Estimation of Prehistoric Values: Cracked Pot Ideas in Archaeology. *In* Expanding Archaeology, edited by J. M. Skibo, W. H. Walker, and A. E. Neilsen, pp. 92–110. University of Utah Press, Salt Lake City.

Shanks, Michael, and Christopher Tilley
- 1987 Re-Constructing Archaeology: Theory and Practice. Cambridge University Press, Cambridge.

Shepard, Anna O.
- 1968 Ceramics for the Archaeologist. 6th edition. Carnegie Institution of
- [1954] Washington, Washington, DC.

Shrarer, Robert J., Andrew K. Balkansky, James H. Buron, Gary M. Feinman, Kent V. Flannery, David G. Grove, Joyce Marcus, Robert G. Moyle, T. Douglas Price, Elsa M. Redmond, Robert G. Reynolds, Prudence M. Rice, Charles S. Spencer, James B. Stoltman, and Jason Yaeger.
- 2006 On the Logic of Archaeological Inference: Early Formative Pottery and the Evolution of Mesoamerican Societies. Latin American Antiquity 17:90–103.

Sigaud, Lygia
- 2002 The Vicissitudes of the Gift. Social Anthropology 10:335–358.

Sigler-Eisenberg, Brenda, Ann Cordell, Richard Estabrook, Elizabeth Horvath, Lee Newsom, and Michael Russo
- 1985 Archaeological Site Types, Distribution, and Preservation within the Upper St. Johns River Basin. Miscellaneous Project and Report Series Number 27, Department of Anthropology, Florida State Museum, Gainesville.

Skibo, James M.
- 1992 Pottery Function: A Use-Alteration Perspective. Plenum, New York.

Skibo, James M., Tamara C. Butts, and Michael Brian Schiffer
- 1997 Ceramic Surface Treatment and Abrasion Resistance: An Experimental Study. Journal of Archaeological Science 24:311–317.

Skibo, James M., Michael B. Schiffer, and Kenneth C. Reid
- 1989 Organic-Tempered Pottery: An Experimental Study. American Antiquity 54:122–146.

Smith, Betty A.
- 1975 The Relationship between Deptford and Swift Creek Ceramics as Evidenced at the Mandeville Site, 9Cla1. Southeastern Archaeological Conference Bulletin 18:195–200.
- 1979 The Hopewell Connection in Southwest Georgia. *In* Hopewell Archaeology: The Chillicothe Conference, edited by D. S. Brose and N. Greber, pp. 181–187. Kent State University Press, Kent, OH.

1998 Neutron Activation Analysis of Ceramics from Madeville and Swift Creek. *In* A World Engraved: Archaeology of the Swift Creek Culture, edited by M. Williams and D. T. Elliott, pp. 112–129. University of Alabama Press, Tuscaloosa.

Smith, Bruce D.
 1986 The Archaeology of the Southeastern United States: From Dalton to de Soto. *In* Advances in World Archaeology, vol. 5, edited by F. Wendorf and A. Close, pp. 1–92. Academic Press, Orlando, FL.

Smith, Greg C., and Brent M. Handley
 2002 Addendum To: Archaeological Data Recovery and Mitigation at 8DU5544/5545, Queen's Harbour Yacht and Country Club, Duval County, Florida. Report on file, Division of Historical Resources, Tallahassee.

Smith, Karen
 1999 From Pots to Potters: Ceramic Manufacture at Fairchild's Landing, Seminole County, Georgia. M.A. thesis, Department of Anthropology, University of Alabama, Tuscaloosa.

Smith, Marion F., Jr.
 1988 Function from Whole Vessel Shape: A Method and Application to Anasazi Black Mesa, Arizona. American Anthropologist 90:921–922.

Smith, Robin L.
 1978 An Archaeological Survey of Kings Bay, Camden County, Georgia. Manuscript on file, Department of Anthropology, University of Florida, Gainesville.

Smith, Robin L., Chad O. Braley, Nina T. Borremans, and Elizabeth Rietz
 1981 Coastal Adaptations in Southeast Georgia: Ten Archaeological Sites at Kings Bay. Report submitted to the U.S. Department of the Navy, Kings Bay, Georgia.

Smith, Robin L., Bruce Council, and Rebecca Saunders
 1985 Three Sites on Sandy Run: Phase II Evaluation of Sites 9CM183, 184, 185 at Kings Bay, Georgia. Report submitted to the U.S. Department of the Navy, Kings Bay, Georgia.

Snow, Frankie
 1975 Swift Creek Designs and Distributions: A South Georgia Study. Early Georgia 3:38–59.
 1977 An Archaeological Survey of the Ocmulgee Big Bend Region: A Preliminary Report. Occasional Papers from South Georgia, Number 3. South Georgia College, Douglas.
 1998 Swift Creek Design Investigations: The Hartford Case. *In* A World

Engraved: Archaeology of the Swift Creek Culture, edited by Mark Williams and Daniel T. Elliott, pp. 61–98. University of Alabama Press, Tuscaloosa.

2007   Swift Creek Design Catalog. Report on file, South Georgia College, Douglas.

Snow, Frankie, and Keith Stephenson

1998   Swift Creek Designs: A Tool for Monitoring Interaction. *In* A World Engraved: Archaeology of the Swift Creek Culture, edited by M. Williams and D. T. Elliott, pp. 99–111. University of Alabama Press, Tuscaloosa.

Spaulding, Albert C.

1954   Reply (to Ford). American Anthropologist 56:112–114.

Stark, Miriam T.

1998   Technical Choices and Social Boundaries in Material Culture Patterning: An Introduction. *In* The Archaeology of Social Boundaries, edited by Miriam T. Stark, pp. 1–11. Smithsonian Institution Press, Washington, DC.

Stephenson, Keith, Judith A. Bense, and Frankie Snow

2002   Aspects of Deptford and Swift Creek on the South Atlantic and Gulf Coastal Plains. *In* The Woodland Southeast, edited by David G. Anderson and Robert C. Mainfort Jr., pp. 318–351. University of Alabama Press, Tuscaloosa.

Steponaitis, Vincas, M. James Blackman, and Hector Neff

1996   Large-Scale Compositional Patterns in the Chemical Composition of Mississippian Pottery. American Antiquity 61:555–572.

Steponaitis, Vincas, M. James Blackman, and Russell Weisman

1988   Chemical and Mineralogical Characterization of Mississippian Pottery. Paper presented at the 53rd Annual Meeting of the Society for American Archaeology, Phoenix, AZ.

Stoltman, James B.

1989   A Quantitative Approach to the Petrographic Analysis of Ceramic Thin Sections. American Antiquity 54(1):147–160.

1991   Ceramic Petrography as a Technique for Documenting Cultural Interaction: An Example from the Upper Mississippi Valley. American Antiquity 56(1):103–120.

2001   The Role of Petrography in the Study of Archaeological Ceramics. *In* Earth Sciences and Archaeology, edited by Paul Goldberg, Vance T. Holiday, and C. Reid Ferring, pp. 297–326. Kluwer Academic/Plenum Publishers, New York.

Stoltman, James B., and Robert C. Mainfort Jr.
   2002   Minerals and Elements: Using Petrography to Reconsider the Findings of Neutron Activation in the Compositional Analysis of Ceramics from Pinson Mounds, Tennessee. Midcontinental Journal of Archaeology 27:1–33.

Stoltman, James B., Joyce Marcus, Kent V. Flannery, James H. Burton, and Robert G. Moyle
   2005   Petrographic Evidence Shows that Pottery Exchange between the Olmec and Their Neighbors Was Two Way. Proceedings of the National Academy of Sciences 102:11213–11218.

Stoltman, James B., and Frankie Snow
   1998   Cultural Interaction within Swift Creek Society: People, Pots, and Paddles. *In* A World Engraved: Archaeology of the Swift Creek Culture, edited by M. Williams and D. T. Elliott, pp. 130–153. University of Alabama Press, Tuscaloosa.

Stoner, Wesley D., Christopher A. Pool, Hector Neff, and Michael D. Glascock
   2008   Exchange of Coarse Orange Pottery in the Middle Classic Tuxtla Mountains, Southern Veracruz, Mexico. Journal of Archaeological Science 35:1412–1426.

Strathern, Marilyn
   1988   The Gender of the Gift: Problems with Women and Problems with Society in Melanesia. University of California Press, Berkeley.

Struever, Stuart
   1964   The Hopewell Interaction Sphere in Riverine—Western Great Lakes Culture History. *In* Hopewellian Studies, edited by Joseph Caldwell and Robert Hall, pp. 86–106. Scientific Papers 12, Illinois State Museum, Springfield.

Struever, Stuart, and Gail L. Houart
   1972   An Analysis of the Hopewell Interaction Sphere. *In* Social Exchange and Interaction, edited by E. N. Wilmsen, pp. 47–79. Anthropological Papers of the Museum of Anthropology, University of Michigan, No. 46, Ann Arbor.

Sturtevant, William C.
   1979   Black Drink and Other Caffeine-Containing Beverages among Non-Indians. *In* Black Drink: A Native American Tea, edited by Charles M. Hudson, pp. 150–165. University of Georgia Press, Athens.

Sykes, Karen
   2005   Arguing with Anthropology: An Introduction to Critical Theories of the Gift. Routledge, London.

Taussig, Michael T.
- 1993 Mimesis and Alterity: A Particular History of the Senses. Routledge, London.

Tesar, Louis D.
- 1980 The Leon County Bicentennial Survey Report: An Archaeological Survey of Selected Portions of Leon County, Florida. Miscellaneous Project Report Series 49, Bureau of Historic Sites and Properties, Florida Division of Archives, History and Records Management, Florida Department of State, Tallahassee.

Thomas, David H., and C. S. Larsen, eds.
- 1979 The Anthropology of St. Catherines Island 2: The Refuge-Deptford Mortuary Complex. Anthropological Papers of the American Museum of Natural History 56, New York.

Thomas, Julian
- 1993 The Politics of Vision and the Archaeologies of Landscape. *In* Landscape Politics and Perspectives, edited by Barbara Bender, pp. 19–48. Berg, Oxford.
- 1999 Economy of Substances in Earlier Neolithic Britain. *In* Material Symbols: Culture and Economy in Prehistory, edited by John E. Robb, pp. 70–89. Occasional Paper No. 26. Center for Archaeological Investigations, Southern Illinois University, Carbondale.

Thomas, Nicholas
- 1991 Entangled Objects: Exchange, Material Culture, and Colonialism in the Pacific. Harvard University Press, Cambridge.

Thomas, Prentice M., Jr., and L. Janice Campbell, eds.
- 1993 Technical Synthesis of Cultural Resources Investigations at Eglin Santa Rosa, Okaloosa and Walton Counties. Report of Investigations 192, New World Research, Fort Walton Beach, FL.

Thunen, Robert L.
- 1998 Defining Space: An Overview of the Pinson Mounds Enclosure. *In* Ancient Earthen Enclosures of the Eastern Woodlands, edited by Robert C. Mainfort Jr. and Lynne P. Sullivan, pp. 57–67. University Press of Florida, Gainesville.

Thunen, Robert L., and Keith H. Ashley
- 1995 Mortuary Behavior along the Lower St. Johns: An Overview. The Florida Anthropologist 48(1):3–12.

Tilley, Christopher
- 1999 Metaphor and Material Culture. Blackwell, Oxford.

van der Leeuw, Sander E., Dick A. Papousek, and Anick Coudart
- 1992 Technological Traditions and Unquestioned Assumptions: The Case of Pottery in Michoacan. Techniques et Culture 16–17:145–173.

Vincentelli, Moira
- 2000 Women and Ceramics, Gendered Vessels. Manchester University Press, Manchester.
- 2004 Women Potters: Transforming Traditions. Rutgers University Press, New Brunswick, NJ.

Waggoner, James C.
- 2006 A Techno-Functional Analysis of Fiber-Tempered Pottery from the Squeaking Tree Site (9Tf5), Telfair County, Georgia. Early Georgia 34:3–16.

Walker, William H.
- 1995 Ceremonial Trash? *In* Expanding Archaeology, edited by James S. Skibo, William H. Walker, and Axel E. Neilsen, pp. 67–79. University of Utah Press, Salt Lake City.

Wallis, Neill J.
- 2004 Perpetuating Tradition on the Lower St. Johns: Pottery Technology and Function at the Mayport Mound (8DU96). The Florida Anthropologist 57(4):271–298.
- 2006a The Case for Swift Creek Paddles as Totemic Symbols: Some Anthropological Considerations. The Florida Anthropologist 59:55–61.
- 2006b The Production of Meaning in Swift Creek Iconography. Paper presented at the 71st Annual Meeting of the Society for American Archaeology, San Juan, Puerto Rico.
- 2007 Defining Swift Creek Interaction: Earthenware Variability at Ring Middens and Burial Mounds. Southeastern Archaeology 26(2): 212–231.
- 2008 Networks of History and Memory: Creating a Nexus of Social Identity in Woodland Period Mounds on the Lower St. Johns River, Florida. Journal of Social Archaeology 8(2):236–271.

Wallis, Neill J., Mathew T. Boulanger, Jeffrey R. Ferguson, and Michael D. Glascock
- 2010 Woodland Period Ceramic Provenance and the Exchange of Swift Creek Complicated Stamped Pottery in the Southeastern United States. Journal of Archaeological Science 37:2598–2611.

Wallis, Neill J., Ann S. Cordell, and Lee A. Newsom
- 2005 Petrographic Analysis of Charcoal-Tempered Pottery from Northeastern Florida. Poster presented at the 70th Annual Meeting of the Society for American Archaeology, Salt Lake City, UT.

Walthall, John A., and Brad Koldehoff
  1998   Hunter-Gatherer Interaction and Alliance Formation: Dalton and the Cult of the Long Blade. Plains Anthropologist 43:257–273.
Waring, Antonio J., Jr., and Preston Holder
  1968   The Deptford Ceramic Complex. In The Waring Papers: The Collected Works of Antonio J. Waring, Jr., edited by S. Williams, pp. 135–151. Peabody Museum of Archaeology and Ethnology. Harvard University, Cambridge.
Washburn, Dorothy
  1995   Perception, Geometry, and Style. In Style, Society, and Person, edited by Christopher Carr and J. Neitzel, pp. 101–122. Plenum Press, New York.
Wayne, Lucy B.
  1987   Swift Creek Occupation in the Altamaha Delta. Early Georgia 15:46–65.
Weigand, Phil C., Garman Harbottle, and Edward V. Sayre
  1977   Turquoise Sources and Source Analysis: Mesoamerica and the Southwestern U.S.A. In Exchange Systems in Prehistory, edited by T. K. Earle and J. E. Ericson, pp. 15–34. Academic Press, New York.
Weiner, Annette B.
  1976   Women of Value, Men of Renown: New Perspectives in Trobriand Exchange. University of Texas Press, Austin.
  1992   Inalienable Possessions: The Paradox of Keeping-While-Giving. University of California Press, Berkeley.
  1994   Cultural Difference and the Density of Objects. American Ethnologist 21:391–403.
Welch, Paul D.
  1991   Moundville's Economy. University of Alabama Press, Tuscaloosa.
Wharton, Charles
  1978   The Natural Environments of Georgia. Georgia Department of Natural Resources, Atlanta.
Wiessner, Polly
  1982   Beyond Willow Smoke and Dogs' Tails: A Comment on Binford's Analysis of Hunter-Gatherer Settlement Systems. American Antiquity 47:171–178.
  1983   Styles and Boundaries in Kalahari San Projectile Points. American Antiquity 48:253–276.
  1985   Style or Isochrestic Variation? A Reply to Sackett. American Antiquity 50:160–166.
  1989   Style and Changing Relations between the Individual and Society. In

The Meaning of Things: Material Culture and Symbolic Expression, edited by Ian Hodder, pp. 56–63. Unwin Hyman, London.

Willey, Gordon R.
1945  The Weeden Island Culture: A Preliminary Definition. American Antiquity 10:225–254.
1949  Archaeology of the Florida Gulf Coast. Smithsonian Miscellaneous Collections 113. Smithsonian Institution, Washington, DC.

Williams, Mark, and Daniel T. Elliott (editors)
1998  A World Engraved: Archaeology of the Swift Creek Culture. University of Alabama Press, Tuscaloosa.

Williams, Mark, and Jennifer Freer Harris
1998  Shrines of the Prehistoric South: Patterning in Middle Woodland Mound Distribution. *In* A World Engraved: Archaeology of the Swift Creek Culture, edited by Mark Williams and Daniel Elliott, pp. 36–47. University of Alabama Press, Tuscaloosa.

Wilson, Rex L.
1965  Excavations at the Mayport Mound, Florida. Contributions of the Florida State Museum 13, Gainesville.

Wing, Elizabeth, and L. McKean
1987  Preliminary Study of the Animal Remains Excavated from the Hontoon Island Site. The Florida Anthropologist 40:40–46.

Wobst, H. Martin
1977  Stylistic Behavior and Information Exchange. *In* For the Director: Research Essays in Honor of James B. Griffin, edited by Charles E. Cleland, pp. 317–342. Anthropological Papers No. 61, Museum of Anthropology, University of Michigan, Ann Arbor.

# Index

agency of objects, 15, 20–22
Alicia mounds, 81, 157, 159, 162, 197
Alligator Bayou Stamped pottery, 30
Alt, Susan, 21–23
Altamaha River: archaeological sites on, 72–75; chemical constituents of clays near, 101–102; environmental setting of, 54–55
Altamaha spiny mussel shells, 41
Amelia Island, 58, 65, 125; archaeological sites on, 68, 71, 81, 109, 195; clay samples from, 93, 118
Anderson, David, 37, 74
Annawakee Creek site, 37
apotropaic function of designs, 201–202
Appadurai, Arjun, 15–17
archaic: cultures, 39–40; gifts, 14
architecture, 22: at Hartford site, 38; at Swift Creek ring middens, 39
arsenic, 98, 101, 104
artifact distribution patterns. *See* chemical groups; mineralogical groups; paddle matches
Ashley, Keith, 59–60, 72, 88

barrier islands, 54–55
Basin Bayou Incised pottery, 163
beakers, 168–169. *See also* vessel form: summary of dimensions

Beauclerc mounds, 81, 85, 150, 162–163, 167, 197
Bernath site, 39, 70
*bilums*, 26
biography of objects, 15–16, 180, 190, 197–198. *See also* genealogy of material practice
Block-Sterns site, 37, 43
Boas, Franz, 48
boat-shaped bowls, 164–166. *See also* vessel form: summary of dimensions
bowls. *See* boat-shaped bowls; double bowls; open bowls; restricted bowls; shallow bowls; small cups and bowls
Brown mound, 81
Broyles, Bettye, 41–42, 45
burial mounds. *See* mortuary mounds

calcium, 94–98, 130. *See also* shell middens
carbon dates: from northeast Florida, 62; from southeast Georgia, 63. *See also* old wood problem
Carrabelle Punctuated pottery, 90, 109, 114, 163
Cartersville archaeological culture, 30, 35
Cathead Creek site, 72–73, 77, 89, 96, 108, 110, 112, 117, 128, 174
cemetery: in village plaza, 39, 70. *See also* mortuary mounds

central plaza: and ring middens, 39–40. See also cemetery: in village plaza; middens: ring
ceramic ecology, 94, 205
ceramic paste: and cooking, 139, 184–189; natural and cultural constituents, 119–128. See also methods: technofunctional analysis; temper
ceramic vessels: estimating form from sherds, 143–145; function of, 138–140. See also manufacture of ceramic vessels; vessel lip form; vessel orifice diameter; vessel rim thickness
ceremonial centers, 21, 24, 29, 36–39
Chapman, John, 16. See also enchainment
charcoal-tempered pottery: chemical characterization of, 104, 114; mineralogical characterization of, 65, 122–123, 129–130; spatial distribution of, 64; symbolism in, 193; temporality of, 60–65
chemical groups, 98–101, 103–105, 108–113, 126–130, 133
chiefdoms, and tribute systems, 25
chromium, 96, 101, 104–107, 111, 130–131, 135
chronology: of Swift Creek archaeological culture, 32–34; of Swift Creek on the Atlantic coast, 60–66. See also genealogy of material practice
circular villages. See middens: ring
citation, 9, 17, 22–23, 192, 195, 197–198, 204, 206–207. See also Jones, Andrew
civic-ceremonial centers. See ceremonial centers
clay resource groups, 120–125. See also mineralogical groups
coastal sector, 53–55
cobalt, 98, 101, 104–107, 111, 130–131, 133, 135
Cold Springs site, 37
collared jars, 157–160. See also vessel form: summary of dimensions
Colorinda pottery, 59
continuous-use mounds, 76
Cook, Fred, 64
cooking: and the suitability of vessel forms, 145–172

copper artifacts, 14, 28, 38, 40, 75, 193
Cordell, Ann, 65, 116, 118
cups. See small cups and bowls

daub, 39
Dent Mound site, 61, 75–77, 81, 89, 108, 110, 117, 128, 168, 180
Deptford: archaeological culture, 34–35; association with Swift Creek, 29–30, 32, 40–41, 61, 86, 192–194; Atlantic coastal, 56–60; check-stamped pottery, 90, 104, 154
descent: groups and exchange, 8, 11, 29, 45–46, 51, 53, 200–207; lines of material forms, 20
design 34, 77, 79, 110, 128–129
design 36, 77, 80, 81, 110, 128–129
design 38, 81, 82, 112, 128–129
design 151, 85
design 291, 84, 112, 128–129
designs, Swift Creek, 5, 30–33; differences between Early and Late, 195; distribution of, 7, 28–30; flaws in, 4, 41; meaning of, 47–52, 197–207; regional distinctions in, 194. See also paddle matches; Snow, Frankie; split representation; stamping
diagenesis, 97, 115
diatoms, 116, 118–120, 124, 127
distributed object, 9, 17, 198–199
distributed person, 18, 198–203, 207
dividual, 19–20.
double bowls, 166–167. See also vessel form: summary of dimensions
double-globed jar, 169–170. See also vessel form: summary of dimensions
Dunns Creek Red pottery, 57, 75, 90, 109, 114, 149, 151, 161, 165–166, 180, 190

Early Swift Creek: chemical group assignments, 104, 114; interactions, 76–77, 197; paddle matches, 81; phase, 30, 38, 41, 60–62, 182, 187, 194, 196, 197; pottery, 33, 44, 64–66, 193, 195–197; rim thickness, 182; vessel form, 151, 154, 161, 166, 168, 181
enchainment, 16, 198

*enchainment organique*, 142. *See also* Mauss, Marcel
Espenshade, Christopher, 187
Evelyn site, 37, 64, 72, 74, 77, 89, 108, 113, 117, 174, 194, 204; Mound B, 72, 74, 204; Mound C, 72, 74, 113, 204
exchange: contexts of, 23; functionalist interpretations of, 23–25; of Swift Creek vessels, 197–207; of utilitarian objects, 25–26. *See also* prestige goods

Fairbanks, Charles, 29, 32, 59, 76
faunal remains, 69–70; Hartford site, 38; as seasonality indicators, 39, 73
feasting, 24, 45
flattened-globular bowls, 154, 156–157. *See also* vessel form: summary of dimensions
food: in mortuary contexts, 18; preparation in ceramic vessels, 4–5, 151, 154, 160, 169, 171, 203; residue on vessels, 139–140; sharing as reciprocity, 2
Fortson Mound, 38
functionalism. *See* exchange: functionalist interpretations of

Garden Creek site, 37
gathering centers. *See* ceremonial centers
Gell, Alfred, 17, 21, 48, 51, 199, 201
gender, 22; and exchange, 25; and political economy, 2; and vessel production, 202
genealogy of material practice, 6, 9, 20–23, 27; in Swift Creek contexts, 192–197
Georgia Bight, 54, 183
gift: exchange of, 1–3, 8; inalienability of, 14–15; and reciprocity, 13–14. *See also* Mauss, Marcel; social life of things; Weiner, Annette
Goggin, John, 56, 59
gorget, 40, 74
Gosden, Chris, 16, 20, 22–23
Grant site, 77, 79, 89, 93, 108, 118, 124, 155, 163, 165; low mounds A and E, 75–76, 155, 157, 159, 161–165, 167, 169–170
Greenfield site #7, 69, 89, 108, 117, 174, 182, 187, 188

Greenfield site #8/9, 39, 46, 70, 76, 89, 96, 108, 117, 128, 174, 182, 188
Green Point Complex, 41, 193
grit temper, 56, 112–13, 119, 121–123, 125, 129, 187, 189, 194
Group 1. *See* chemical groups
Group 2. *See* chemical groups
Gulf Coast: chronology, 33; and Hopewell Interaction Sphere, 38, 41; and Swift Creek interactions, 65, 77, 86, 104, 109, 112, 114, 193–194, 196–197, 205; vessel form, 145, 166, 170, 172, 190

*habitus*, 142
hafnium, 129, 133, 205
Harris, Jennifer, 37–38
Hartford site, 33, 36, 38, 42–43, 110
*hau*, 14
heating effectiveness: and temper, 139; and vessel thickness, 183
Hopewell Interaction Sphere, 40–41, 56–57, 75
Horseshoe Bayou site, 39
household middens. *See* middens: household

indexicality, 9, 17, 18, 22, 23, 138, 198, 199, 206–207. *See also* citation
Instrumental Neutron Activation Analysis, 10, 43–44, 87–114; methods, 92–95; results, 95–114; sampling, 88–93. *See also* chemical groups
interaction: and Swift Creek Complicated Stamped pottery, 4–8, 40–46. *See also* exchange; Hopewell Interaction Sphere; Kula ring
Interregional Hopewell. *See* Hopewell Interaction Sphere

jars, 152, 156. *See also* double-globed jar; small jars
Jennings, Jesse, 32
Jones, Andrew, 22–23

Kelly, Arthur, 32–33
Kelvin archaeological culture, 64, 66, 72–73
Kings Bay site, 46, 64, 71–72, 77, 81, 84, 90, 108, 182, 187, 206

Kirshenblatt-Gimblett, Barbara, 18
Knight, Vernon, 33
Kolomoki site, 32–34, 37, 42–43, 45–46
Kula ring, 1, 16–18, 198–199
Kwakwaka'wakw, 17

Larson, Lewis, 56
Late Swift Creek: chemical group assignment, 112–114; interactions, 197–207; paddle matches, 77–86; phase, 41, 72, 74, 76–77, 194–198, 203; pottery, 10, 33, 61, 64–67, 182, 195; rim thickness, 182–184; vessel form, 149, 151, 153, 158, 163
Latour, Bruno, 21
Levi-Strauss, Claude, 13, 48–51, 200
Lewis Creek site, 72–73, 77, 81, 89, 108, 110, 112, 117, 128, 175, 204
Linton, Ralph, 138
lip form. *See* vessel lip form
lithics, 2, 18, 35, 40, 57, 72, 75
Lower St. Johns River. *See* St. Johns River

Mahalanobis distance, 95, 101, 104
Mainfort, Robert, 43–44
Malinowski, Bronislaw, 1–2, 13
Mallard Creek site, 46, 71, 84
Mandeville site, 32–33, 37, 42–43
Mann site, 44
manufacture of ceramic vessels: and gender, 2, 4; as meaningful practice, 198, 202; and stamping, 31. *See also* ceramic vessels; production; provenance; temper
Marksville archaeological culture, 30, 40. *See also* Santa Rosa–Swift Creek
Marshall, Yvonne, 16
masking cultures, 49–50
masks, 17; in Swift Creek designs, 31, 47–48, 50. *See also* designs; masking cultures; split representation
Mauss, Marcel, 3–4, 12–13, 142
Mayport Mound site, 61, 75–76, 81, 89, 108, 112, 117, 128, 160, 180–181
McArthur Estates site, 71, 89, 108, 117, 174, 187
McKeithen site, 37, 169

mend holes, 145, 148, 171–172, 180–181, 190. *See also* vessel form
Meskell, Lynn, 22
methods: Instrumental Neutron Activation Analysis, 92–95; petrographic analysis, 116–119; technofunctional analysis, 143–145. *See also* sampling
mica: as constituent of ceramic paste, 119–121, 123–124, 127–128; sheets, 28, 38, 72, 75
middens: household, 46, 69–71; ring, 36, 38–40, 70. *See also* shell middens
middle-range societies, 25
Middle St. Johns River, 58–59; as provenance of nonlocal vessels, 60, 104, 109, 114, 166, 196, 205. *See also* St. Johns River
Milamo site, 38, 42–43
Milanich, Jerald, 28, 35, 59, 76, 156
mineralogical groups, 119–127; compared to chemical groups, 128–136
minimum number of vessels (MNV), 144
Mississippian, 21, 37, 47
Mistovich, Timothy, 33
MNV. *See* minimum number of vessels
mobility, 39, 76; residential, 44; seasonal, 36. *See also* post-marital residence patterns
Moore, Clarence B., 56, 59, 74–76, 81, 166, 168, 170; mounds excavated by, 74–76
mortuary mounds: citational practices at, 197–198, 204; distribution of, 6, 9, 38, 40, 53, 64, 67, 70, 73–76; pottery assemblages at, 8, 30, 145–170. *See also* continuous-use mounds
mounds. *See* continuous-use mounds; mortuary mounds; platform mounds
multi-compartment trays, 166–168. *See also* vessel forms: summary of dimensions
Myers, Fred, 18

net impressed pottery, 90
Neutron Activation Analysis. *See* Instrumental Neutron Activation Analysis
Newsom, Lee, 65

object agency. *See* agency of objects
object biography. *See* social life of things
Ocean Reach site, 71
Ocmulgee Big Bend, 36, 44
Oconee River, 42
old wood problem, 61
open bowls, 145, 150–151. *See also* vessel form: summary of dimensions
open pots, 154–155. *See also* vessel form: summary of dimensions

paddle matches, 5–6, 10, 41–46; explanations for, 40–45; on the Atlantic coast, 77–86
panpipes. *See* copper artifacts
Papua New Guinea, 18
partibility, 19. *See also* distributed object
paste. *See* ceramic paste
Pauketat, Timothy, 21–23
petrographic analysis, 10, 42–44, 65, 115–136, 197, 205; methods, 116–119; results, 119–28; sampling, 116–117. *See also* clay resource groups
phytoliths, 116, 118–121, 123–125
Pickwick Complicated Stamped pottery, 30
Pinson mounds, 43–44
platform mounds, 37–38. *See also* Evelyn site: Mound B
Pluckhahn, Thomas, 46
plummets, 40
Point La Vista mounds, 75–76, 163, 167
Polanyi, Karl, 13, 24
post-marital residence patterns, 44, 143
posts, 21–22, 70
pottery. *See* ceramic vessels
pottery manufacture. *See* manufacture of ceramic vessels
prestige goods, 24–25
principle components, 95, 102–103, 132–135
production: domestic mode of, 2–4, 25; of persons, 20; of pottery, 4–8, 25, 44, 64, 86, 135, 138, 192, 202–203
provenance: and bulk chemical composition, 94–95, 115; and mineralogy, 115, 119

quartz temper, 10, 66, 109, 129–130, 133, 135–136, 187, 190

reciprocity, 2, 13; generalized, 23
recontextualization, 22, 138, 203, 206
Rein, Judith, 44
residential mobility. *See* mobility: residential
restricted bowls, 151–152. *See also* vessel form: summary of dimensions
restricted pots, 152–154. *See also* vessel form: summary of dimensions
Rice, Prudence, 138, 141
rim thickness. *See* vessel rim thickness
ring middens. *See* middens: ring
Ruby, Brett, 44
Russo, Michael, 160

Sabarl axes, 18
Sadlers Landing site, 64, 72, 74, 77, 84
Sahlins, Marshall, 2–3, 13, 24
sampling, 88–93, 116–118, 143–144. *See also* methods
sand mounds. *See* mortuary mounds
sand-tempered plain pottery: in determining MNV, 144; in Lower St. Johns chronology, 59–60, 65–66; nonlocal, 104, 110, 113, 205. *See also* temper
Santa Rosa Punctuated, 30
Santa Rosa Stamped, 30
Santa Rosa–Swift Creek, 30, 35, 36, 38–39, 41, 161
Satilla River, 55, 60
Saunders, Rebecca, 46, 182
Savannah River, 35, 55
Sears, William, 29, 41, 59, 60, 65, 156, 190
seasonal mobility. *See* mobility: seasonal
settlement patterns, 34–36; on the Altamaha, 71–73, 76; on the St. Johns, 68–71, 76
shallow bowl, 169. *See also* vessel form: summary of dimensions
shell middens: and diagenesis in pottery, 97; and preservation, 36, 68. *See also* middens
Shriner, Christine, 44

Sidon Plantation site, 72–74, 77, 89, 96, 108, 110, 117, 175
small cups and bowls, 158, 160–161. *See also* vessel form: summary of dimensions
small jars, 161–164. *See also* vessel form: summary of dimensions
small-scale societies, 2, 12, 24–25
Smith, Betty, 43
Snow, Frankie, 31–32, 36, 41–42, 43, 44, 45, 47, 77, 205
social life of things, 15–20
soot. *See* carbon dates; use alteration
split representation, 9, 48–52, 199–200
sponge spicules: as natural constituent of clay, 116, 118–121, 123–125, 127–128, 184; as temper, 56, 61, 109, 185, 188
Stallings culture, 40
stamping: in the Southeast, 30; and tools of vessel manufacture, 31–32. *See also* designs
St. Catherines Island, 56
St. Johns Plain pottery, 30, 57, 59, 60, 75, 90, 109, 114, 149, 151, 153, 161, 169, 180
St. Johns River: archaeological sites on, 57, 66–71; chemical constituents of clays near, 97, 101–106; environmental setting of, 55. *See also* Middle St. Johns River
St. Marys region, 60
St. Marys River, 55, 71
Stephenson, Keith, 45
Stoltman, James, 42–43, 115–116
Strathern, Marilyn, 19
strontium, 94–97. *See also* shell middens
style, 140–141. *See also* technological style
Sun City Complicated Stamped pottery, 65
Swift Creek archaeological culture: mound building, 37–39; and regionalization, 35–37; type site, 32–33. *See also* middens: ring; Swift Creek Complicated Stamped pottery
Swift Creek Complicated Stamped pottery: manufacture, 30–32; spatial distribution, 7, 28–30. *See also* chronology; designs: Swift Creek; vessel form

tattoos, 49–51, 199
technofunction: definition of, 138–140; methods of analysis of, 143–145
technological style, 6, 137, 142–143, 190
temper: as aspect of tradition, 187–189; varieties of, 122–123, 184–187. *See also* charcoal-tempered pottery; heating effectiveness and temper; vessel rim thickness
Thomas, David Hurst, 56
Thomas, Nicholas, 22. *See also* recontextualization
Tillie Fowler site, 68, 89, 96, 108, 117, 174, 182
trays. *See* multi-compartment trays
Trobriand Islands, 18. *See also* Kula Ring

use alteration, 138–140, 145, 172–181. *See also* vessel form

vessel form, 144–172; summary of dimensions, 146–149. *See also* cooking: and the suitability of vessel form
vessel function, 140. *See also* technofunction
vessel lip form, 144; as temporally diagnostic, 61
vessel orifice diameter, 10, 144, 146, 150–172; among paddle-matching vessels, 81; average in mound assemblages, 173; average in village assemblages, 174–176; as proxy for vessel size, 172
vessel rim form, 33, 64, 144, 195. *See also* vessel lip form
vessel rim thickness, 144, 181; averages among mound assemblages, 173; averages among vessel form, 146; averages among village assemblages, 174–175; correlated with temper size, 187–189; as related to habitual styles, 142–143, 182–184, 190, 195

Weeden Island culture, 29–30, 169, 197
Weeden Island Incised pottery, 90, 109, 112, 114, 117, 149, 156, 161
Weeden Island Red pottery, 90, 109, 112, 114, 117, 149, 152, 154, 156, 166, 168, 184, 197

Weiner, Annette, 14–15, 18
Willey, Gordon, 33; and vessel form, 145–172
Williams, Mark, 37–38
wood carvings, 31, 45, 51, 202. *See also* designs
Wood-Hopkins Midden, 59
Woodland period: Middle, 28–30; Late, 30. *See also* ceremonial centers; Hopewell Interaction Sphere; middens: ring

Yent Complex, 41, 193

zirconium, 129, 133, 205